# TESTING FOR TEACHERS
## Second Edition

### HENRY E. GARRETT
#### University of Virginia

**VAN NOSTRAND REINHOLD COMPANY**
New York  Cincinnati  Toronto  London  Melbourne

VAN NOSTRAND REINHOLD COMPANY Regional Offices:
Cincinnati New York Chicago Millbrae Dallas

VAN NOSTRAND REINHOLD COMPANY International Offices:
London Toronto Melbourne

Copyright © 1965 by Litton Educational Publishing, Inc.

All rights reserved. Certain portions of this work
copyright © 1959 by Litton Educational Publishing,
Inc. No part of this work covered by the
copyrights hereon may be reproduced or used
in any form or by any means—graphic, electronic,
or mechanical, including photocopying, recording,
taping, or information storage and retrieval systems
—without written permission of the publisher.
Manufactured in the United States of America.

Published by VAN NOSTRAND REINHOLD COMPANY
450 West 33rd Street, New York, N.Y. 10001

15 14 13 12 11 10 9 8 7 6 5

# PREFACE

In *Testing for Teachers, Second Edition,* I have updated materials wherever desirable and have expanded the sections on teacher-made tests. Since teachers generally have reported success in using the text, I have not changed its basic design or dimensions.

The book is written primarily for prospective teachers who want to know how mental tests can be of help in their school work. It will serve also as a guide for teachers in service. The first seven chapters describe the varieties of mental tests and point out the usefulness and limitations of each sort. The last three chapters deal with the writing of objective items, with the construction of classroom tests, and with some of the ways in which tests can be profitably employed in guidance and counselling. Chapter 2 covers in summary fashion the statistical terms and procedures most often found in mental tests. I do not believe it possible to describe mental tests intelligently without using relevant statistical terms. At the same time, I think that the classroom teacher need not be a psychometrician or testing specialist in order to use standard tests in school. For those who want to go further into test construction, there is an Appendix which treats statistical method more fully.

I have found it profitable to teach Chapter 2 before taking up a discussion of mental tests themselves—to use it, that is, as a foundation for later chapters. An alternate method, which also works well, is to refer specifically to the sections of Chapter 2 whenever the need for the various statistical terms arises.

I believe that the book will be found to contain ample material for one term's work. This is especially true when the laboratory exercises and questions at the ends of the chapters are covered in class discussion, and when reports on relevant literature are required.

HENRY E. GARRETT

December 1964

# TABLE OF CONTENTS

1. MENTAL TESTS IN THE SCHOOLS  1
2. STATISTICS IN MENTAL TESTING  14
3. INDIVIDUAL INTELLIGENCE SCALES  46
4. GROUP TESTS OF INTELLIGENCE  84
5. EDUCATIONAL ACHIEVEMENT TESTS  108
6. APTITUDE TESTS  141
7. PERSONALITY TESTS  168
8. OBJECTIVE-TEST ITEMS AND SHORT-ANSWER TECHNIQUES  198
9. CONSTRUCTING THE OBJECTIVE TEST  223
10. SOME PROBLEMS IN THE EVALUATION OF TEST SCORES  244

Appendix A: Statistical Supplement  257
Appendix B: Publishers of Mental Tests  272
Glossary  273
Subject Index  277
Author Index  280

## TABLES

2-1 Frequency Distribution of Fifty Scores on a Test of English Grammar 15
2-2 Frequency Distribution and Cumulated Frequencies of Fifty Scores on an English Grammar Test 26
2-3 Frequency Distribution of 180 Scores Achieved on a Clerical Aptitude Test 35
2-4 $M$'s and $\sigma$'s Earned on Five Objective Tests of Educational Achievement Given in the Sixth Grade 37
3-1 Illustrative Tests from Stanford-Binet Scale for Years IV, X, XIV, and Average Adult 50–51
3-2 Numbers of Children in the School Population to Be Expected at Various IQ Levels 57
3-3 Educational Expectation in Relation to IQ Level 58
3-4 Intelligence Classification for WISC IQ's 75
9-1 Item Analysis of the First Five Items of a Test Made on Two Criterion Groups, the Highest and the Lowest 25 Percent in Total Score 239
10-1 Differential Aptitude Scores (Ninth-Grade Class) 245
10-2 Sociometric Tabulation 253
A-1 Frequency Distribution of Forty Scores on a Social Studies Test 258
A-2 Computation of the Mean from a Frequency Distribution 263
A-3 Computation of the Median and Q from a Frequency Distribution 265
A-4 Computation of the Standard Deviation ($\sigma$) from a Frequency Distribution 269
A-5 Correlation Between Reading and Arithmetic in the Fifth Grade 270

## FIGURES

2-1 Frequency Polygon of Fifty Scores Achieved by Seventh-Grade Children on a Test of English Grammar 16
2-2 Histogram of Fifty Scores Achieved by Seventh-Grade Pupils on a Test of English Grammar 17
2-3 The Normal Curve 18
2-4 Negatively Skewed Curve 19
2-5 Positively Skewed Curve 19
2-6 Two Distributions with the Same Mean but Differing Markedly in Range (Variability) 22
2-7 Areas Under the Normal Curve 24
2-8 Use of Normal Curve Model to Show Distribution of Sixty Scores on a Reading Text 25
2-9 Ogive or Cumulative Frequency Curve 27
2-10 Cumulative Frequency Polygon (Ogive) of 180 Scores Achieved on a Clerical Aptitude Test 36

TABLE OF CONTENTS vii

FIGURES

2–11 Profile of the Percentile Ranks in Various Subjects for a Given Child   36
3–1 Distribution of IQ's on the Stanford-Binet Scale for Nearly 3,000 Children, 2–18 Years Old   56
3–2 Test Materials Used in the Stanford-Binet Scale   Facing 56
3–3 Items from the Performance Part of the Wechsler Adult Intelligence Scale   Facing 56
3–4 Performance Tests Found in the Arthur Point Scale   Facing 57
3–5 Age-Progress Curves for the Stanford-Binet Scale   66
4–1 Illustrative Items from the Pinter-Cunningham Primary Test   87
4–2 Profile for the California Test of Mental Maturity   91
4–3 Sample Items from the Lorge-Thordike Intelligence Tests, Level 3, Form A, Non-Verbal Battery   95
4–4 Sample Items from the Terman-McNemar Test of Mental Ability (Form C)   97
4–5 Norms for Various Occupational Groups on the Army General Classification Test   105
5–1 Sample Items from the Stanford Achievement Test, Primary Battery, Form K   114
5–2 Profile Chart for the Metropolitan Achievement Tests   116
5–3 Student Profile to Illustrate the Use of Percentile Bands   123
5–4 Sample Items from Metropolitan Readiness Tests   129
5–5 Sample Multiple-Choice Items from the Cooperative Mathematics Test for Grades 7, 8 and 9   132
5–6 Sample Multiple-Choice Items from the Cooperative Science Test for Grades 7, 8 and 9   134
6–1 Sample Items from the MacQuarrie Test of Mechanical Ability   145
6–2 Samples from Bennett Mechanical Comprehension Test   147
6–3 Sample Items from the Differential Aptitude Tests   152
6–4 Sample Items from the Meier Art Judgment Test   Facing 152
6–5 Profile of a High-School Boy on the Differential Aptitude Tests   154
6–6 Sample Items from the Minnesota Paper Form Board Test   155
7–1 Sample Items from Various Graphic Rating Scales   171
7–2 Sample Items from the California Test of Personality, Elementary, Grades 4–5–6–7–8, Form AA   178
7–3 Specimen Items from a Study of Values   187
8–1 Objective-Test Items Represented by Picture, Drawing, or Diagram   200–201
9–1 Item Analysis Data for Test File   236
10–1 Sociogram for Twenty-One Kindergartners, Thirteen Boys and Eight Girls   255
A–1 Frequency Distribution of the Forty Scores in Table A–1   260
A–2 Histogram of the Forty Scores in Table A–1   261

## Chapter 1

# MENTAL TESTS IN THE SCHOOLS

### THE TEACHER AND MENTAL TESTS

The widespread use of standardized tests in today's schools render it increasingly necessary for the classroom teacher to be familiar with these devices, with what they are and what they do. Teachers often are required to administer and score tests and frequently to use these scores in the evaluation of pupil capabilities and future promise. This is essential, of course, if the standardized test is to have value in the work of the school. Most teachers, however, have no desire to become testing specialists or psychometricians, and many have little knowledge of modern statistical method. For these reasons, books dealing chiefly with the statistics of test construction and with other technical problems, while a necessary part of the training of school and clinical psychologists, often are not very useful to the teacher. In fact, they may leave him more confused than enlightened.

This book is planned to present a brief but comprehensive account of mental tests to teachers and other workers in education who do not plan to become specialists in this field. It is not a book on statistical method; it does not deal broadly with the history of testing, or with the applications of tests to problems of business and industry. Instead, it describes the various kinds of standardized tests, their uses and abuses, and how they supplement and aid the work of the classroom. It deals with the methods of constructing teacher-made tests and improving classroom examinations. Statistical terms necessary to an understanding of the tests themselves are defined and illustrated, but detailed calculations are not included in the text. The book's usefulness will be enhanced if the exercises and topics at the ends of the chapters are carefully worked through. It is highly desirable, too, that the instructor have the class examine, take, and score a number of tests. The discussion in a chapter will be clarified if there is actual familiarity with the tests described.

### What Mental Tests Are

In a mental test, the examinee is confronted with a variety of tasks—questions to be answered, problems to be solved, directions to be followed, and so on. Answers may be given orally, in writing, or sometimes by marking or manual manipulation, such as fitting blocks into apertures. Mental tests differ from physical tests, though there is a large overlap in the two kinds of measurement. Both varieties of tests require previous learning and both present problems, but the mental test—to a greater degree than the physical—demands verbal abstraction rather than action, ideas rather than muscles. Tests of physical fitness—of height, weight, and physical strength, for example—differ most markedly from mental tests; in other words, they are the most physical. Tests which require speed and accuracy of hand-eye or hand-ear coordination or which demand manual dexterity and skill (called sensory-motor tests) are both mental *and* physical. But none of these tests is as "mental" as the intelligence test or school examination in algebra or history, since none of them depends to so large a degree on verbal symbols.

The term *mental test* is sometimes restricted to the measurement of intelligence or aptitude, examinations in school subjects being classified as educational achievement tests. The reasoning here is that the mental test—the intelligence test, for example—tells us how much a child *can* learn, whereas the school examination tells us what he *has* learned. To some extent this is true, but the distinction between the two sorts of measurement is one of degree rather than of kind. No mental test measures potential ability except by way of performance. We possess no microscope by which we can discover the inherited qualities of a childs' brain or nervous system. The general intelligence test, to a greater degree than the school examination, measures potential ability because it draws more on native alertness than on routine school learning. But the school examination also draws on native alertness *as expressed in school learning,* and both sorts of test demand the use of symbols—words, diagrams, numbers, pictures. Accordingly, in this book the term *mental test* will be used to describe both sorts of examination.

The primary objective of a mental test is to detect individual differences—that is, to discover how one child compares or "stacks up" against another child of the same age, sex, or grade classification. This knowledge, as we shall see later, is useful in many ways in school and out. A second objective of the mental test is to discover *intra*-individual differences or the variations in performance *within* an individual. The scores made by an examinee, when put in comparable units and represented on a profile, provide a useful record of the examinee's strengths and weaknesses.

## A Classification of Mental Tests

In beginning the study of mental tests, it will be helpful to draw up a list of the different varieties of tests. Most widely used tests are *standardized* for procedure and results. A standardized educational achievement test, for example, is one that has been constructed in accordance with the best principles of test-making and has been administered to hundreds of pupils in those grades for which the test is suitable. Tests are always given and scored in a prescribed way. Results from standardized tests are expressed as *norms*. These are typical scores earned by large groups of children chosen to be representative of various ages and grades. For example, a score of 45 on a standard reading test may be the norm for children 9 years, 0 months old, or for children who are beginning the fourth grade.

The following outline gives some idea of the field to be covered and at the same time furnishes an overview of the chapters to follow.

VARIETIES OF MENTAL TESTS

I. Intelligence Tests
   (1) individual: administered to one examinee at a time
   (2) group: administered, like a school examination, to many examinees at the same time
   (3) performance: make little or no use of language, in contrast with the paper-and-pencil tests used in (1) and (2)

II. Educational Achievement Tests
   (1) survey: comprehensive examinations used to determine general academic standing
   (2) subject: examinations in specific fields—for example, physics, Spanish
   (3) diagnostic: cover a wide range of academic skills (in reading or arithmetic, for example) and are designed to reveal specific weaknesses and strengths

III. Aptitude Tests
   (1) general: for example, of mechanical ability or clerical ability
   (2) special: aptitude for school subjects—for example, chemistry or foreign languages; differential aptitudes
   (3) professional: for example, in law, medicine, engineering, teaching
   (4) talent: aptitude in such fields as art or music

IV. Test of Various Aspects of Personality
   (1) personal adjustment questionnaires: surveys of worries, fears, social inadequacies
   (2) attitude surveys: on, for example, social, economic and political questions
   (3) inventories of interests as related to various occupations
   (4) environmental factors related to personality; questionnaires covering socio-economic background and other variables
   (5) projective techniques: subtle and indirect measures of dominant motivational trends

All of these varieties of mental test will be treated in subsequent chapters. The following sections of this chapter provide a brief outline of the development of psychological testing in order to clear the ground for later work. For a more complete discussion of the historical development of mental tests, the student should consult references at the end of this chapter.

THE BEGINNINGS OF MENTAL TESTS

Interest in psychological testing developed in Germany and France about the middle of the last century. This interest grew out of the acute need for a better understanding of feeblemindedness and the various forms of insanity. Tests were devised for the purpose of determining *what* the feebleminded person can learn, *how much* he can learn, and in what respects he differs most drastically from the normal. In the case of the insane and the mentally deteriorated, brief tests were drawn up for assessing loss of memory, distortions of perception, distractibility, mental fatigue, and changes in such sensory-motor functions as speed and accuracy of motor responses.

In England, interest in mental testing arose from the study of individual differences in mental and physical functions. The leader in this movement was Sir Francis Galton, an eminent geneticist, who set up a testing laboratory in London in 1882. Here, for a small fee, a person could have the keenness of his vision and hearing tested, as well as his muscular strength and speed and coordination of response. Galton's tests were quite brief, and sampled rather narrow aspects of behavior. In fact, they were *sensory-motor* rather than strictly mental in character. One of the first American psychologists to become interested in mental testing was James McKeen Cattell. Cattell introduced mental tests of the Galton type in this country at the turn of the century.

**INTELLIGENCE TESTS: INDIVIDUAL**

The individual intelligence test as we know it today grew out of the work of Alfred Binet, a French psychologist, who was director of the laboratory for physiological psychology at the Sorbonne. In 1904 Binet was asked to devise a mental test for detecting slow learners in the schools of Paris. The test was to be used not only to sift out the subnormal children in the grades but also to provide a better understanding of *degrees* of feeblemindedness, with a view to improving the education of these children. In 1905, Binet and a collaborator, Théophile Simon, brought out the first scale for measuring intelligence. This scale consisted of thirty problems and questions arranged in order from easy to difficult. A second edition of Binet's Scale appeared in 1908, and a third and final edition in 1911. These tests differed sharply from those of Galton. Binet was interested in determining the intellectual level of school children, not, as was

Galton, in studying differences among individuals in fairly narrow mental and sensory-motor functions. In order to measure intelligence, Binet believed he must get tests which would measure a child's memory, comprehension, judgment, and insight. He avoided questions which demanded specific and routine school learning. For example, instead of asking the examinee the product of 6 × 3 or the name of the largest city in France, Binet asked the child to repeat four digits (single numbers) or the words of a sentence (heard only once); to tell the "thing to do" in specific problem situations; to criticize ("see through") an absurd statement or fallacy; to give differences between, for instance, a president and a king; to define abstract words like *justice* and *loyalty*.

Binet's famous tests became the basis for the widely used Stanford Revision of the Binet-Simon Scale, described in Chapter 3. To Binet belongs the credit for having set up the first *age scale*—that is, a test series in which items are arranged or grouped by age levels. A child's "score" on an age scale is determined by the level attained and is expressed by a mental age (MA), which denotes the child's maturity.

The Binet-type intelligence scale with its mental age units has been most widely used in the United States. The first Stanford Revision was in 1916, the second in 1937, and a third "edition," made up of best items in the second revision, in 1960. Millions of these tests have been given in schools.

Children of preschool age are unable to do tests which require reading and word knowledge. For these children, therefore, as well as for children handicapped in speech, vision, or hearing, and for the non-English speaking, *performance* tests must be used. In a typical performance test, the child is asked to identify common objects, string beads, build towers of blocks; or he may be asked to fit blocks into cutouts, arrange pictures in sequence, match the colors of cubes. Performance tests have been devised for use with illiterate and less intelligent adults as well as with children.

INTELLIGENCE TESTS: GROUP

When intelligence tests are administered to large groups of examinees at the same time, they are appropriately called "group tests." The first group tests were developed (in 1917) during World War I. Together with other information, these tests were used by the Army (1) in accepting or rejecting men, (2) in the classification of those accepted, (3) in the assignment of draftees to various types of service, and (4) in determining admission of candidates to officer training schools. Actually, there were two tests, the Army Alpha and Army Beta. The first was intended for soldiers who could read and write. It required that an examinee follow fairly involved directions, solve "mental arithmetic" problems, know the meanings of words, and perceive relations (for example, in an analogies test the question might be as follows: *Hand is to foot as glove is to ....?...* ). Army Beta was a non-language or non-verbal test. It made use only of diagrams, pictures, and numbers and was answered by a simple system of marking. Army Beta was administered to the illiterate and the foreign-born. Directions were given in pantomime for the benefit of those soldiers who did not understand English.

During World War II, a group intelligence test called the Army General Classification Test (AGCT) was administered to some 12 million men. AGCT, a verbal or language test, includes three sorts of materials: verbal (vocabulary), numerical (arithmetic problems), and spatial (for example, problems in spatial relations presented by pictures of block piles to be "counted" by the examinee). No specific "school" questions were asked, since the test was designed to measure mental alertness in dealing with symbolic materials apart from specific training. Both Alpha and AGCT are still used in the testing of adults.

Between World Wars I and II, scores of group tests of intelligence were constructed and used widely in the schools and colleges. These and other mental tests (aptitude, personality) have been widely employed in business and industry as an aid in the selection and placement of personnel.

In most group intelligence examinations, items are answered by marking one of several possible solutions (multiple-choice), by selecting one of two answers (true-false), or by checking or underlining the appropriate reply among several options. These answer techniques are called "objective" (page 198), because in scoring such tests the judgment of the examiner does not enter in—or does so to a very slight degree. Group tests of intelligence are treated in Chapter 4.

## Educational Achievement Tests

Since World War I, a number of tests of educational achievement have been constructed on objective principles. These tests are used to determine general educational level or standing, as well as knowledge of a given subject field—for example, geometry or French. The general survey test, when used in the elementary school, is a comprehensive examination of the student's knowledge of reading, spelling, arithmetic, grammar and literature, history, and elementary science. Tests in separate subjects —history or physics, for example—are also available for secondary school and college. Educational achievement tests are called *diagnostic* when they are used to reveal a student's weaknesses in a particular area such as arithmetic or reading. Diagnostic tests must of necessity cover a wide range of information and skills in a given subject. Educational achievement tests are described in Chapter 5.

## Aptitude Tests

Tests designed to discover whether a student is "gifted" in music or mathematics, say, or whether a young man has the knack for dealing with tools and mechanical contrivances are called aptitude tests. Aptitude may be inferred (1) from the degree of mastery attained in a "new" subject after a period of study. Aptitude for a foreign language, for instance, is demonstrated in the ease with which the subject (Spanish, for example) is acquired after a term's work. Achievement tests, given after a period of "exposure," reveal this aptitude directly. Aptitude is also inferred *before* a period of study by testing (2) to see whether an examinee possesses those abilities and skills judged to make for success in a given subject (for example, physics), or in a profession (for example, medicine or law). Aptitude for physics is gauged by finding how well the student has learned the mathematics necessary for work in physics; aptitude for law is judged by the student's ability to read difficult prose, comprehend fairly involved legal arguments, and follow a line of reasoning to a conclusion. What are called "differential aptitude tests" are designed to assess a student's strengths and weaknesses in certain fundamental abilities believed to be crucial in a number of activities—in and out of school.

Tests of general mechanical aptitude sample performance in a number of activities believed to demonstrate mechanical knowledge and skill. Factors measured by these tests include familiarity with tools, insight into mechanical relations (pulleys, levers, and the like), ability to solve problems expressed in diagrams of machines and mechanical contrivances, and interest in mechanical things, as shown by the reading of popular science, building radios, tinkering with cars, and so on. Manipulative tasks and mechanical gadgets have been employed to test for special abilities in a variety of situations. Among the traits studied are manual dexterity, sensory-motor skills, and visual and auditory acuity, all of which are needed in many jobs in industry and in the armed forces.

Clerical aptitude tests assess the knowledge and skills needed in a business office. Tests of this kind provide scores which can be used to predict an examinee's ability to carry out the written work of an office—to write reports, check records, read and write easily and accurately. Clerical ability embraces a wide range of activities, from the high level work of the confidential secretary to the routine duties of the relatively unskilled office clerk. No single test, of course, covers the gamut of clerical aptitude. Such tests are most useful when combined with other tests (intelligence, educational achievement, personality), the difficulty and level of the test combination depending on the requirements of the job.

Aptitude tests of a special sort have been devised for judging talent in art and music. In music, for instance, many of the factors needed for success can be measured: "ear" for music, rapid and accurate reading of music at sight, and knowledge of harmony and other technical matters. In art, "taste" for color, form, symmetry, and other artistic dimensions are determined by comparing a student's judgments with those of acknowledged experts. Knowing whether a person possesses talent in art or music is often highly important in educational and vocational guidance. Aptitude tests are treated in Chapter 6.

## Personality Tests

Psychologists have used the questionnaire or inventory to determine personality factors in three areas: (a) personal adjustment, (b) attitudes, and (c) interests. In addition, questionnaires have been used in the social sciences to survey socio-economic, home, and community phenomena. "Tests" of personality are in reality standard interviews designed to reveal characteristic ways of behaving. The personal adjustment questionnaire or personal data sheet inquires into a person's fears, worries, anxieties, and home and work adjustments. Such inventories are often appropriately called "trouble sheets." In some cases, the questions are direct and undisguised: "Are you afraid of high places?" "Can you stand the sight of blood?" "Do your parents treat you right?" In other adjustment inventories, questions are disguised and indirect, so that the *intent* of the question may not be understood by the examinee. A technique often used in such inventories is that of "forced choices" (page 182).

Attitude questionnaires attempt to reveal systematic ways of behaving or thinking about social, religious, or political matters. Can a student be classified as narrow- or broad-minded, religious or irreligious, or somewhere between these extremes? Attitude inventories try to answer these questions.

Interest inventories survey a person's interests in books, sports, people, occupations, social activities, and the like. An examinee's pattern of interests may serve to identify him with some well-defined occupational group—for example, lawyers or chemists. Or a young man's interests may identify him with some *area* of interests, such as science, business, or social service. Interest tests are especially valuable in counseling, since interest, as much as ability, may determine a student's educational or vocational choices.

Another group of personality tests makes use of what have been called "projective" techniques. Projective tests are disguised interviews in which an examinee is asked what he "sees" in some neutral situation—an ink blot or a picture, for example. These tests are perhaps most useful in the diagnosis of disturbed mental states. They must be administered by an expert and are employed mostly by psychiatrists and clinical psychologists in severe behavior problems.

The techniques of the personality questionnaire have been widely used in polls conducted to assess public opinion about such things as political issues and social questions. Inventories also have been employed to survey systematically the association between items in a constellation of attitudes or opinions—for instance, between social and economic background factors, preferences for political candidates and so on, and views about social and economic issues. In sociological studies in which environmental factors loom large, the kind of home from which a child comes, the educational and occupational status of the parents, and the character of the community may be revealed by a systematic survey of background variables. Personality tests are treated in Chapter 7.

## How Mental Tests Are Used in the Schools

As we have said, the primary function of the mental test is to reveal individual differences. More specifically mental tests are useful to the teacher in three ways. *First,* mental tests aid in the evaluation of class performance in relation to established norms (page 124). *Second,* tests reveal the strengths and weaknesses of individual pupils, that is, are useful in educational diagnosis (page 125). *Finally,* tests enable the teacher to discover whether a pupil possesses aptitude for a given subject or course of study, and to predict his probable success in college or professional school. We shall consider these three objectives in the chapters to follow.

## SUGGESTIONS FOR FURTHER READING

Comprehensive accounts of the development of mental testing and of the application of tests in various areas will be found in the references below:

ANASTASI, A. *Psychological Testing.* 2nd. ed.; New York: Macmillan, 1961.
FREEMAN, F. S. *Theory and Practice of Psychological Testing.* Rev. ed.; New York: Holt, 1955.
ROSS, C. C. and STANLEY, J. C. *Measurement in Today's Schools.* 3rd ed.; New York: Prentice-Hall, 1954.
THORNDIKE, R. L. and HAGEN, ELIZABETH. *Measurement and Evaluation in Psychology and Education.* 2nd ed.; New York: Wiley, 1961.

## Chapter 2

## STATISTICS IN MENTAL TESTING

The purpose of this chapter is to acquaint the prospective user of mental tests with those statistical terms and techniques most often used in testing. Throughout the chapter stress will be placed on the meaning and significance of symbols and terms rather than on the mechanics of computation. For the latter, the student should consult the Appendix (pages 257–271) as well as the books on statistical method listed at the end of this chapter.

Perhaps the best advice that can be offered to the teacher who is planning to use mental tests is that he first take a course in statistics. For students who have been wise enough to do so, the present treatment will constitute simply a brief review and summary. For those who have had no statistical training, it will provide the minimum essentials for understanding and evaluating the mental tests themselves.

## THE FREQUENCY DISTRIBUTION

DRAWING UP A FREQUENCY DISTRIBUTION

Suppose that a teacher has administered a test of English grammar to fifty children in the seventh grade. The papers have been marked and the names and scores of the children recorded. Two questions arise: (1) What is the *typical* performance of the class, and (2) What is the *range of talent* in the class? To answer these questions, we may organize and present the fifty scores in several ways.

Table 2–1 is a systematic tabulation of the fifty English grammar scores into what is called a *frequency* distribution. The scores have been arranged from high to low into sets of five under the heading "Scores." In the frequency column headed "f" are listed the numbers of scores which fall into each subgroup. For example, five children score in the interval 60–64, eight in the interval 55–59, and so on down to four who score in the bottom interval, 30–34.

A test score is always taken to represent the distance along some scale of ability running from low to high. Thus, a score of 46 covers the span from 45.5 to 46.5, 46.0 itself being the middle

*TABLE 2–1*

*Frequency Distribution of Fifty Scores on a Test of English Grammar*

| Scores | f |
|---|---|
| 60 – 64 | 5 |
| 55 – 59 | 8 |
| 50 – 54 | 10 |
| 45 – 49 | 12 |
| 40 – 44 | 6 |
| 35 – 39 | 5 |
| 30 – 34 | 4 |
|  | $N = 50$ |

of the score interval. Other scores have the same meaning: in each case the score covers the distance .5 unit *below* to .5 unit *above* the face value of the given score. This definition of a score means, of course, that the interval 30–34 begins at 29.5 and ends at 34.5, that interval 35–39 begins at 34.5 and ends at 39.5, and so on. For convenience in writing, the intervals in Table 2–1 are the score limits rather than the exact limits. In each case, however, the exact limits of the intervals are understood.

### GRAPHIC REPRESENTATION OF THE FREQUENCY DISTRIBUTION

A frequency distribution may be represented graphically by a *frequency polygon,* as shown in Figure 2–1. In the construction of a frequency polygon, scores are laid off along the baseline, or X-axis, at equal intervals, and the frequencies ($f$'s) are plotted on the vertical or Y-axis. Each $f$ is plotted directly above the midpoint of the interval on which it falls. The four scores falling in the first grouping, 30–34, are plotted above 32, the midpoint of the interval. In the other intervals (reading up), five scores are plotted above 37, midpoint of 35–39, six above 42, twelve above 47, and so on. The points are joined with short straight lines to give the outline of the frequency polygon.

Figure 2–1   *Frequency Polygon of Fifty Scores Achieved by Seventh-Grade Children on a Test of English Grammar*

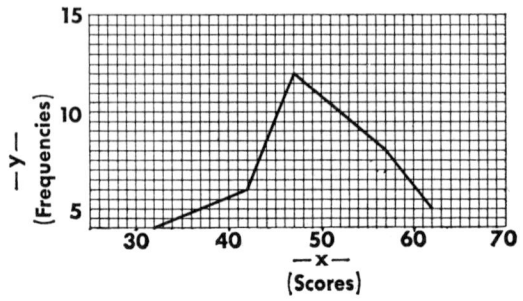

GRAPHIC REPRESENTATION OF THE FREQUENCY DISTRIBUTION  17

A frequency polygon shows graphically how the scores are spread over the test scale from low to high. From Figure 2–1 it is apparent that more children scored in the middle of the scale (see, for example, the 12 on interval 45–49) than at either extreme. Rules for constructing a frequency polygon that will provide a good picture of the test data will be found in the Appendix.

Another way of representing a frequency distribution graphically is the histogram. Figure 2–2 represents the $f$'s on the score intervals by small rectangles set up over each interval. For the first interval the rectangle is four Y-units high, for the second interval five Y-units high, and so on. The highest rectangle, twelve units on the Y-axis, is above interval 45–49.

The histogram and frequency polygon represent the same facts, and there is little to choose between them. Frequency polygons are to be preferred to histograms when two distributions are plotted on the *same axes*, since in the histogram the vertical and horizontal lines often coincide, making the figures difficult to disentangle.

Figure 2–2   *Histogram of Fifty Scores Achieved by Seventh-Grade Pupils on a Test of English Grammar*

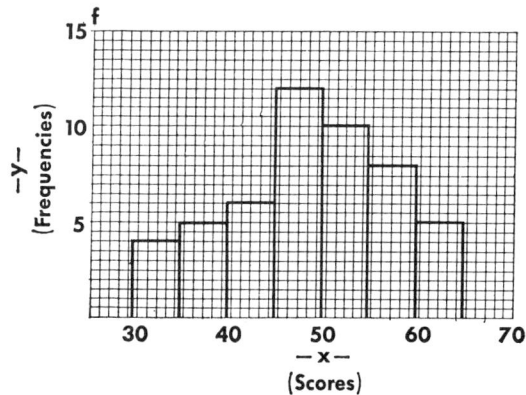

## The Normal Curve

The symmetrical bell-shaped graph shown in Figure 2–3 is the well-known *normal curve*. This "ideal" frequency polygon is the mathematical model which many distributions of actual scores approximate. (See, for example, Figure 2–1.) The normal curve is often called the *normal probability curve* because it shows the probability of occurrence of scores of different size when these are determined by a large number of independent and randomly combined factors.

The normal curve has played an important role in the development of mental measurement. Among its uses in testing may be mentioned the following:

1. **Selecting the Items of a Test.** When the distribution of test scores for a class is badly off-center or "skewed," as shown in Figure 2–4 and 2–5, the test is not suitable for the group. In Figure 2–4 the test is too easy—there are too many high scores; and in Figure 2–5 the test is too hard—there is a disproportionate number of low scores. When the test maker takes the normal curve as his model, questions and problems are carefully se-

Figure 2–3  *The Normal Curve*

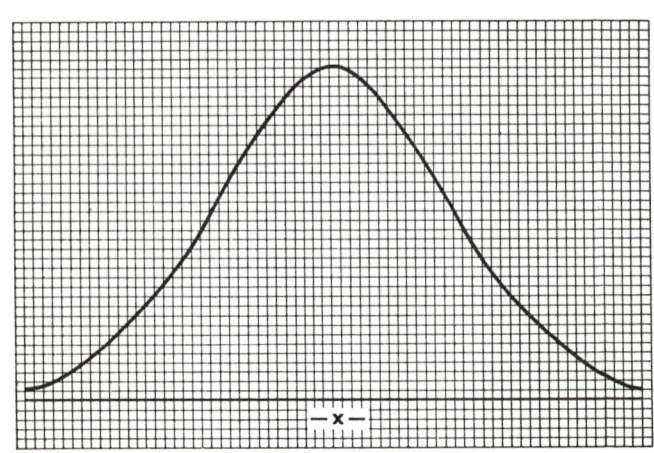

*Figure 2–4  Negatively Skewed Curve*

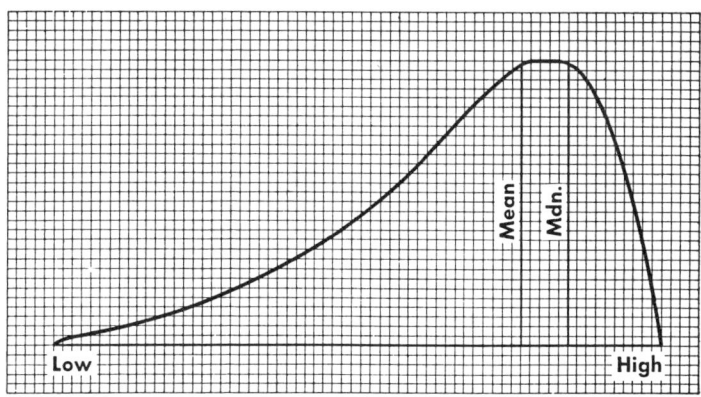

*Figure 2–5  Positively Skewed Curve*

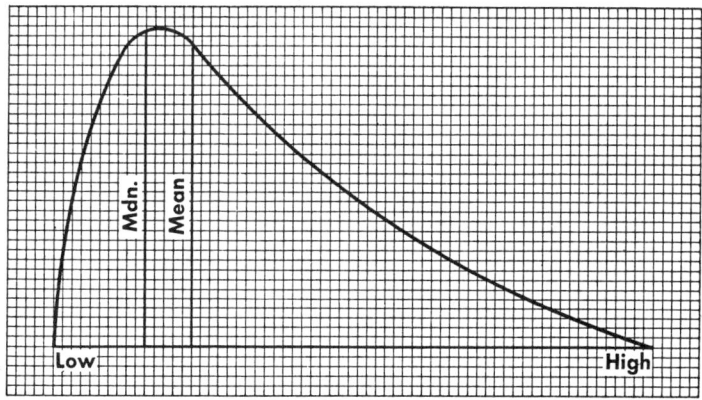

lected and their scoring adjusted to give a symmetrical arrangement of test scores like that of the normal curve. This means that a majority of pupils score at the middle of the scale and a smaller number score at the high and low ends. Note that, according to the criterion of normality, the frequency polygon in Figure 2–1 shows the English grammar test to be generally satisfactory, though perhaps a bit too easy.

**2. Scaling the Obtained Scores from a Test.** Raw scores (scores obtained on a test) are usually expressed by an arbitrary number of points. Scores of this sort do not represent equal steps or equal units along some ability scale; and since there is no zero point, a score of 40 is not twice as good as a score of 20. When point scores are transformed into deviations from the average or mean and expressed in units of the standard deviation (page 37) of the group, they are called *sigma-scores*. The unit of deviation (the standard deviation) is usually represented by the Greek letter $\sigma$ (sigma). Sigma-scores may later be converted into standard scores (page 38). Many educational achievement and aptitude tests publish norms (page 42) on the basis of standard scores. These scores are comparable from test to test when distributions are normal, or approximately so.

Point scores may also be changed over directly into equal-unit scores in a normal distribution. Such "normalized" scores have several advantages (page 41).

**3. Determining the Stability of a Test Score.** An obtained score on a test—for example, a group test IQ—can be expected to vary up or down to some degree when the test is administered a second time. The variation to be expected in a score—that is, its probable stability—can be predicted from formulas and from tables of the normal probability curve (page 24).

## AVERAGES

After a frequency distribution has been tabulated, we are ready to compute a typical measure or average. There are three sorts of averages—also called measures of central tendency—in common use.

### THE MEAN ($M$)

Given a set of ten scores, 10, 9, 10, 12, 8, 6, 4, 7, 5, and 4, the mean is simply 7.5—found by adding the scores (75) and dividing this sum by their number (10). The $M$ is popularly called the average. When scores have been grouped into a frequency distribution, as shown in Table 2–1 on page 15, a slightly different method is employed in finding the $M$ (see Appendix), but the $M$ is always essentially the sum of the scores divided by their number.

### The Median ($Mdn$)

When scores are arranged in order of size, another sort of average, the *median* ($Mdn$), can be found. This is the *point* in the distribution obtained by counting off one-half of the scores from either end of the series. We usually start with the low end. For example, for the five scores 7, 8, 9, 10, and 12, the median or mid-score is 9; there are two scores above and two below it. When the number of scores is even—for example, 5, 7, 8, 9, 10, and 12—the median is midway between the two middlemost scores, or 8.5. There is no mid-score. When scores are grouped into a frequency distribution, as shown in Table 2–1 on page 15, the median is still the 50 percent point—the point found by counting 50 percent of the way into the distribution. For a method of computing the median, see the Appendix.

### The Mode

That score or set of scores which occurs most frequently is called the *crude mode,* or the modal score. The crude mode is a third sort of average. In Table 2–1 the crude mode is taken at 47, midpoint of the interval which contains the largest frequency. The mode can be computed more exactly, but usually we simply take the most often recurring score as the crude mode without further refinement. In most cases, the mode is a preliminary measure of central tendency. It does not need to be computed so precisely as the mean or median.

## MEASURES OF VARIABILITY

THE RANGE

It is sometimes more important to know the variability of a set of scores than to know the mean or median. Suppose, for example, that two sections of Grade 7 have the same mean but differ markedly in spread of talent, as evidenced in the variability of scores around the mean. Figure 2–6 shows two distributions of this sort: the scores in A range from 40 to 60, and the scores in B range from 20 to 80. The difference between the high and low scores in the A distribution is 20 points; in the B distribution it is 60 points. The *range* is the most general index of variability. Other more exact measures are the standard deviation (written as SD or $\sigma$) and the quartile deviation (written as Q).

THE STANDARD DEVIATION ($\sigma$)

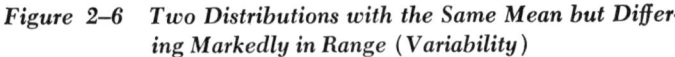

The mean of the set of five scores—12, 10, 8, 6, and 4—is 8. If 8 is subtracted from each score, we have $12 - 8 = 4$, $10 - 8 = 2$,

Figure 2–6   *Two Distributions with the Same Mean but Differing Markedly in Range (Variability)*

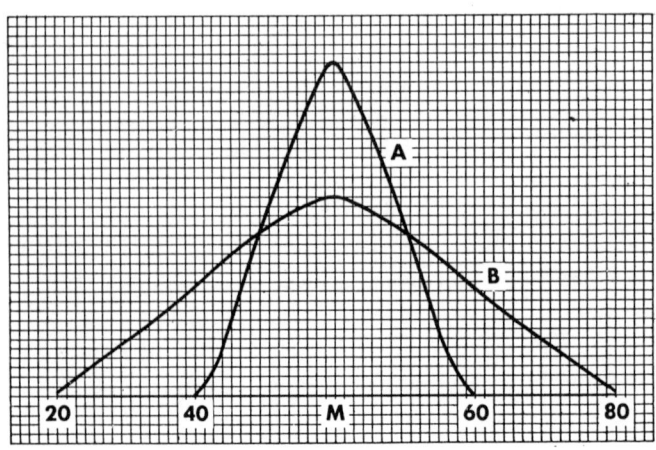

$8 - 8 = 0$, $6 - 8 = -2$, and $4 - 8 = -4$. The *size* of a deviation from $M$ tells the extent to which the individual score deviates from the common mean; and the *sign* of the deviation indicates its direction from $M$. If each deviation is now squared, we have $4^2 = 16$, $2^2 = 4$, $(-2)^2 = 4$, and $(-4)^2 = 16$. The square of 0 is, of course, 0. The sum of these squared deviations is 40, and $\sigma$, the standard deviation, is defined as

$$\sigma = \sqrt{\frac{(\text{deviations})^2}{N}}$$

or, in our example,

$$\sigma = \sqrt{40/5} = \sqrt{8}$$
$$\sigma = 2.83^1$$

Squaring the separate deviations around the $M$ eliminates the minus signs and gives extra weight to extreme deviations. A SD or $\sigma$ is judged to be large or small (to reflect much or little variation) in relation to other SD's computed for the same test. For example, if thirty-five boys and forty-two girls have the same $M$ on a history test but the boys' $\sigma$ is 10 and the girls' $\sigma$ is 6, we know that the boys' scores spread more than the girls' up and down the scale—in both directions from the mean.

In the normal curve, $\sigma$ provides valuable information concerning the way in which the separate measures fall around the common mean. In Figure 2–7, for example, $3\sigma$ is seen to include virtually all the measures above the $M$, and $-3\sigma$ all of the measures below the $M$. The total area of the normal curve is taken as $N$. From tables of the area of the normal curve, we know that approximately 34 percent of the measures (actually 34.13 percent) are between $M$ and $1\sigma$; and that 34 percent of the measures are between $M$ and $-1\sigma$. The two "halves" of the curve are equal. Hence we find about 68 percent of the measures—roughly two thirds—between $M$ and $\pm 1\sigma$. Furthermore, from tables we find that 14 percent of the measures fall between $1\sigma$ and $2\sigma$ in the normal curve and about 2 percent between $2\sigma$ and $3\sigma$. The same proportions hold, of course, for the half of the

[1] For calculation of $\sigma$ from a frequency distribution, see Appendix.

*Figure 2–7   Areas Under the Normal Curve*

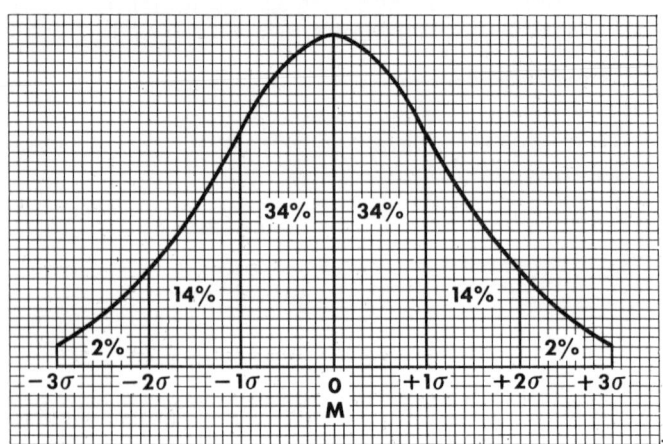

curve to the left of the *M*, since the *M* divides the area of the normal curve into two equal parts.

The relations of $\sigma$ to the total area ($N$) in the normal curve model hold approximately for distributions which resemble the normal curve in form. Figure 2–8 will make clear how the normal curve model is used in such cases.

Suppose that on a reading test administered to sixty children in the fifth grade, the $M = 62$ and $\sigma = 8$; and suppose further that the frequency polygon of these scores closely resembles the normal curve in form. Taking the normal curve as our model, then, we can say that approximately two thirds of the scores (that is, forty) fall between 54 and 70 ($62 \pm 8$). Moreover, about 14 percent of the scores, or about 8, will fall between 70 and 78 (between $1\sigma$ and $2\sigma$), and about 2 percent or 1 or 2 will fall between 78 and 86 (that is, between $2\sigma$ and $3\sigma$). In the lower half of the distribution, 14 percent, or 8 scores, will fall between 54 and 46, and 2 percent between 46 and 38. These relationships are shown in Figure 2–8. Note that *M*, the reference point, is 62 and $\sigma$ is eight units on the test scale.

*Figure 2–8 Use of Normal Curve Model to Show Distribution of Sixty Scores on a Reading Test*

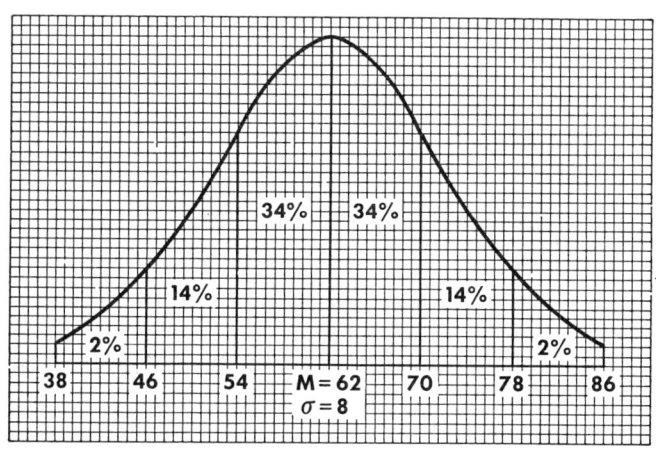

## THE QUARTILE DEVIATION (Q)

Just as we compute the median by counting off 50 percent of the scores, so we can count off 25 percent of the scores from the low end of the distribution (that is, 25 percent of $N$) to locate $Q_1$, the first quartile point. Similarly, we can count off 75 percent of the scores from the low end of the distribution to locate $Q_3$, the third quartile. The gap between $Q_3$, the third quartile, and $Q_1$ is called the interquartile range, or range of the middle 50 percent. Q, the semi-interquartile range, is computed as follows:

$$Q = \frac{Q_3 - Q_1}{2}$$

Like $\sigma$, Q is a measure of variability but, unlike $\sigma$, it is found by counting into the distribution, whereas $\sigma$ is computed from the squared deviations taken around the $M$. When the median is the measure of central tendency, we generally use Q; when $M$ is the measure of central tendency, we use $\sigma$.

Methods of computing Q from a frequency distribution will be found in the Appendix. Here we are concerned primarily with the meaning of Q as a measure of variability. Q's usefulness will become clearer when we have computed the percentile curve, or *ogive*.

## PERCENTILES AND PERCENTILE RANK

Table 2–2 shows the frequency distribution of Table 2–1, with the addition of two columns in which the $f$'s have been cumulated. In column (3), scores have been added progressively—cumulated—from the bottom to the top of the distribution. On the first interval, 4 is the entry; $4 + 5$ on the next interval gives 9; $9 + 6$ on the third interval gives 15; and so on. In column (4), these cumulated scores are expressed as percentages of $N$. In Figure 2–9, cumulated $f$'s in percentages have been plotted against the score-intervals laid off along the baseline. As scores are added over each interval, each percent cum.$f$ is plotted just above the *upper* limit of the interval in which it falls. The resulting S-shaped curve is called an *ogive*, or cumu-

*TABLE 2–2*

*Frequency Distribution and Cumulated Frequencies of Fifty Scores on an English Grammar Test*
(*Data are the fifty scores in Table 2–1.*)

| (1) Scores | (2) $f$ | (3) cum.$f$ | (4) % cum.$f$ |
|---|---|---|---|
| 60 – 64 | 5 | 50 | 100 |
| 55 – 59 | 8 | 45 | 90 |
| 50 – 54 | 10 | 37 | 74 |
| 45 – 49 | 12 | 27 | 54 |
| 40 – 44 | 6 | 15 | 30 |
| 35 – 39 | 5 | 9 | 18 |
| 30 – 34 | 4 | 4 | 8 |
|  | $N = 50$ |  |  |

*Figure 2–9  Ogive or Cumulative Frequency Curve*

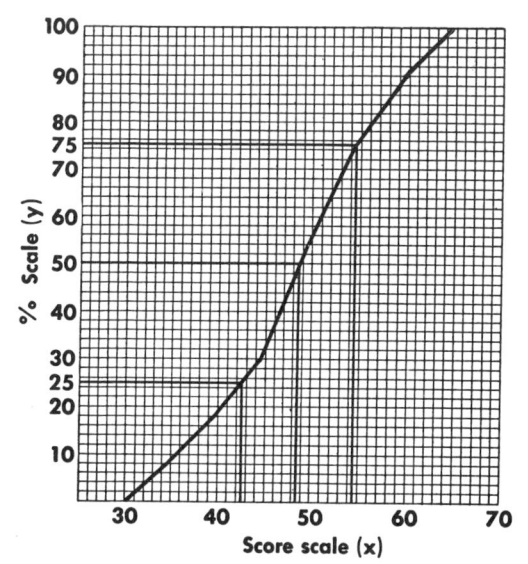

lative frequency graph. The ogive constricts or expands the scale of scores into a scale of one hundred points, called a *percentile scale*. The median and the Q's can be read from the ogive almost as accurately as they can be computed from a frequency distribution. To illustrate: if a line is run from the 50 percent point on the Y-scale across to the curve, a perpendicular dropped from this point to the score-scale locates *Mdn* at approximately 49. (The computed value is 48.66.) The twenty-fifth percentile, or Q1, is located from the ogive at approximately 42; and the seventy-fifth percentile, or Q3, at about 55. Other percentile points (for example, $P_{38}$ or $P_{63}$) can be located in the same manner by going from the appropriate point on the vertical percentage scale across to the ogive and dropping a perpendicular to the baseline. Note that the distance from Q3 to Q1 (that is, 55–42) is the interquartile range or range of the "middle 50." One-half of this distance is 13/2, or 6.5, which is the quartile deviation, or Q. The larger the Q of a distribution, the greater the spread of the middle 50 percent of scores along the scale and the larger the variability.

A pupil's percentile rank (PR) is the position on the percentile scale (on a scale of one hundred points) to which his score entitles him. Suppose that Tom Brown achieves a score of 40 on our English grammar test. What is his PR? Going out to 40 on the score-scale on the baseline, up to the curve, and then across to the Y-scale, we locate Tom's PR at about 20. This PR tells us at once that about 20 percent of the pupils scored lower than Tom. If Mary Green scores 58 on the grammar test, her PR is read at approximately 84—and 84 percent of the class made lower scores than she did. Scores achieved on tests expressed in different units—for example, a reading test and an arithmetic test—cannot be compared directly. But relative positions (PR's) of a child in his classes can be quickly determined and compared when both sets of scores have been converted into a common percentile scale. Moreover, several PR's may be combined to give a general index.

## CORRELATION[2]

The relationship between two sets of test scores can be described mathematically by the coefficient of correlation between them. Correlation is expressed by a decimal fraction (called $r$), which may vary along a scale from 0.00 to ± 1.00. Suppose that tests in English grammar and in history have been administered to the same seventh-grade class. Suppose further that children who score high in the English test tend to score high in history, and that children scoring fairly high or quite low in English tend to score fairly high or quite low in history. When this happens, the coefficient of correlation between the two sets of scores will be marked or substantial—for example, .60 to .70. Now suppose that most pupils who score high in English gram-

[2] See Appendix for computation of a correlation coefficient.

mar score only average in arithmetic. The correlation between these two areas will be low—perhaps no more than from .20 to .30. If those pupils who score high in English grammar tend to earn very low scores on a test in shop work, the correlation will be close to zero, or perhaps negative.

Positive coefficients of correlation run from .00 to + 1.00; good scores in the one test go with good scores in the other. Negative coefficients of correlation run from .00 to − 1.00 (denote inverse relationship), and good scores in the first test go with poor scores in the second. Zero correlation denotes no relationship between two variables.

Whether a correlation coefficient is to be regarded as high or low depends upon a number of factors. The correlation of height with weight in school children is generally high—around .70 for a given age level. The correlation of a good intelligence test and school grades will fall typically between .50 and .70; and the correlations between personality traits (from questionnaires) and school achievement are usually low and often negative. The following table will aid in interpreting coefficients of correlation:

| | |
|---|---|
| $r$'s from  .00 to ± .20 | very low; negligible |
| $r$'s from ± .20 to ± .40 | low; present but slight |
| $r$'s from ± .40 to ± .70 | substantial or marked |
| $r$'s from ± .70 to ± 1.00 | high to very high |

When computing the correlation between two forms of the same test (the self-correlation of the test), we demand much higher $r$'s than are found typically between different variables.

### The Reliability of a Test

**The Reliability Coefficient.** One important application of correlation to mental testing is in the determination of the reliability of a test. Test reliability refers to the stability of test scores. If a child achieves a score of 48, for example, on a highly reliable test of general science, subsequent scores earned by this pupil on equivalent forms of this test should not differ greatly from the initial score of 48. If the test is unreliable, however, in repeated testing the score may vary widely from its first determination.

The reliability coefficient of a test is found by computing the self-correlation of the test. Suppose that a reading examination has been given to five sixth-grade classes and that two weeks later the same test or an equivalent form is administered to the same classes. If the correlation between these two administrations of the test is high (and a *reliability* coefficient must be .90 or more to be considered high), we may feel confident that scores earned by pupils in this class are reasonably accurate measures of "true" ability.

Test reliability is sometimes determined by repeating a test and correlating the second set of scores against the first set. This method is followed when there is only one form of the test. More often, an equivalent or parallel form of the test is given, and the reliability coefficient is the $r$ between the test and its alternate form. The reliability coefficients of many standard educational tests have been determined in this way. Other means of determining test reliability will be found in the references at the end of the chapter. Usually the authors of standard tests will specify what method has been used in computing the reliability of their tests.

**The Standard Error of a Score.** The accuracy or *precision* of an individual score is perhaps best expressed by the *standard error of a score*, which is also called the standard error of measurement. The SE (standard error) is calculated by the following formula:

$$\text{SE (score)} = \sigma \sqrt{1 - r_{11}}$$

where $\sigma$ is the standard deviation of the test scores and $r_{11}$ is the reliability coefficient of the test. Suppose that the $\sigma$ of a set of test scores is 10 and the reliability coefficient ($r_{11}$) is .95. Then the SE of a score on this test is SE = 10 $\sqrt{1 - .95}$ or 2.2. This may be interpreted to mean that if a child takes this test a second time, the chances are good (about 7 in 10) that his "new" score will not diverge by more than ± 2 points from the true determination. The SE of a Stanford-Binet IQ is 4.5 points for IQ's from 90 to 110. In other words, if the test is repeated, we can expect a child's IQ to stay within 4 to 5 points of its true value.

Reliability coefficients of standard intelligence and educational achievement tests are generally above .90 for large groups of pupils. The size of the reliability coefficient depends on several factors: the variability of the group, the length of the test, the method used in determining reliability. A reliability coefficient of .50 in a single grade or class may indicate as much stability of score as a reliability coefficient of .90 in a large group. The great advantage of the SE of a score is that it takes account of both the reliability coefficient *and* the variability (SD) in the group. (See page 59.)

### The Validity of a Test

A mental test is a valid testing device when it measures what it claims to measure. Tests are not valid for all areas and all situations, but are valid in certain defined situations and for certain behaviors. A group intelligence test, for example, is not a valid measure of emotional control or of delinquent behavior. Validity may be classified, for convenience, into three types: *experimental, content,* and *predictive*. The validity of an intelligence test is determined experimentally by computing the test's correlation with various criteria: school grades, ratings for mental alertness, and other measures of intellect. Many of the best tests of general intelligence have been validated against the Stanford-Binet, the best known individual intelligence test (page 49). Aptitude tests—for example, those of clerical and mechanical aptitudes—are validated against demonstrated proficiency in office work or in mechanical tasks. Independent measures against which tests are validated are called *criteria*.

Criteria do not represent entirely adequate or completely sufficient determinations of a trait. Insofar as criteria incorporate valuable aspects of the behavior we are studying, they represent variables with which a test, to be valid, must correlate positively.

Tests of educational achievement in history, mathematics, languages, and the like possess *content validity* in that test questions sample the subject matter areas directly. Content validity is not alone a sufficient index of a test's usefulness. Such considerations as choice of items, extent of sampling, form of items, and level of difficulty are also very important. But content validity is a necessary first step. Intelligence and aptitude tests possess content validity insofar as the items in them fulfill the author's definition of what he is measuring. Such asserted or "face" validity, however, is never as convincing as is the content validity of the educational achievement test. Generally, tests of intelligence and of aptitude must depend for their validity on correlations with independent criteria judged to be dependable indices of the trait under study.

*Predictive validity* is the degree to which a test battery is related to some criterion of future performance or measure of success which will become available in the future. The predictive validity of a good group intelligence test for school performance ranges from about .40 to .60. (See page 56.) Many short tests have low correlations with a criterion, but when put with other tests into a team they combine forces to raise the correlation of the battery with the criterion. Validity coefficients do not run as high as do reliability coefficients, since no test can correlate higher with other tests than with measures of itself.

Personality questionnaires, interest blanks, and attitude scales have content validity insofar as choice of items is concerned. Such instruments are usually validated experimentally against objective expressions of interest, indices of neurotic behavior, and the like.

#### Further Considerations in the Choice of a Test

There are a number of factors which enter into the choice of a mental test besides validity and reliability. Some of the more important are the following:

1. Appearance: Is the test format good? Are the items attractively presented and arranged?
2. Administration: How much time is required to give and score the test? What is the cost?
3. Manual: Does the author give full accounts of reliability and validity—how found, on what samples, on what kind of samples? Are instructions clear?
4. Norms: Are the test norms readily interpreted? Are age and grade equivalents given? What type of scaling is used?

## SCALING TEST SCORES

The purpose of scaling is (1) to revamp the raw test scores into a scale of equal units, and thus (2) to enable us to combine subtests into a single index. It is sometimes important (especially with aptitude tests) to compare relative performances, and this can be done only when test scores are expressed in equal units. The score on a test when expressed simply in number of items done correctly is an aggregate of arbitrary points. Pupils can be ranked in order of merit for such aggregates, but such "scores" do not constitute a scale. There are several methods for scaling raw scores.

#### The Age Scale

When scores are put into MA (mental age) units, they form an age scale. Mental age is the chronological age which corresponds to or is typical of a given test score. The MA of 9–6, for example, represents the performance of the average child who is 9 years and 6 months old. Thus if Dick achieves an MA of 9–6 on the Stanford-Binet, this mental age is a measure of his intellectual status or degree of mental growth.

If Dick's life age (CA) is 10–4, his IQ is 92. IQ = MA/CA, and in our example it is 114 mos/124 mos (the decimal is dropped). IQ is a measure of a child's brightness relative to that of other children of his age. When MA and CA are equal, the IQ is 100, the brightness index of the average child. Dick's IQ of 92 means that he is somewhat less bright than the typical child of his age level. IQ's above 100 are achieved by bright children—those whose mental growth runs ahead of their years. IQ's below 100 indicate that a child is below normal, and very low IQ's (70 or below) imply feeblemindedness.

The age scale is used in most individual intelligence scales and by many group tests of general intelligence. The MA and IQ were first widely used to measure performance on the Stanford-Binet test, which was constructed to meet the requirements for a constant ratio score, or IQ. Many group tests do not meet these requirements. It is wise, therefore, to accept IQ's from group tests as tentative indices of brightness which are not always closely related to IQ on the Stanford-Binet.

### The Percentile Scale

We have already seen (page 26) how obtained scores can be fitted into a scale of one hundred units to yield a percentile scale. The *PR* (percentile rank) of a score—its position on the percentile scale—can be computed from the frequency distribution of scores. But the simplest plan is to plot an ogive (see Figure 2–9, page 27) and read the *PR* from the graph. The *PR* of any score then becomes the percentage of the distribution which lies below the score. This method is not accurate beyond the first decimal, but it is sufficiently precise for most purposes. It is easy to apply and requires a minimum of calculation.

Table 2–3 gives the frequency distribution of 180 scores on a clerical aptitude test earned by students enrolled in several courses in a business college.

## TABLE 2–3

**Frequency Distribution of 180 Scores Achieved on a Clerical Aptitude Test**

| Scores | Midpoints | f | cum.f | % cum.f | PR's of midpoints |
|---|---|---|---|---|---|
| 194 – 196 | 195 | 3 | 180 | 100 | 99 |
| 191 – 193 | 192 | 10 | 177 | 98 | 95 |
| 188 – 190 | 189 | 27 | 167 | 93 | 85 |
| 185 – 187 | 186 | 30 | 140 | 78 | 69 |
| 182 – 184 | 183 | 40 | 110 | 61 | 50 |
| 179 – 181 | 180 | 35 | 70 | 39 | 29 |
| 176 – 178 | 177 | 18 | 35 | 20 | 14 |
| 173 – 175 | 174 | 10 | 17 | 9 | 7 |
| 170 – 172 | 171 | 7 | 7 | 4 | 2 |
|  |  | N = 180 |  |  |  |

The ogive in Figure 2–10 has been constructed from the percent cum.f's in Table 2–3 following the method outlined on page 26. In the last column the PR's of the midpoints of the successive score-intervals are entered. The midpoints reading down are 195, 192, 189, 186, 183, 180, 177, 174, and 171. Any student who earns a score of 191, 192, or 193—who falls, that is, in the interval next to the top—receives a PR of 95, the PR of the midpoint of this interval. These midpoint PR's constitute *norms* for the test. PR's can be read with a high degree of accuracy from the ogive.

PR's have several advantages over raw scores. Suppose that a child has taken tests in arithmetic, science, English, history, and spelling. If his PR's in each of these tests are known, they can be represented comparatively on a profile, like that shown in Figure 2–11. This graph permits a comparison of the child's achievement in the five subjects. It is clear that he is satisfactory in arithmetic ($PR = 60$) and science ($PR = 55$), above average in history ($PR = 60$), average in English ($PR = 50$), and below

36　　　　　　STATISTICS IN MENTAL TESTING

*Figure 2–10　Cumulative Frequency Polygon (Ogive) of 180 Scores Achieved on a Clerical Aptitude Test*

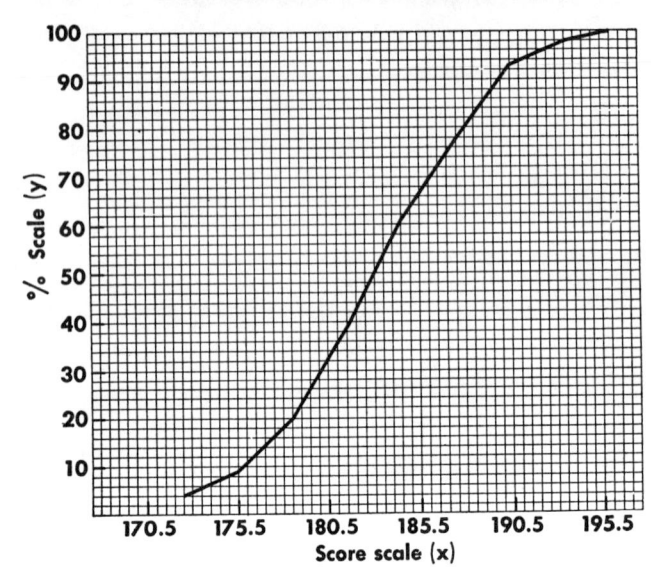

*Figure 2–11　Profile of the Percentile Ranks in Various Subjects for a Given Child*

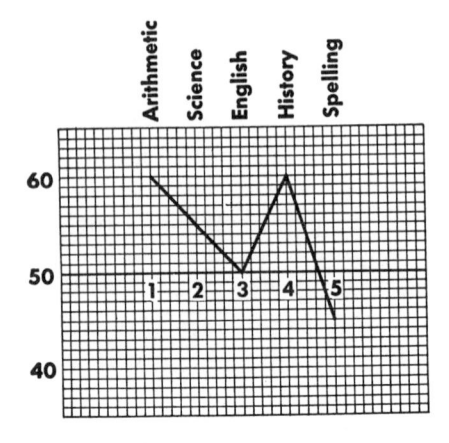

average in spelling ($PR = 45$). Comparisons of this sort cannot be made from raw scores. One disadvantage of the $PR$ scale is the fact that units are not equal at the extremes of the scale. When $PR$'s are below 20 or above 80, they must be compared (or combined) with caution. (See references on page 44.)

### Sigma-Scores and Standard Scores

We have seen that one way of converting raw scores into a scale is by using percentile ranks. Another method of scaling is to express the deviation of each test score from the common mean in units of SD, thus putting all scores into $\sigma$-units. Such "deviation" scores are called $\sigma$-scores and sometimes $z$-scores. The following is an illustration of the method of converting obtained scores into $\sigma$-scores.

Table 2–4 gives the $M$'s and the $\sigma$'s earned by fifty sixth-grade pupils on five objective educational achievement tests. At the bottom of the table are listed the scores achieved by two children, Mary and Howard.

From an inspection of these scores, it is clear that Mary is below the class mean in arithmetical reasoning, arithmetical computation, and science, but above the mean in reading and grammar. Howard, on the other hand, is exactly on the mean in arithmetical reasoning, above the mean in computation and

TABLE 2–4

*M's and σ's Earned on Five Objective Tests of Educational Achievement Given in the Sixth Grade*

|  | (1) Arith. Reas. | (2) Arith. Comp. | (3) Reading | (4) Grammar | (5) Science |
|---|---|---|---|---|---|
| Mean | 62 | 124 | 43 | 28 | 46 |
| $\sigma$ | 10 | 20 | 7 | 4 | 8 |
| Mary's scores | 57 | 119 | 50 | 31 | 36 |
| Howard's scores | 62 | 144 | 41 | 26 | 49 |

science, and slightly below the mean in reading and grammar. These comparisons are useful, but because of differences in the units in which test scores are expressed, we cannot compare Mary's and Howard's scores in the several tests, except to point out that they are above or below the mean, or combine either pupil's scores into a single meaningful index of academic achievement. Conversion of test scores into $\sigma$-units will permit us to carry out both these operations.

The formula for a $\sigma$-score or $z$-score is

$$z = \frac{(X-M)}{\sigma} \text{ or } z = \frac{x}{\sigma}$$

where $(X-M) = x$. Mary earned a score of 57 in arithmetical reasoning. This score deviates $-5$ points from the mean ($57 - 62 = -5$). If we divide this deviation of $-5$ by 10 (the $\sigma$), we have $-.50$ as Mary's $\sigma$ score in arithmetical reasoning. In Test 2, arithmetical computation, Mary's $\sigma$-score is $(119-124)/20$ or $-.25$. Her other $\sigma$-scores are computed in the same way; those that are plus are above the mean, the minus below the mean. Mary's five $\sigma$-scores are

| Test | (1) | (2) | (3) | (4) | (5) |
|---|---|---|---|---|---|
| Mary's $\sigma$-scores | $-.50$ | $-.25$ | 1.00 | .75 | $-1.25$ |

Howard's $\sigma$-scores are found in the same way. In Test 1, his score of 62 is exactly on the mean, and his $\sigma$-score is .00. In Test 2, arithmetical computation, Howard's $\sigma$-score is $(144-124)/20$ or 1.00. Howard's scores are below the mean in Tests 3 and 4, and his $\sigma$-scores are minus. His scores are tabulated below:

| Test | (1) | (2) | (3) | (4) | (5) |
|---|---|---|---|---|---|
| Howard's $\sigma$-scores | .00 | 1.00 | $-.29$ | $-.50$ | .38 |

It is apparent that $\sigma$-scores are simply plus or minus deviations from the test mean expressed in $\sigma$-units. A practical disadvantage of such scores is that they are small decimal fractions and are about as often plus as minus. For greater convenience, therefore, $\sigma$-scores are usually converted into a distribution of standard scores with an assigned $M$ and $\sigma$. $M$'s and $\sigma$'s often selected are $M = 100$, $\sigma = 20$, $M = 500$, $\sigma = 100$, $M = 10$, $\sigma = 3$.

If Mary's and Howard's scores are converted into a standard score distribution with $M = 100$ and $\sigma = 20$, we have

| Test | (1) | (2) | (3) | (4) | (5) | Total | Mean |
|---|---|---|---|---|---|---|---|
| Mary's standard scores | 90 | 95 | 120 | 115 | 75 | 495 | 99 |
| Howard's standard scores | 100 | 120 | 94 | 90 | 108 | 512 | 102 |

In the first test, Mary's $\sigma$-score is $-.50$, or $-.50$ of $\sigma$ below the $M$. In our new distribution ($M = 100$, $\sigma = 20$), the equivalent standard score is one-half of $\sigma$ below 100, or 90. In Test 2, Mary's standard score is ¼ of $\sigma$ below the mean of 100 or 95 (¼ of 20 is 5). A formula for converting obtained scores directly into standard scores with an $M = 100$ and a $\sigma = 20$ is

$$X' = \frac{20}{\sigma}(X - M) + 100$$

in which $X' = $ standard score in the "new" distribution.

$X = $ original or raw score
$M = $ mean of the raw score distribution
100 and 20 are the $M$ and $\sigma$ of the new distribution
$\sigma = $ SD of the original or raw scores

Substituting for Mary's raw score of 50 in Test 3, we have

$$X' = 20/7 \; (50 - 43) + 100$$
$$= 120$$

Howard's standard scores in the new distribution are found from the same formula. In Test 4, for example, Howard's obtained score is 26 and from the formula we have

$$X' = 20/4 \; (26 - 28) + 100$$
$$= -10 + 100 \text{ or } 90$$

The formula will convert any pupil's raw scores into standard scores when the M of the standard score distribution is 100 and σ is 20.

When put in standard score form, Mary's and Howard's scores can be compared directly; and the five scores of each child can be combined with equal weights. On the five tests, Mary's average is 99 and Howard's 102.

Raw scores are converted into standard scores by what is called a linear transformation. This means that the relationship between raw and standard scores can be described by a straight line; one score is converted into the other by direct proportion, just as inches are changed into feet. If the distribution of raw scores is skewed, so is the distribution of standard scores.

### The IQ as a Standard Score

When raw scores are converted into standard scores in a distribution with a mean of 100 and a σ of 15, these new scores are often called "deviation IQ's" (page 70). In the Wechsler Adult Intelligence Scale, for example, IQ's are determined by this method. A WAIS IQ of 115 is 1σ above the mean of the group; an IQ of 85 is − 1σ below the mean of the group.

A general formula for transforming obtained scores into standard scores with any given mean and σ is

$$X' = \frac{\sigma'}{\sigma}(X - M) + M'$$

where

$X'$ = standard score in new distribution
$X$ = obtained score (usually in points)
$\sigma'$ = SD of the new distribution
$\sigma$ = SD of obtained score distribution
$M'$ = M of standard score distribution
$M$ = M of raw score distribution

This formula may be used to compute deviation IQ's. Suppose that Arthur J., thirty-two years old and a veteran, earns a score of 86 on an intelligence test for which the mean of his age-group is 80 and the $\sigma$ is 10. What is Arthur J.'s deviation IQ? Substituting in the formula, we have

$$X' = 15/10\ (86 - 80) + 100$$
$$= 109$$

## Normalized Standard Scores, or T-Scores

When raw point scores are transformed into *PR*'s and the resulting *PR*'s are converted into equivalent "scores" in a normal distribution, the final scores are said to be "normalized." If the normal scaling distribution into which the scores are converted has an $M = 50$ and $\sigma = 10$, the normalized scores are called T-scores. Converting raw scores into T-scores can be done easily with the aid of tables prepared for this purpose. First, the *PR*'s of the scores (or of the midpoints of the successive intervals) are read from an ogive. The T-scores (normalized scores) corresponding to these *PR*'s are then read from the tables.

Theoretically T-scores range from 0 to 100, practically from about 15 to 85. (The method of computing T-scores for a given distribution will be found in detail in the references. T-scores, or normalized standard scores, unlike ordinary standard scores are *not* related to raw scores by a straight line. If the distribution of raw scores is skewed, the distribution of T-scores will be normal, and hence several sets of test scores are directly comparable when expressed as T-scores.

For this and other reasons, T-scaling is theoretically the soundest method of converting raw scores into an equal-unit scale. Many of the widely used educational achievement tests make use of some variety of T-scaling. T-scores can be added or averaged; they have the same meaning and denote the same relative achievement.

## NORMS

Norms are scores which are typical or characteristic of pupils of a given age or grade. To provide comparable norms, scores on group tests are expressed in PR's, standard scores, or normalized scores. Performance tests and individual intelligence scales have norms expressed in MA's and IQ's. Many group intelligence tests also have their raw scores put into MA and IQ terms. Such MA's and IQ's are rarely comparable to the MA's and IQ's of the Stanford-Binet.

Educational achievement tests usually provide both age and grade norms. From a table of norms, a teacher can tell if his class is up to grade level and how individual pupils in the class stand in relation to each other on the subtests of the battery. Suppose that Carl W., age 11 years, 2 months, who is just entering the sixth grade, earns a score of 18 on an arithmetical problems test of the Metropolitan Achievement Test. From the table of norms we find that Carl has a PR of 68 on the test. Furthermore, we find that his age-equivalent is 12–4 and his grade equivalent is 6.9. Carl's score is typical of children about a year older than he, and his knowledge of arithmetic equals that of children who are completing the sixth grade. His PR, of course, reflects performance above the average.

The SRA (Science Research Associates) verbal and nonverbal tests are group tests of intelligence. Norms are given in PR's and IQ's. If a child achieves a score of 34 on the verbal section, for example, his PR from the table of norms is 40 and his IQ (really a standard score) is given as 96. The Stanford Achievement Test provides age and grade equivalents to obtained scores. Raw scores from nine subtests are converted into an equal-unit scale, in accordance with which a profile is drawn up (page 36). Suppose that Louise M., age 12 years and 6 months in the last quarter of the seventh grade, earns a raw score of 40 on the science test of the battery. From tables of norms we find that this score has a grade equivalent of 8.3 and an age equivalent of 13–4. Thus Louise's score in science places her above her age and grade levels. Her *PR* on the science test is 60.

Many aptitude tests supply scaled score norms for various groups of workers differing in experience, training, and skill. Interest inventories are scored to reflect an applicant's interests in a large number of occupations. Thus if the vocational-interest blank is scored with the key for lawyer interests, we can tell whether the applicant has the interests of a lawyer and to what extent. Scores from personality questionnaires serve to identify a subject as "dominant," "introverted," or "neurotic" in relation to the norms given for these classifications.

Teachers use test norms for a number of purposes, which will be discussed in detail in later chapters. Among the most important objectives are the following:

1. To estimate group achievement. Performance of the class as a whole can be evaluated against national, state, or local norms (page 122).
2. To evaluate individual achievement. A pupil's score on an educational achievement test is always considered in connection with his native capacity or mental alertness. A slow or dull child may be working up to his limit, while a bright child may be performing below expectation.
3. To evaluate family and cultural background. The achievement of a class or of an individual will always depend on his socio-economic status, family background, and opportunities.
4. To evaluate curriculum effects. A pupil's achievement must be judged as good or poor in the light of the content, emphasis, and objectives of the school.
5. To measure individual differences. There are always wide differences in academic achievement within a group or class. These differences are due in part to differences in native ability and in part to differences in environmental opportunities.

## SUGGESTIONS FOR FURTHER READING

GARRETT, H. E. *Statistics in Psychology and Education.* 5th ed.; New York: Longmans, Green, 1958.

MANUEL, HERSCHEL T. *Elementary Statistics for Teachers.* New York: American Book, 1962.

NOLL, V. H. *Introduction to Educational Measurement.* Boston: Houghton Mifflin, 1957.

ROSS, C. C. and STANLEY, J. C. *Measurement in Today's Schools.* 3rd ed.; New York: Prentice-Hall, 1954. Part 1.

THORNDIKE, R. L. and HAGEN, E. *Measurement and Evaluation in Psychology and Education.* 2nd ed.; New York: Wiley, 1961.

## QUESTIONS FOR DISCUSSION

1. A fifty-item multiple-choice test in science, administered to ninety pupils, showed scores ranging from 16 to 48. Fifty scores fell between 35 and 48. What is the distribution like? Is it skewed? What measure of central tendency is most suitable?

2. In question 1, what do you conclude about the suitability of the test for the group?

3. Explain the implications of each of the following correlation coefficients:
   (a) The correlation between height and arithmetic test score is .04.
   (b) Ratings of pupils for social intelligence and aggressiveness show a correlation of − .65.
   (c) The correlation between term grades and scores on an intelligence test is .70.

4. Rank the following twenty-three scores in order of size: 35, 40, 31, 29, 35, 23, 32, 34, 28, 34, 15, 14, 34, 40, 22, 32, 30, 39, 50, 19, 40, 27, 37. Compare the "mid-score" with the mean. What is the crude mode?

5. Karl's *PR* on a Biology Test is 48. What does this mean?

6. Margaret has taken five tests. What would be the advantage of having her scores on these tests expressed in *PR*'s?

7. From the ogive in Figure 2–10, read the *PR*'s for the scores of 38, 54, and 68.

8. Given the following:

|  | Paragraph Reading | Arithmetic |
|---|---|---|
| Mean = | 51.7 | 38.6 |
| $\sigma$ = | 9.2 | 6.5 |

William achieves a score of 56 on the first test and 35 on the second. Convert these raw scores into $\sigma$-scores. Into a distribution with a mean of 50 and SD of 10.

9. A test has a reliability coefficient of .91 in a sample of 450 children and an SD of 10. What is the Standard Error ($SE$) of a score on this test? Interpret it.

10. How are age and grade norms obtained? Which is more useful in determining a child's placement in school?

11. Two classes earn about the same mean on a test, but Class A's SD is twice as large as Class B's. What do you conclude from this fact?

12. How can you validate a teacher-made test in American history?

Chapter 3

# INDIVIDUAL INTELLIGENCE SCALES

This chapter will consider four individual intelligence scales or test batteries.[1] These are (1) the Stanford-Binet (1937 or revised form)[2] designed for children from age two through adolescence; (2) the Wechsler Adult Intelligence Scale (WAIS) for use primarily with adults; (3) the Wechsler Intelligence Scale for Children (WISC); and (4) the Arthur Performance Scale, useful from about age four to maturity. These four scales —one for adults and three for children—are representative of the best individual intelligence scales now available. They are carefully constructed, widely used, valid, and dependable. Ordinarily, the individual intelligence test is not administered by the classroom teacher. Nonetheless, the teacher must be familiar

[1] A test battery is a group of carefully selected tests designed to operate as a team.
[2] The full name is Stanford Revision of the Binet-Simon Scale.

with the makeup of these scales and with their role in the school program if he is to make good use of the test findings.

The individual intelligence examination should not be administered by a novice. Giving such a test—and more important interpreting it—requires special training in mental measurement and in clinical psychology, plus a sound knowledge of psychological theory. In addition, at least six months giving and scoring these tests under supervision is desirable if one is to have a minimum of "clinical experience." Unfortunately, directions and materials for giving the individual scales are readily available in the manuals, and the beginner is tempted to try his hand at administering the tests. Much undeserved criticism of the individual intelligence test—and of the MA and IQ—has resulted from the faulty administration and interpretation of these scales by unskilled amateurs.

### The Concept of General Intelligence

Before examining the individual intelligence scales in detail, we must get a clearer notion of what the tests are attempting to measure. This means that we must formulate a definition of what is meant by "general intelligence."

Definitions of general intelligence have run the gamut from such comprehensive biological descriptions as adjustment to the environment to the fairly narrow designation of aptitude for academic work. The French psychologist Alfred Binet defined intelligence as (1) the ability to take and maintain a definite direction—that is, to carry through a course of action once begun; (2) adaptability to new situations and new requirements; and (3) the power to evaluate and criticize one's own acts (not present in the feebleminded). Other psychologists, agreeing in the main with Binet, have stressed adjustment to life and capacity to learn. In contrast with these broad formulations, Lewis M. Terman, author of the Stanford-Binet, has defined intelligence simply as the ability to carry on abstract thinking.

Definitions of general intelligence must be broad when they stress biological adaptability to life. Such definitions are hardly incorrect, but neither are they useful. Indeed, any attempt to encompass such a comprehensive function as general adaptability is an almost impossible task. On the other hand, a definition of intelligence simply as the ability to do school work is certainly too narrow. Proficiency in everyday activities in business and the professions, where aptitude displayed in school finds ready application, should be included.

In order to give greater precision to the concept of intelligence, the educational psychologist Edward L. Thorndike has suggested that we recognize at least three broad areas of intelligent behavior. These "intelligences" he called *abstract, mechanical,* and *social.* He defined abstract intelligence as the "ability to understand and manage ideas and symbols, such as words, numbers, chemical or physical formulas, legal decisions, scientific principles and the like. . . ." In the case of students, this is very close to what commonly is called scholastic aptitude. Mechanical intelligence includes "the ability to learn, to understand and manage things and mechanisms, such as a knife, a gun, a mowing machine, an automobile, a boat, a lathe. . . ." Social intelligence is "the ability to understand and manage men and women, boys and girls, to act wisely in human relations."

We should expect to find high abstract intelligence in scholars, scientists, executives in business and government; high mechanical intelligence in mechanics, builders, expert carpenters and plumbers; and high social intelligence in politicians, salespeople, leaders in society. Presumably the successful civil engineer possesses high abstract as well as high mechanical intelligence; the successful criminal lawyer abstract as well as social intelligence; and the machinery salesman mechanical and social intelligence. These "intelligences" are positively, but not always highly, correlated. Hence, a high level of one "intelligence" may accompany a fairly low degree of another. A nuclear physicist (high in abstract intelligence) may be socially inept, and the man successful in business or politics may be mediocre in mechanical skills. Perhaps the jack-of-all trades can be expected to rate well, but not necessarily very high, in all three areas.

On examining the individual intelligence test, we find that it presents a variety of problems which demand the ability to utilize ideas and symbols—for example, words, numbers, diagrams, pictures, geometrical figures. When used with young children, general intelligence tests are primarily measures of mental alertness on the abstract level. For adults, such tests are measures of the aptitude for those occupational and other tasks which draw on abilities operative in school work. In short, the individual intelligence test measures abstract or scholastic ability primarily and is rarely a gauge of mechanical aptitude or of social competence. The evidence for this view comes from an analysis of the tests themselves, as well as from many studies in which individual intelligence tests have been used.

## THE STANFORD-BINET INTELLIGENCE SCALE (1937 Revision)

Because of the time required to administer the Stanford-Binet (forty minutes to an hour) and the training demanded of the examiner, this test rarely is given routinely in most schools. The classroom teacher must be generally familiar with the Stanford-Binet, however, in order to know what can be expected of it— that is, how it can add to his knowledge of a given pupil. The Stanford-Binet is a valuable supplement to a group intelligence test or to an educational achievement examination when (1) a child has a severe reading disability or some physical handicap (for example, in sight, hearing, or muscular coordination); (2) when a pupil exhibits marked emotional stress or emotional disturbance; and (3) when other test results or school marks do not jibe with the teacher's estimate of the pupil's ability. For purposes of routine classification and placement, the group intelligence test is about as satisfactory as the Stanford-Binet, but the latter will provide a more accurate, detailed, and comprehensive appraisal of intellectual level and is more useful in diagnosis and prediction.

**Description.** The 1937 edition of the Stanford-Binet represents a careful and thorough reworking of the earlier 1916 scale. The number of test items was increased from 90 to 129, and the scale was extended to lower age levels and was much strengthened at the upper age levels. Two equivalent forms of the scale, called L and M, were constructed. Table 3–1 contains a selection of items at different age levels. Note that at a lower age

*TABLE 3–1    Illustrative Tests from Stanford-Binet Scale*

**Year IV**
1. Picture Vocabulary — Child must recognize and name everyday objects seen in the pictures.
2. Naming Objects — Child is shown small toys representing common objects. These he names, or they are named for him. Later he must recall from memory the name of each object.
3. Picture Completion — Child must finish the incompleted drawing of a man.
4. Pictorial Identification — Pictures of objects on cards to be identified.
5. Discrimination of Forms — Recognition and identification of simple geometrical forms.
6. Comprehension — Sensible answers to "why" questions.
Alternate: Memory for Sentences — Repetition of short sentences read aloud to the child.

**Year X**
1. Vocabulary — The examinee must give definitions of eleven words in a standard vocabulary list.
2. Picture Absurdities II — Must recognize what is "foolish" in a presented picture.
3. Reading and Report — Reads a selection and reports from memory what is read.
4. Finding Reasons — Gives sensible reasons to explain cause-and-effect relations in familiar situations.
5. Word Naming — Names as many words as he can in one minute; a measure of word fluency.
6. Repeating Six Digits — The lists are read aloud at a rate of about one a second.

level, such as IV, the test situations make use of objects and pictures and require that the child understand and carry out oral directions. At the upper age levels, X, XIV, and Average Adult, the test items are more abstract and bookish; the problems require verbal and numerical manipulation, reasoning, logical selection, choice, and good judgment. Memory for numbers and for sentences occurs throughout the scale. Questions

*for Years IV, X, XIV, and Average Adult*

Year XIV

| | | |
|---|---|---|
| 1. | Vocabulary | Larger vocabulary required than at year X. |
| 2. | Induction | Tests ability to grasp and apply a general rule. |
| 3. | Picture Absurdities III | Must recognize what is "foolish" in a picture; more difficult than at Year X. |
| 4. | Ingenuity | Tests ability to solve problems mentally. |
| 5. | Orientation: Direction I | Must be able to solve problems involving space relations by following fairly complex directions. |
| 6. | Abstract Words II | Must define words like "loyalty" and "justice." |

Average Adult

| | | |
|---|---|---|
| 1. | Vocabulary | Larger vocabulary than at Year XIV. |
| 2. | Codes | Must learn two codes and write messages in them. |
| 3. | Differences Between Abstract Words | Tests ability to generalize; makes use of fairly difficult concepts. |
| 4. | Arithmetical Reasoning | Requires solution of mental arithmetic problems. |
| 5. | Proverbs | Interpretation of proverbs and fables. |
| 6. | Ingenuity | Solution of problems requiring "mental manipulation." |
| 7. | Memory for Sentences | Tests ability to reproduce rather long and involved sentences heard once. |
| 8. | Reconciliation of Opposites | Must tell how words denoting opposite states are alike. Tests ability to grasp abstract relations. |

dealing with specific facts learned in and out of school are excluded, but many common-knowledge questions are included on the reasonable assumption that what a person has learned in everyday living is a good index of what he can learn—and will learn—later. Some Stanford-Binet test materials are shown in Figure 3–2, facing page 56.

**Scope.** The placement of test items at a given age level was made to depend on the responses of one hundred children at each age level below six, two hundred children at ages six to fourteen inclusive, and one hundred children at ages fifteen through eighteen. In all, about three thousand children constituted the standardization group.

Terman and his co-workers selected children whose parents constituted a good cross-section of occupational levels in the United States for the year 1930. The Stanford-Binet, like the original Binet Scale, is an *age-scale*. (See page 33.) It begins at two years and items are grouped at one-half year intervals (at 2, 2½, 3, 3½, 4, 4½) up to five years. Mental growth at the lower age levels is so rapid that the authors of the scale thought it wise to narrow the gaps between age levels over this range. From five to fourteen years, test items are grouped by year intervals; and beyond fourteen there is an average adult level and three superior adult levels. The Stanford-Binet is most useful over the age range from about six to fourteen—that is, the range of the elementary grades.

**Scoring.** The Stanford-Binet assigns a mental age (MA) to a child in accordance with his ability to progress up the age scale. As shown in the examples on page 53, two children may earn the same MA on the Stanford-Binet in different ways.

James, who is 9–3 or 111 months old, earns an MA of 8–10, or 106 months, by scattering his answers up the scale from age VII to age XIII. Robert also earns an MA of 106 months, but does not scatter as much as James. MA is a measure of mental maturity or status. Children differ in the way in which they answer the test items, but by and large a child comes out with an MA which indicates his ability to perform mental-manipulative tasks like those of the Scale.

*Test record of James Brown, chronological age 9–3, or 111 months**

| Year Level | Tests Passed and Failed | Months Credit Per Test | Total Year | Credit Month |
|---|---|---|---|---|
| VII | all passed |  | 7 |  |
| VIII | four passed | 2 months |  | 8 |
| IX | three passed | 2 months |  | 6 |
| X | two passed | 2 months |  | 4 |
| XI | one passed | 2 months |  | 2 |
| XII | one passed | 2 months |  | 2 |
| XIII | all failed |  |  | 0 |
|  |  |  | 7 | 22 |

* The expression 9–3 means 9 years and 3 months.

MA = 8–10 or 106 months
James' IQ = MA/CA × 100 = 106/111 × 100 = 95 (decimal point dropped)

*Test record of Robert Green, chronological age 8–4, or 100 months*

| Year Level | Tests Passed and Failed | Months Credit Per Test | Total Year | Credit Month |
|---|---|---|---|---|
| VII | all passed |  | 7 |  |
| VIII | five passed | 2 months |  | 10 |
| IX | four passed | 2 months |  | 8 |
| X | two passed | 2 months |  | 4 |
| XI | all failed |  |  | 0 |
|  |  |  | 7 | 22 |

MA = 8–10 or 106 months

Robert's IQ = 106/100 = 106

The intelligence quotient, or IQ, is found by dividing the child's MA by his CA (chronological age). It is a measure of brightness or dullness. James has an IQ of 106/111, or 95, and Robert, who is 11 months younger, has an IQ of 106/100, or 106. Both boys have the same mental maturity, but Robert is brighter than James because he has reached the maturity level of 8–10 at an earlier age. The two measures, MA and IQ, are complementary, each providing distinctive information. A child of eight and a man of forty may each earn an MA of eight years on the Stanford-Binet—that is, have the same mental status on the basis of the tests—but the child has an IQ of 100 (8/8) and is normal, while the man is feebleminded with an IQ of approximately 53. (From the tables in the test manual.)

The IQ is a developmental ratio which inevitably loses its value as a child grows older and mental maturity is approached. There is little difference in mean performance on the Stanford-Binet at ages fifteen, eighteen, and twenty, and a correction table is provided in the test manual which adjusts the CA divisors in order to make the older person's IQ comparable to that of the child. There is no specific age at which intelligence can be said to "mature" or reach its peak, but fifteen is taken somewhat arbitrarily to be the MA of the average adult on Stanford-Binet. For any person over sixteen, therefore, the corrected divisor is fifteen years. The highest MA which can be earned on the Stanford-Binet by passing all of the tests in the Scale is 22¾ years. This MA yields a maximum IQ for adults of 152— found by dividing 273 months by 180 months—that is, by 15 years.

## THE STANFORD-BINET INTELLIGENCE SCALE
### (1960 edition)

In 1960, a third edition of the Stanford-Binet was published. This "revision" contained no new material. It was composed of items from the two forms (L and M) of the 1937 scale and is in reality a selection of best items rather than a new version. The major innovation in the 1960 Stanford-Binet is the introduction of a deviation IQ,[3] to be used as an alternative to the ratio IQ employed in the earlier editions. Stanford-Binet deviation IQ's are standard scores with a Mean = 100 and SD = 16 (the same

---
[3] See also page 70.

mean and SD in the ratio IQ).[4] To expedite the calculation of IQ's, tables are provided in the Manual from which, knowing a child's MA and CA, his IQ can be read easily.

There are two recurring difficulties in the ratio IQ which renders it less useful than the deviation IQ. For one thing, the SD's of the IQ distributions from different age levels vary in size, despite great care in scale construction. This introduces instability in the IQ's of children who differ widely in age. Again, systematic corrections need be made to the ratio IQ (MA/CA) to prevent it from falling with increases in CA. The Stanford-Binet deviation IQ avoids both of these difficulties.

The new deviation IQ represents a real improvement over the ratio IQ. However, the IQ as MA/CA has been associated with the Stanford-Binet Scale for nearly a half century and is firmly entrenched in the testing literature. Hence, the ratio IQ will probably continue to be used for a long time. But it seems certain that eventually it will give way to the deviation IQ.

## STANFORD-BINET IN THE SCHOOLS

The evaluation of pupils from their school grades or from subjective impressions of cleverness or brightness often is misleading. A teacher may describe a conscientious, amiable girl of ten who is one year overage for grade as "bright" when her IQ turns out to be relatively modest. And, a rude, inattentive youngster may be rated as "about average" or even below average when his IQ is in reality well above normal. Judgments of intelligence are always influenced by personality traits and social behaviors. It is not strange, therefore, to find that two pupils must in general differ by as much as twenty points of IQ before a teacher is forced to lay other criteria aside and admit that the badly behaved youngster is brighter than the courteous, hardworking one.

[4] See p. 56.

Teachers should know certain facts about the IQ, what it is and how best it can be used, in order to make maximum use of the information provided by the test. More specifically, the classroom teacher should know (1) the range of IQ's to be expected in the school population, (2) the dependence to be placed on the IQ as a measure of intelligence, (3) to what extent the IQ has diagnostic value, and (4) the limitations of the IQ and the precautions to be observed in making interpretations based on it.

### RANGE OF IQ'S IN THE SCHOOL POPULATION

The frequency polygon in Figure 3–1 shows the distribution or spread of IQ's for the nearly three thousand children from two to eighteen years old who made up the standardization sample. The frequency polygon is close to the normal curve model (page 18). IQ's center at 100 and range about equally above and below this value. The $\sigma$ of the IQ distribution is about sixteen points (exactly 16.4). This means that the middle 2/3 of school children will earn IQ's between 84 and 116. About

Figure 3–1  *Distribution of IQ's on the Stanford-Binet Scale for Nearly 3,000 Children, 2–18 Years Old*

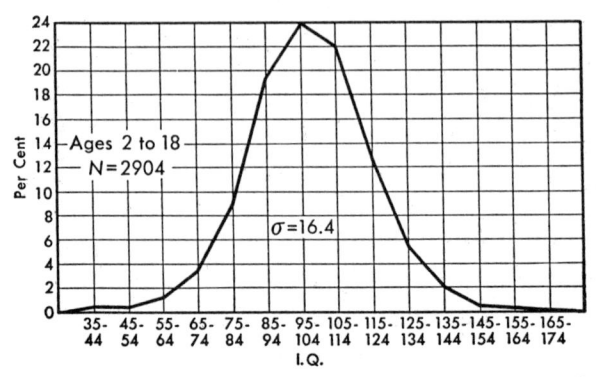

From Terman, Lewis M., and Merrill, Maud A., *Measuring Intelligence*. Reproduced by permission of Houghton Mifflin Company.

*Figure 3–2   Test Materials Used in the Stanford-Binet Scale*

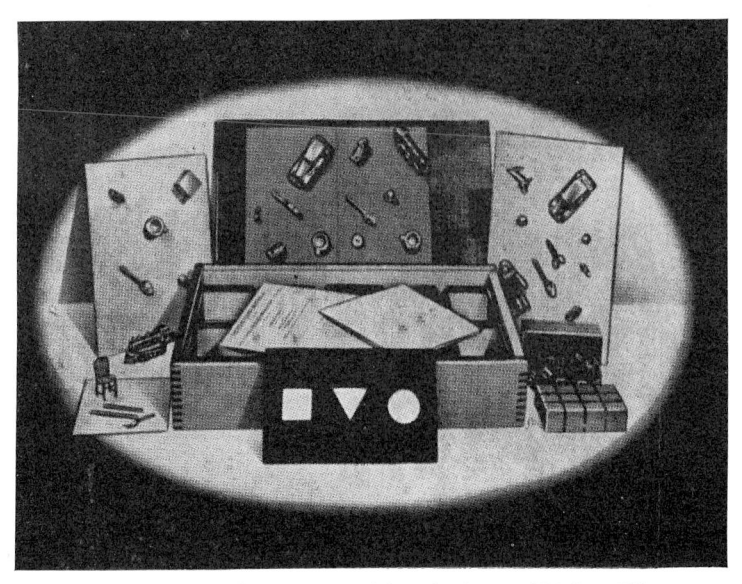

Reproduced through the courtesy of C. H. Stoelting and McGraw-Hill.

*Figure 3–3   Items from the Performance Part of the Wechsler Adult Intelligence Scale*

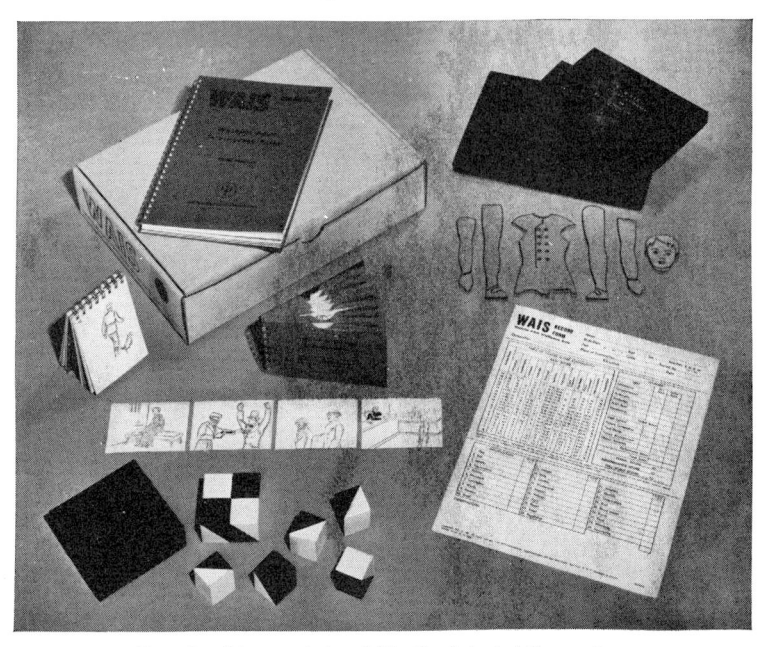

Reproduced by permission of The Psychological Corporation.

Figure 3-4  Performance Tests Found in the Arthur Point Scale

Reproduced by permission of The Psychological Corporation.

1/6 of the children will have IQ's above 116 and 1/6 will have IQ's below 84. (See Figure 2-7.) The percentage of school children who can be expected to occupy the different IQ levels may be summarized as follows:

*TABLE 3-2*

*Numbers of Children in the School Population to Be Expected at Various IQ Levels*

| IQ Level | Description | Percent of Children in Each Category |
|---|---|---|
| 130 and above | Superior or gifted | 3 – 5 |
| 110 – 129 | Above average to high | 25 |
| 90 – 109 | Average or normal | 45 – 50 |
| 70 – 89 | Low normal to dull | 20 – 25 |
| Below 70 | Dull to feebleminded | 2 – 3 |

The number of children found in any group (especially in the two extreme groups) will vary somewhat with the social and economic conditions of the community and with the standards established for defining the different intelligence levels.

The IQ is useful in setting educational expectations. Suppose that William Butler, a fifth-grade pupil in a large school system, has a chronological age of 10–2 and a Stanford-Binet IQ of 116. William reads at fifth-grade level, is somewhat above average in his other subjects, and is excellent in arithmetic. He is a quiet, well-behaved boy who seldom becomes angry or annoyed. William makes friends readily and is accepted as a member of his group. What are William's educational expectations?

Table 3–3 will be of help in answering this question. William falls in the upper 16 percent of school children. He should have no trouble completing elementary and high school. If he is industrious, emotionally stable, and has intellectual interests, William may be encouraged to go to college. It might be wise to advise William to choose a college of medium standards, if the boy lacks self-confidence, and to enlist his parents' enthusiastic support.

## TABLE 3-3
### Educational Expectation in Relation to IQ Level

| IQ Level (Stanford-Binet) | Educational Expectation |
|---|---|
| 120 + | Can do acceptable work in a first-class college if properly motivated. |
| 115 – 119 | Should do acceptable but not outstanding college work. Would probably do best in a small college where the work is individual and standards not too high. |
| 105 – 114 | Should complete high school, and may do well in the less difficult college courses. Will have trouble with science and mathematics. |
| 90 – 104 | This group constitutes about fifty percent of the elementary-school population. If not retarded by illness or other causes should complete the eighth grade on schedule. Some of these pupils do fairly well in high school. |
| 80 – 89 | Usually one to two years overage for grade. Acceptable high-school work very unlikely for IQ's below 90. A child of IQ 80 will complete the eighth grade—if at all—two or three years behind schedule. |
| 75 – 79 | These children may reach the fifth grade. Will rarely go beyond unless given much individual attention. |
| Below 75 | If one of these children reaches the fifth grade he will be fourteen–fifteen years old. Unable to do fifth grade work; but because of chronological age is likely to be pushed ahead after repeating each grade two or three times. May be promoted far beyond his mental capacity because of age. |

Mary, age 12–0 with an IQ of 83, presents a very different picture. Mary is doing barely passing work in the fifth grade, though she is about two years overage for the grade. Since her MA is not more than ten years,[5] she is perhaps doing all we can reasonably expect of her. It would be manifestly unfair to scold

[5] Since MA/CA = IQ, Mary's MA is 12 × .83, or about 10 years.

Mary and insist that she "try harder." Mary's educational expectation (see Table 3–3) is no higher than the eighth grade, if that.

## STABILITY OF THE IQ

When a second form of the Stanford-Binet is administered to a child, his second IQ will often vary somewhat up or down from the first determination. Norman's IQ, for example, may be 109 today, though it was 112 six months ago, and it may very well be back at 106 in six months. The stability of a test score when the test is repeated or another form given, is called the *reliability* of the test (page 29). Stanford-Binet is one of our most dependable mental examinations, with reliability coefficients which are usually well over .90 (page 30). Despite this fact, fluctuations in individual IQ's can still be expected when the test is repeated or a second form administered.

The reliability of a test is conveniently expressed by the standard error ($SE$) of a test score (page 30). The $SE$ gives the allowable (one might almost say the inevitable) changes to be expected when a second form of the test is given. The $SE$ of the Stanford-Binet IQ is four to five points[6] for IQ's between 90 and 110. The $SE$ is slightly higher for high IQ's and somewhat lower for low IQ's. Expressed as chances or probability of change, a $SE$ of five points means that the odds are roughly 2:1 that an IQ of 102, for example, will not be higher than 107 (102 + 5) nor lower than 97 (102 − 5) on retest. The $SE$ represents the amount of fluctuation to be expected in most cases. The change in a few individual cases may be somewhat greater than five points or somewhat less than five points.

Fluctuations in IQ from time to time arise from many causes: changes in the testing situation and changes in the child being tested. When a child's mental or physical health or his home or

---

[6] When $SE_{IQ} = 16\sqrt{1 - .90}$, we have 5 as the approximate value of the $SE$. This is a slight overestimation since the reliability coefficient is usually above .90.

school environment changes radically between tests, fluctuations in IQ can be expected. Mental measurement is never as precise as physical measurement: a child is a much more variable "object" than a piece of metal, for example. Changes in IQ from one test to another rarely shift a child from one classification to another, however (see Table 3–2)—that is, from normal to superior or from dull to normal. The consensus, in fact, is that the IQ is extremely hard to change and that we can accept an IQ as a reliable appraisal of a child's general mental level if it has been expertly determined.

### THE STANFORD-BINET IQ IN DIAGNOSIS OF CHILD BEHAVIOR

Children who achieve the same mental age will differ in IQ when their chronological ages differ (page 53). Furthermore, even when the IQ is the same, two children may differ sharply in various aspects of mental development, as shown by the sorts of tests passed and failed and by the degree of scatter over the scale. The Stanford-Binet is primarily a standard test-interview designed to furnish a cross-sectional view of a child's intellectual capacities—that is, to give the level at which the child normally functions. At the same time, the school psychologist, in writing an account of a child's performance on the test, will usually note irregularities in development and learning ability, and these observations can provide the teacher with valuable clues to an understanding of the child. Visual handicaps, incoordinations, and other physical handicaps may be noted, as may be deficiencies in arithmetic skills, in word comprehension, in reasoning, and in current information. The subtests of the Stanford-Binet call for fairly specific performances and are not sufficiently numerous or comprehensive to permit the final judgment that "John is weak in number work, but excellent in rote memory," or that "Sarah's verbal facility far exceeds her manipulative skills." But the *pattern* of a child's responses and the relative strengths and weaknesses displayed on groups of items will provide useful information.

Parents are often puzzled when, at the same time, a child who is a discipline problem is described as above normal in intelligence. The reason, of course, is that Stanford-Binet is not a measure of social intelligence or of emotional stability but of general verbal or abstract level (page 48). At the same time, the observant psychologist will note and record characteristic emotional and temperamental behavior displayed as the child takes the test. The rude or indifferent youngster, who doesn't care and doesn't cooperate, the spoiled and petulant "brat," who gives up and pouts at the first failure, the timid, insecure child, who inquires eagerly "Is that right?" after answering each item—all reveal their distinctive personality traits by the manner in which they handle the test. Standards of behavior in the home, ideals of conduct, values, and attitudes are often exhibited clearly, if indirectly, in the course of a mental examination. At Year VII, for example, is the question "What's the thing to do if another boy (or girl, depending on the sex of the examinee) hits you without meaning to do it?" The child who is immature socially or reared in a rough-and-tumble community will answer promptly "Hit him back." The seven-year-olds who are better trained in acceptable social practices will qualify their replies, or suggest that forgiveness may be in order if the blow is truly accidental.

The following case histories will illustrate how qualitative analysis of a child's test performance can help the classroom teacher who refers him to the psychologist.

Case I. SM, a boy; CA = 10–2, MA = 8–2, IQ = 80.

This boy was referred by his teacher because of unsatisfactory work in the fourth grade. He is a good-looking, polite lad, normal in appearance and in social manner. Anyone unacquainted with his school work might judge SM to be average in intelligence, or perhaps above average. On the Stanford-Binet, SM's vocabulary was childish with definitions based on use. He passed the vocabulary test only at year VI. His answers to the picture and verbal absurdities were halting, poorly phrased, and uncomprehending. He had inaccurate and meager responses to "seeing relations" items—differences and similarities. He was poor in number relations; his coordination and rote memory were fair. SM is a dull boy who may reach the eighth grade, but is not likely to go beyond. It was recommended that SM undertake vocational training.

Case 2. RW, a girl; CA = 11–2, MA = 11–3, IQ = 100.

RW is a well-developed girl, apparently calm and self-possessed. She was referred by her teacher because of poor work in the sixth grade. She is described as being inattentive and given to daydreaming. RW seemed indifferent to the test but did not refuse to cooperate. She often asked that a question be repeated, and the examiner suspected slight deafness. She became more interested as the test proceeded, especially when she got the answers to several questions. Her vocabulary is at Year X, but her verbal ability is about normal, as shown by her ability to deal with pictures and verbal absurdities, name words, define abstract terms, and handle similarities. Her attention was somewhat variable and she was easily distracted. She showed uncertainty in using number relations—for example, in making change. RW is normal in intelligence and should be able to do satisfactory work in the sixth grade. It is suspected that her daydreaming is, in part, a consequence of puberty. It was recommended that the classroom teacher check on RW's friends, outside activities, and home conditions.

Case 3. HP, a boy; CA = 6–5, MA = 9–6, IQ = 148.

The second-grade teacher is not sure what to do with HP; he seems to know everything she is teaching. HP's father is a prominent surgeon. This boy entered school at 6–1 and was put in the second grade. He is well-mannered, normal in play and social activities, and gets along well with his classmates. HP whizzed through the tests for Years VI, VII, and VIII. His vocabulary is at Year X. He defined an orange as "a citrus fruit, round and yellow, comes from Florida." His coordination is not up to his verbal level, but his memory and perception of differences and likenesses are excellent. HP is a very bright youngster. He should be ready for high school by age twelve or earlier. He should now be in the fourth grade, if he is ready for it socially. If promotion is not feasible, a program of outside reading and some special attention is suggested.

### Precautions To Be Taken in Interpreting the IQ

Some of the factors which may influence a child's IQ have been touched upon in preceding paragraphs. To what extent the IQ is an index of "innate ability" will depend on the cooperation and motivation of the examinee, and on how expertly the test has been administered. Several factors which may affect the reliability of an IQ are the following:

*Physical conditions:* Sensory defects, deafness, poor eyesight. Malnutrition and illness are also important.

*Examiner:* The personal equation of the examiner may be crucial. Mental test examiners who are poorly trained, have harsh and unpleasant voices, peculiarities of manner or dress, or who are supercilious or arrogant in their relations with the child get poor cooperation and uncertain test results.

*Testing conditions:* Test results are likely to be unreliable when the examination room is bare, too cold or too warm, or over-decorated. Coaching on the tests must always be watched for, since the tests have been widely distributed.

*Environmental surroundings:* The degree of stimulation received in the home, the school, and the community will markedly affect the test performance. Children from homes broken by divorce or by drunkenness will often show IQ increases of as much as twenty points after several months of kind treatment. On the other hand, children from good homes who have been transferred to a deprived and restrictive environment (for example, in war) may show sharp drops in IQ.

Because of the many factors which may affect its determination, a Stanford-Binet IQ should not immediately be denounced as worthless if there is a large shift in a second rating. Instead, a drastic change in IQ should be taken as a challenge, and the causes ferreted out if possible. The neglected dull-normal child will often show an increase in measured IQ when taken into a good home, as will a child adopted into a good family. By the same token, a normal child will do poor school work if he is insecure and unhappy. It seems very unlikely that even sharp changes in IQ reflect a real alteration in a child's aptitude. All of the environmental factors must be considered before this conclusion is reached.

### Constancy of the IQ over the Age Range

Suppose that Bob White, who is seven years old, has an MA of eight years on Stanford-Binet and an IQ of 8/7, or 114. When Bob is fourteen years old, his MA must be sixteen years if his IQ is to remain constant at 114 (16/14 = 114). The IQ is a measure of brightness or dullness relative to a child's age group. Hence, should an IQ fluctuate widely—for example, from 114 to 85 or to 140—the ratio MA/CA becomes valueless. We have said earlier (page 59) that when the IQ of a child has been determined by an expert, it is a highly dependable index. But whether the IQ remains constant over the years from six to fourteen (during elementary school, for example) will depend, for one thing, on the way in which the test has been constructed. It is appropriate to ask therefore "Is the Stanford-Binet so constructed that a constant IQ is probable or even possible?"

There are three conditions which an intelligence test must meet if the IQ (defined as the ratio, MA/CA)[7] is to remain constant over the age-scale. These are:

---

[7] The IQ may also be defined as a standard score (page 40). The conditions for IQ constancy, given above, apply only to age-scales, that is, wherein IQ = MA/CA.

1. Increased spread of MA's (larger SD's) as we go up the age-scale.
2. Homogeneity of mental function over the age range covered by the scale. Homogeneity means that the test measures the same "intelligence" for example, from age two to age eighteen.
3. Zero correlation between chronological age and IQ.
These conditions are met to a high—though not perfect—degree by the Stanford-Binet. They are not met, even approximately, by most group intelligence tests (page 104).

Let us examine each condition further.

1. The SD of the Stanford-Binet MA distributions increases fairly regularly with chronological age. At Year VII, for example, the SD of the mental age distribution is 1 year; at Year X the SD is 1.6 years; at Year XIII it is 2.3 years; and at Year XVI it is 2.6 years. This means that if Bob White has a CA of 7 years and is *one* SD above the mean for his age (that is, at 8 years), his IQ will be 8/7, or 114. If Bob maintains his rate of mental growth, at age 10 his MA will be 1 SD above the mean, or at 11.6 years (10 + 1.6). Bob's IQ is now 11.6/10 or 116. At year 13, should Bob stay 1 SD above the mean, his MA will be 15.3 (13 + 2.3) and his IQ 117. And at age 16, should Bob maintain his rate of growth, his MA should be 18.6 (16 + 2.6) and his IQ 18.6/16 or 116. Figure 3–5 shows that when a child maintains an accelerated rate of growth, his IQ (like Bob's) will remain approximately constant—that is, within 2 to 3 points.

Figure 3–5 shows that when a child is below the mean for his age, his IQ will again remain approximately constant should he maintain his slower rate of growth. If a child has an MA of 6 and a CA of 7—1 SD *below* the mean for his age—his IQ will be 6/7, or about 86. Should this child maintain his slower rate of growth, at Year XIV his MA will be 11.8 (14 − 2.2), and his IQ will be 11.8/14, or 84. It is the increasing spread of MA's with increasing CA which keeps the ratio MA/CA constant within 2 to 3 points, provided, of course, that the child maintains a constant rate of growth. (See Figure 3–5.)

*Figure 3–5  Age-Progress Curves for the Stanford-Binet Scale [Note that the spread of MA's becomes greater with increasing chronological age.]*

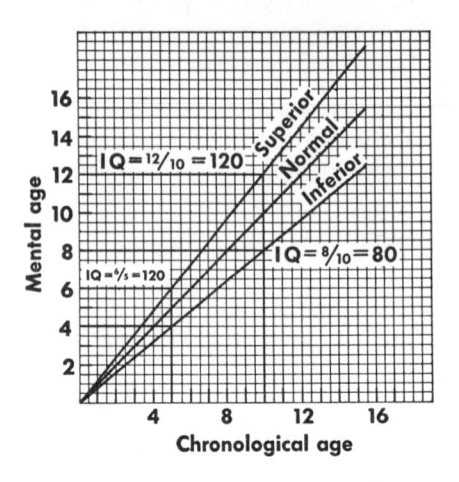

2. Statistical analysis has shown that the correlation between successive MA levels is very high, and that the Stanford-Binet is measuring essentially the same "intelligence" as it goes up the age-scale.

3. When a child reaches the upper teens, mental growth changes as shown by the Stanford-Binet fail to keep pace with chronological age. When this happens, the curves in Figure 3–5 lose altitude and bend over to become parallel with the baseline. Failure of the MA to increase with CA leads inevitably to a falling IQ among older children and, if uncorrected, to a negative correlation between CA and IQ. (Negative correlation follows because the CA continues to increase, whereas the IQ no longer does—see page 54). To overcome this fault in the age-scale, the authors of Stanford-Binet provide a steadily decreasing CA divisor from age thirteen and above. This procedure bolsters up the IQ by lessening the denominator (CA) and thus balancing the decreasing numerator (MA). This means that a child's IQ

does not *have* to decrease as the child grows older—and that there is no systematic correlation (positive or negative) between CA and IQ. (See page 29).

## THE WECHSLER ADULT INTELLIGENCE SCALE (WAIS)

**Description.** The Stanford-Binet is sometimes used to measure the intelligence of adolescents and adults, but it is not well suited to these groups, since the items of the test were selected to appeal primarily to children. An examination better suited for measuring adult intelligence is the Wechsler Adult Intelligence Scale (WAIS), an individual intelligence test designed especially for adults.

The Wechsler Adult Intelligence Scale (WAIS) was published in 1955. It is a revision and restandardization of the older Wechsler-Bellevue Intelligence Scale (1939). WAIS makes use of the same principles of construction, scoring, and IQ derivation as those of the Wechsler-Bellevue. The WAIS is a carefully made test. The group employed in standardizing the test battery —that is, the sample on whose answers the scoring and norms depend—consisted of young people and adults from each age level, chosen to match the 1950 census distribution for sex, region of the country, urban-rural, race, occupation, and education. The standardization of the WAIS is superior to that of the Wechsler-Bellevue, which was carried out on a sample drawn mostly from New York City and New York State.

The WAIS consists of two parts, a Verbal Scale and a Performance Scale. Language is required in the first scale, but is not demanded in the actual solution of the problems in the performance scale. Directions, however, are given orally so that the second scale is not exclusively manipulative. What is called the Full Scale is a combination of the Verbal and Performance sections. The Verbal Scale is made up of six tests.

## VERBAL SCALE

1. Information: Twenty-nine questions covering a wide range of common information and dealing with facts which all normal adults have presumably had a chance to learn. Questions are graded in difficulty from easy to hard. The maximum score is 29.
2. Comprehension: Fourteen questions in each of which the examinee is asked to tell what should be done in certain situations, or why certain practices should be followed. Questions are planned to call out practical judgment, common sense, and understanding. The maximum score is 28 (two points for each question).
3. Arithmetic: Fourteen mental arithmetic problems. Each problem is presented orally and must be solved without use of paper or pencil ("in the head"). The maximum score is 18 (extra points are allowed for certain problems solved within given time limits).
4. Similarities: Thirteen word-pairs, each pair alike in some way. The examinee must say in what way the two words are alike. Maximum score 26 (two points for each item).
5. Digit Span (Digits forward and backward): Memory span for digits presented one at a time and ranging in number from 3 to 9. In the second part (digits backward), the examinee is asked to give a list of numbers ranging from 2 to 8 in reverse order. Maximum score 17 (8 + 9).
6. Vocabulary: A list of forty words graded in difficulty to be defined orally. Maximum score 80 (two points per word).

## PERFORMANCE SCALE

1. Digit Symbol: A simple association-learning test. Nine symbols are matched with nine numbers in accordance with a key. Maximum score 90.
2. Picture Completion: Twenty-one cards, each containing a picture from which some part is missing. The examinee must find the missing part. Maximum score 21.
3. Block Design: Sixteen small cubes (blocks) colored red, white, and red-and-white on the sides. Examinee is to arrange blocks to match ten designs presented on test cards. Designs increase in complexity. Maximum score 48.
4. Picture Arrangement: Eight sets of pictures, each set containing three to six separate pictures. The examinee is asked to arrange

the pictures in a given set in sequence to tell a story. Maximum score 36.
5. Object Assembly: Four "jigsaw puzzle" forms—the Manikin, the Profile, the Hand and the Elephant. The parts of each "puzzle" must be put together to form a complete object. Maximum score 44.

Samples of the items from the performance section of the WAIS are shown in Figure 3–3. These tests are "performance" in the sense that the examinee, in solving each problem, must manipulate the pieces—for example, pictures, forms, blocks, symbols. But "ideas" are certainly not excluded, nor is spoken language. Accordingly, Wechsler's performance tests are measures of abstract intelligence to a considerable degree, as well as measures of motor and mechanical activities. This is shown by a correlation between the two scales (Verbal and Performance) of .77 in an unselected group of 300 persons, ages 25 to 34. The Full Scale correlates .95 with the Verbal and .92 with the Performance Scale.

**Scope.** The WAIS provides scores in the form of "IQ's." Norms are from age sixteen up, but the scale's principal value is over the age range from about twenty to sixty years. Beyond sixty, IQ's are not always dependable, owing in part to the selected character of the samples at advanced age levels. Age-level scores on the Full Scale show a gradual decline after age twenty, the drop from age 20 on being greater for the Verbal than for the Performance tests.

**Scoring.** Following the directions laid down in the Manual, the examiner first adds up the items done correctly in each of the eleven subtests. Scores on each subtest are then converted into normalized standard scores (page 41). The age-group twenty–thirty-four served as the normative or reference group. The mean of each subtest was set at 10 for this group with $SD = 3$. This gives a range of converted scores from about 1 to 19 (page 24). Conversion of the separate subtest scores into a common normalized standard score scale allows the examiner to combine the tests into a single index, and furthermore to compare the ups and downs in performance from test to test.

WAIS does not ordinarily yield mental ages since the concept of mental age, though useful with children, has little meaning when applied to normal adults. The Scale does provide for an IQ (called a "deviation IQ") which is essentially a standard score. There are three IQ's, one from the Verbal, one from the Performance, and one from the Full Scale. In each of these, deviation IQ's are computed in the following way. Scaled scores on the subtests (eleven in all for the Full Scale) are added and the total score converted again into a standard score, this time with $M = 100$ and $SD = 15$ (page 40). At each age level, for example, 35, 40, 50, the mean scaled test score got from the subtests is set at 100. Thus a score which is 1 SD above the mean scaled score at *any* age level yields an IQ of 115 (page 24). A score 1 SD below the mean yields an IQ of 85. Putting the mean scaled score for each age level at $IQ = 100$ adjusts for the steady decline in raw score with age.

The same scaled score will denote different degrees of retardation or advancement depending on the person's age level. For example, we read from the tables in the Manual that a man of age thirty-five who earns a scaled score of 77 on the eleven tests of the Full Scale has an IQ of 83, which is considerably below the mean IQ of 100 for his age group. The same scaled score of 77 becomes an IQ of 89 at age forty-five, and an IQ of 100 at age seventy. This means that a total scaled score of 77 on the eleven tests of the Full Scale is "normal" (or "at age") for age seventy, and hence yields an IQ of 100. But the total scaled score of 77 is *below* the mean for ages thirty-five and forty-five and represents, accordingly, IQ's of 83 and 89. For the same reasons, an examinee who achieves a total scaled score of 90 (Full Scale) has an IQ of 88 if he is twenty-seven, an IQ of 90 if he is thirty-seven, and an IQ of 101 if he is sixty-seven. The older person who maintains his early score (shows no decrease) earns a higher IQ.

To summarize, the WAIS reports IQ's which are converted standard scores in a distribution in which the mean is 100 for each age level and the SD is always 15. WAIS IQ's have the same meaning from one age to another in the sense that an IQ of 105 or 95 implies the same relative superiority or inferiority with respect to the examinee's age group. WAIS always is a standard score, whereas the Stanford-Binet is usually a ratio (MA/CA) (page 53). The two indices are highly correlated, but are not equivalent, or interchangeable. To avoid confusion, it helps to write WAIS IQ or Stanford-Binet IQ. Both IQ's are measures of abstract intelligence (page 48).

## THE WAIS IN THE SCHOOLS

The WAIS has been widely used in the individual study of adolescents and older students for whom the content of the Stanford-Binet is inappropriate. The test is most valuable to teachers in the upper grades and in high schools and technical schools.

### RANGE AND STABILITY OF WAIS IQ's

The range of IQ's in the general school population is about the same for the Wechsler Scale as for the Stanford-Binet. Table 3–2 will serve, therefore, as a guide in the interpretation of a test score. Table 3–3 may be taken also as providing a statement of the educational expectations of older students when we know the Wechsler IQ. The reliability of the WAIS, Full Scale, as given by its standard error, is approximately three points. Hence, the IQ from this scale has about the same stability as the Stanford-Binet IQ.

### THE WECHSLER SCALE IN DIAGNOSIS

The Full Scale—like the Stanford-Binet—yields a measure of a student's general mental level and is often used to provide this information. The WAIS and the older Wechsler-Bellevue have been widely employed in mental hospitals and clinics as an aid in the diagnosis of abnormal behavior. The Scale has been useful in the study of variations of performance in schizophrenia and other mental diseases, in senile deterioration, and in assessing the effects of brain damage and the results of brain surgery. The fact that there are eleven separate tests (six Verbal and five Performance) in the Full Scale has led clinical psychologists to attempt to discover the relative efficiency of various mental functions from irregularities in test performance.

The diagnosis of strengths and weaknesses in pupils from the subtests of the Wechsler must always be taken as tentative, though an examination of each of the different subtests can provide valuable clues. The various tests of the Scale are too short and too complex (measure several overlapping abilities) to allow a sweeping judgment to the effect that "Bill has poor planning capacity and poor judgment," or that "Mary has a good memory and adequate concentration." Observations of this sort are valuable only if made cautiously and taken in conjunction with other evidence. The Full Scale is a good index of present mental efficiency, and the difference between the Verbal and Performance IQ's is often believed to be significant of the academic *versus* the non-academic "mind" (page 79). Judgments based on specific subtests with respect to strengths and weaknesses in memory, learning, perception, planning capacity, concentration, emotional blocks, and the like must be taken as suggestive rather than as conclusive.

## WECHSLER INTELLIGENCE SCALE FOR CHILDREN (WISC)

**Description.** The WISC, as it is called, is a scaled down revision of the Wechsler-Bellevue to render the test more suitable for young children. There are ten subtests and two alternates (twelve in all) in the WISC. The subtests have the same form and cover the same content as the Wechsler-Bellevue, except that easier items have been added. Tests are grouped into five Verbal and five Performance as follows:

| Verbal Scale | Performance Scale |
|---|---|
| General Information | Picture Completion |
| General Comprehension | Picture Arrangement |
| Arithmetic | Block Design |
| Similarities | Object Assembly |
| Vocabulary (Digit Span) | Coding (or Mazes) |

The WISC differs in several respects from the WAIS. In the Verbal Scale, "digit-span" proved to be less satisfactory than the other tests and hence became an alternate. Vocabulary became the substitute. In the Performance Scale, coding is a somewhat easier version of the digit-symbol test. Mazes are sometimes given instead of coding, but the second test is usually preferred, since it takes less time to administer. The maze test is the only test not found in the WAIS.

**Scope.** The WISC is a well-made test. To provide norms, one hundred boys and one hundred girls were tested at each age level from five to fifteen. Children in the standardization sample were drawn from eleven states and from three institutions for the feebleminded. The sample was carefully checked to give a cross section of geographic areas, urban-rural groups, and occupational levels of parents.

**Scoring.** As was true of the WAIS, all subtests were first converted into normalized standard scores in a distribution with $M = 10$ and $SD = 3$. Tables are provided for reading scale score equivalents to raw scores for each four-month period from five to fifteen years. These equally weighted subtest scores are added and then converted into "deviation IQ's," with Mean $=$ 100 and $SD = 15$ (page 70). Performance and Full Scale IQ's may be read from appropriate tables in the Manual. Approximately 50 percent of school children can be expected to earn WISC IQ's between 90 and 110.

**Differences Between the WISC and the Stanford-Binet.** The WISC differs from the Stanford-Binet in several important respects. (1) All items of a given sort in the WISC are organized into subtests instead of different kinds of items being placed at successive age levels. WISC is a point scale rather than an age scale. (2) The WISC IQ is a deviation IQ—a standard score in a distribution with Mean = 100 and SD = 15—while the Stanford-Binet IQ is a development ratio or MA/CA (page 53). The two IQ's are closely related (the correlations between the two sorts of scores run from .80 up), but they are not identical (page 71). The SD of the Stanford-Binet distribution of IQ's is 16, as against the WISC SD of 15, and some of the difference between the two IQ's is due to the greater spread of the Stanford-Binet IQ's. Furthermore, the two mental examinations differ in length, variety and difficulty of items. (3) The WISC provides for three IQ's—a Verbal, a Performance, and a Full Scale. There is only one IQ from the Stanford-Binet, based on all of the tests in the scale.

## THE WISC IN THE SCHOOLS

Both the WISC and the Stanford-Binet are widely used with school children, and in most cases there is little to choose between the two examinations. Many psychologists regard the Stanford-Binet as more satisfactory for use with very young children, since the WISC is not always easy to administer when the child is under seven years of age. WISC takes less time to give and to score than does Stanford-Binet, and some examiners prefer it over the age range of the elementary school. The WISC Full Scale IQ has a higher correlation with Stanford-Binet IQ than does either the Verbal or the Performance Scale IQ.

Bright children tend to score higher on the Stanford-Binet than on the WISC, but dull pupils score higher on the WISC. The separate IQ's of the WISC (Verbal and Performance) are often valuable in bringing out differences in verbal and manipulative skills. Sometimes a child (usually a boy) will do better on the performance tests of the WISC than on the verbal, indicating perhaps a greater aptitude for vocational rather than for academic subjects. A bookish youngster who reads a great deal may do much better on the verbal tests. The performance IQ is usually higher than the verbal in severely disturbed adolescents, and this difference often appears also in younger dull students. From the manner in which the child handles the verbal tests, the expert examiner will often note evidences of insecurity, revealed by incoherence, verbosity, poor attention, and defeatism. Poor performance on the manipulative tests often reveals inept planning and defective coordination, while good performance shows concentration and adequate sensory-motor organization.

## Range and Stability of the WISC IQ's

The range of WISC Full Scale IQ's to be expected in the general school population, and the meaning of these "scores" are shown in Table 3-4.

*TABLE 3-4*
*Intelligence Classification for WISC IQ's*

| IQ Ranges | Classification | Percent in Each Group |
|---|---|---|
| 130 – | very superior | 2 |
| 120 – 129 | superior | 7 |
| 110 – 119 | bright normal | 16 |
| 90 – 109 | average | 50 |
| 80 – 89 | dull normal | 16 |
| 70 – 79 | borderline | 7 |
| 69 below | mental defective | 2 |
|  |  | 100 |

It will be seen that these classifications correspond closely to those for Stanford-Binet IQ's.

Reliability coefficients for the WISC are generally above .90.

They are higher for the Full Scale than for either the Verbal or Performance Scales. The standard error of a WISC IQ is 4–5 points.

### MA's from the WISC

The WISC does not ordinarily make use of mental age, but when mental ages are required for clinical or for legal reasons they can readily be determined. The test Manual (Appendix E) provides a table of "test-age equivalents to WISC raw scores." By reference to the table, we find the chronological age of a child for whom a given raw score is typical (or average), and this is the MA corresponding to the score. For example, a score of 12 on the Comprehension test is achieved on the average by children who are ten–six years old. Hence, a score of 12 in Comprehension has an equivalent MA of 10–6. The *mean* of the subtest MA's is computed (Mean Test-Age Method) or the *median* of the MA's (Median Test-Age Method). Either of these determinations gives the final overall MA. A closely equivalent method for determining MA's from the WISC is the use of the formula $MA = IQ \times CA$. A child who achieves an IQ of 110 and who is 8–2 years old has a MA of $110 \times 8$–2, or approximately 9–0 years.

## PERFORMANCE TESTS

### Development of Performance Tests

Performance tests designed to measure general mental ability often have been used in the schools as substitutes for the more verbal tests, and as supplements to the Stanford-Binet and other linguistic scales. Performance and non-language tests must of necessity be employed with pre-school children and with the very dull. Such tests are useful additions to the Stanford-Binet or WISC in the mental examination of children with speech and language defects or of children with visual and auditory impairment. Batteries of performance tests have long been used in psychological clinics and in institutions for the feebleminded. The classroom teacher should know about performance tests, though he will encounter them much less frequently than the WISC or the Stanford-Binet.

The Pintner-Paterson Scale of Performance Tests (1917) was the first organized battery of manipulative and non-language tests. Widely used for many years, this scale has now been replaced to a great degree by other batteries which are based on it. The Pintner-Paterson Scale consists of fifteen separate tests. The ten tests most often used (in what is called the Shorter Scale) include four form boards, three picture completion tests (of the jigsaw-puzzle type), two object assembly tests, and one block-counting test.

Performance scales devised later include the Cornell-Coxe Performance Ability Scale (1934) and the Arthur Point Scale of Performance Tests (1930, revised 1947). These test batteries draw heavily on the Pintner-Paterson, but include important additions and revisions. In addition to these test batteries, there are a number of other performance tests, of which the Porteus Mazes, a graduated series of mazes, is the best known. Widely used types of performance tests are the object assembly (page 68), various form boards, block counting, and block design. Two of these, block design and object assembly, are found in the Wechsler-Bellevue Scales.

Norms are generally available for the individual performance tests, so that one may use one or more tests without having to administer the whole scale.

## The Arthur Point Scale

The Arthur Point Scale has been widely used over the age range of the elementary school. It is made up of performance tests taken from various sources; it was first published in 1930 and was revised in 1947. The later edition is a considerable improvement over the original insofar as standardization is concerned, and the Scale is a good example of a performance battery designed for children. Figure 3–4 shows the five tests in the Arthur Point.

*Knox Cube.* The four cubes (see Figure 3–4) are tapped in a certain order by the examiner, for example, cube 1, cube 4, cube 2, cube 3. The child is told to imitate the tapping order. Tapping sequences become longer and more complex, until they can no longer be done by the child.

*Sequin Form Board.* Ten common geometric forms (Figure 3–4) are to be fitted into the right apertures in the board.

*Porteus Mazes.* The child is told to trace the shortest path from the entrance to the exit in a maze, not lifting the pencil from the paper. If he makes an error by crossing a line or entering a wrong pathway, he is stopped and given a second trial. Mazes increase in difficulty from three-year level to adult.

*Healy Picture Completion II.* As shown in Figure 3–4, the test shows successive scenes in a boy's life during a typical school day. Small pieces or blocks have been cut out of the scene. The child must select the appropriate pieces from the box and fit them in place.

*Arthur Stencil Design Test.* The child must reproduce designs of increasing complexity. Standard designs to be copied are presented on cards. Each design can be reproduced by fitting together stencils in different colors on a solid white card. Several stencils are needed for the more detailed designs.

**Scope.** The Arthur Performance Scale covers an age range from about four years to maturity, but is used chiefly with younger children. The scale is employed mainly as a clinical test supplementary to, or as a substitute for, the Stanford-Binet.

**Scoring.** Scores on the subtests (based on accuracy and time) are first converted into point scores. These are combined and converted into mental ages. MA's are chronological ages which are typical for given combined scores. Thus if the average child of 10–0 scores 31 points, a score of 31 points becomes an MA of 10–0. MA is divided by CA to give a "performance IQ." These IQ's are not equivalent to the IQ's from verbal intelligence scales and are not to be so regarded. Arthur Point Scale IQ's should always be described as "Arthur Scale IQ's."

## Performance Tests in the Schools

Correlations between scores on the Arthur Scale and the Stanford-Binet are fairly high (.50 or more). The two tests are, however, not measuring exactly the same functions, and hence the Arthur IQ is often used as a "performance supplement" to the Stanford-Binet IQ. Arthur IQ's are higher than Stanford-Binet IQ's when the latter are low—that is, below 90—and this discrepancy is especially striking when children are very dull. There is evidence that low performance test scores may be indicative of behavior problems and of emotional instability. This result probably grows out of the disturbed child's poor attention span, poor perception of relations, and ineptitude in manual activities. Emotional involvement may be expressed in bizarre and unusual responses.

For the classroom teacher the main value of a performance test lies, perhaps, in the fact that such tests may reflect poor language development or lack of language training, and are often indicative of cultural and educational handicaps. As pointed out on page 72, a comparison of performance tests with verbal tests may often reveal children whose manual and manipulative skills ("concrete intelligence") run ahead of their verbal facility ("abstract intelligence"). Performance tests also serve to identify the shy and inarticulate child who is brighter than the verbal tests show. Performance tests are not especially useful with normal school children over twelve years of age, and they rarely differentiate significantly among older bright children.

**Case Histories.** The following brief case histories will illustrate how performance tests, when used with verbal tests, can provide a better understanding of a pupil's capabilities. In most cases recommendations must be tentative and subject to possible revision in the light of further information.

Case 1. Donald B.: age, 10–2; WISC IQ, 92; Arthur Scale IQ, 106.

Donald is doing poor work in the fifth grade. His father is a barber, his mother a part-time clerk in a store. Neither parent went beyond the seventh grade. There are three other children in the family, all younger than Donald. There are few books in the home, but the family owns a TV set and a new automobile. Donald reads the sports page and the comics in the daily newspaper, but little else. He talks in brief sentences and is generally unresponsive in school. He is well-developed for his age, is a good athlete, and is well accepted by his classmates. He has never been a behavior problem.

*Recommendation:* Donald's performance IQ is fourteen points higher than his WISC IQ. In view of his relatively meager abstract intelligence, this boy is probably doing as well as we can expect. He may get to high school, but will almost certainly not complete more than one year. Vocational training seems to be indicated. He will continue to have trouble with verbal subjects, but may be very successful at a skilled trade.

Case 2. Joan M.: age, 8–3; Stanford-Binet IQ, 126; Arthur Scale IQ, 109.

Joan is doing excellent work in the fourth grade. Her problem is a social rather than a scholastic one. Her mother, a widow, is a successful dress designer. Joan is an only child and is alone much of the time. She reads a great deal but has few close friends and is often left out of class activities. She has a tendency to daydream and is shy and withdrawn.

*Recommendation:* Joan's low performance IQ, coupled with her high Stanford-Binet IQ, indicates a lack of experience with "concrete" activities, such as running, playing out-of-doors, skipping rope, dancing, and the like. This lack of opportunity to develop manual skills is often found in children reared in a large city. Joan's mother may be encouraged to meet with other classroom mothers, to arrange parties, and to invite Joan's classmates to her home. The aid of the physical education teacher in getting Joan into games should also be sought. The classroom teacher can often see to it, by suggestion and indirection, that Joan is included in class parties and out-of-class activities.

Case 3. Bob W.: age, 9–2; Stanford-Binet IQ, 104; Arthur Scale IQ, 115.

Bob is doing satisfactory work in the fourth grade. He is shy and timid, with a slight tendency to stammer, especially when questioned. He is one of four children, the other three being girls all older than he. Bob's father is a successful lawyer, and his mother is a college graduate and a prominent club woman. The parents have decided that Bob, as the only boy, is to be a professional man, preferably a physician (his grandfather was a well-known surgeon). They are dissatisfied with Bob's marks, and are sure he is intelligent and that the teacher is to blame.

*Recommendation:* Bob is clearly a normal boy. He is not bright, though he probably is brighter than his Stanford-Binet IQ indicates. The parents must somehow be reconciled to the fact that Bob is not of professional caliber, and that a lower vocational goal (one within Bob's intellectual grasp) will make for a happier boy and probably a much happier life. They must be urged not to scold the boy and thus make him feel more inferior than he already does. This is a difficult problem, because it is the parents—not the child—who have to be "sold" on a different program from the one they have planned.

## SUGGESTIONS FOR FURTHER READING

### GENERAL
ANASTASI, A. *Psychological Testing.* 2nd ed.; New York: Macmillan, 1961.
CRONBACH, L. J. *Essentials of Psychological Testing.* 2nd ed.; New York: Harper, 1960.
FREEMAN, F. S. *Theory and Practice of Psychological Testing.* Rev. ed.; New York: Holt, 1955.

### SPECIFIC
ARTHUR, G. A. *A Point Scale of Performance Tests. Revised Form II. Manual for Administering and Scoring the Tests.* New York: Psychological Corp., 1947.
MC NEMAR, Q. *The Revision of the Stanford-Binet Scale: An Analysis of the Standardization Data.* Boston: Houghton Mifflin, 1942.
TERMAN, L. M. and MERRILL, M. A. *Measuring Intelligence.* Boston: Houghton Mifflin, 1937.
TERMAN, L. M. and MERRILL, M. A. *Stanford-Binet Intelligence Scale.* (*Manual for Third Revision, Form L–M.*) Boston: Houghton Mifflin, 1960.
WECHSLER, D. *Wechsler Intelligence Scale for Children Manual.* New York: Psychological Corp., 1949.
WECHSLER, D. *Wechsler Adult Intelligence Scale Manual.* New York: Psychological Corp., 1955.

## SUGGESTIONS FOR LABORATORY WORK

1. Examine the Stanford-Binet items at ages four, eight, and twelve, and Superior Adult. Classify the items at each age level as verbal, numerical, spatial-perceptual (for example, mazes and the like), and performance (manipulative). Add other categories if you need them. Which category has the largest number of items?

2. Have members of the class pair off and test each other on WAIS. Be sure to follow the Manual carefully. Results from this "test" will not be indicative of mental ability, to be sure, but following the procedure is a good way to learn about the test.

3. Repeat (1) and (2) for the Wechsler Intelligence Scale for Children. For (2), sample the items of each test.

4. Go over the Manual of the Arthur Point Scale. If materials are available, administer the Scale to a child before the class.

## QUESTIONS FOR DISCUSSION

1. What importance do you attach to the fact that test items in Stanford-Binet become more "verbal" as we go up the age scale?
2. Which test, Stanford-Binet or Arthur Point Scale, would you expect to prove more effective in the following situations?
   a) selecting children for a special class for the gifted
   b) selecting children for remedial work in a "slow" class
   c) studying children with reading problems
   d) testing children with speech defects
3. A child taken from public school and entered in a private school is reported by his mother to have shown an increase in IQ of 20 points after six months in the "new" school. Assuming the story to be true, what is misleading about it? What might account for the change in the IQ?
4. A high school boy of 16 has a WAIS IQ of 132. What advice would be justified by this fact alone?
5. Look over the items in the WISC. Which do you think depend primarily on schooling? Do the same for the Stanford-Binet. Which test is the more "school centered"?
6. Terman states that the vocabulary test gives the closest approximation to total performance on Stanford-Binet. What does this tell us about the nature of the Stanford-Binet IQ?
7. In deploring the reading interests, TV programs, and voting habits of the American adult, critics have said that the average mental age of the adult is about 14 (sometimes this is 12 or 15). What does mental age signify here, if anything definable?
8. Does a child with an IQ of 80 possess 80 percent of normal intelligence? Explain your answer.
9. Would a marked change in a child's IQ *necessarily* mean that he is brighter or duller?
10. How might the difference between the Verbal and Performance IQ's help us better to understand a shy, inarticulate pupil?
11. A mother protests that her boy's low IQ would improve if the school would teach him to concentrate. Is this argument likely to be valid?
12. What other factors besides IQ should be considered in deciding whether a student is "college material"?

Chapter 4

# GROUP TESTS OF INTELLIGENCE

GROUP AND INDIVIDUAL TESTS OF INTELLIGENCE

Group tests of intelligence are much like individual tests except that (1) they are administered like school examinations, and (2) they are objective in form—that is, they are answered by checking or circling a number or letter or by marking one of several possible responses. Group tests contain both *verbal* and *nonverbal* materials. Items of the first type are expressed in words and numbers; nonverbal test items consist of problems presented in pictures and diagrams. There is a minimum of language and little or no reading required in nonverbal items. Intelligence tests for preschool and first-grade pupils are of necessity nonverbal, though directions are given orally. Intelligence tests in the elementary grades contain both verbal and nonverbal items. At the high-school and college levels, test items are mostly verbal, mathematical, and abstract, but even here many problems are presented in pictorial and spatial forms.

Group tests of intelligence confront the examinee with tasks like those found in the individual intelligence scales. Both types of test minimize routine school learning and emphasize mental alertness by presenting problems which demand reasoning, generalization, and the manipulation of "ideas." But there are differences, too, between the two sorts of tests. In individual intelligence scales, questions are stated orally and are answered orally; moreover, problems are presented one at a time without time limit, or a generous limit is allowed. In group intelligence tests, questions are printed in a booklet, time limits are fixed, and answers are limited to the options provided. The group test is more dependent on reading than is the individual test; it is less flexible in response; and it is often disturbing to children who are easily flustered by a time limit. When a child's school work and/or the teacher's opinion of his abilities do not jibe with his group test score, it may be advisable to check the group test result against the Stanford-Binet. Group tests, like individual scales, are concerned almost entirely with the abstract level of intelligence (page 48).

The first widely used group tests were the two intelligence examinations developed for the army during World War I (1917–1918). Army Alpha consisted of eight subtests: Following Directions, Arithmetic Problems, Best Answers, Disarranged Sentences, Same-Opposites, Number Series Completion, Analogies, and Information. Army Beta made use of diagrams and pictures, and directions were given in pantomime. During World War II, the Army General Classification Test (AGCT) was developed as a measure of general ability. Unlike Alpha, the items in AGCT were not grouped into subtests, but were printed in ascending order of difficulty. A civilian edition of AGCT is now available.

## REPRESENTATIVE GROUP TESTS OF INTELLIGENCE

This section will describe several tests of general intelligence covering the age range from preschool to college. These test batteries have been chosen for illustration because they are well standardized, are widely used in the schools, and are representative of a large assortment of group tests designed to measure general ability. They are not necessarily the best mental examinations for every testing situation or for every school. Selection of a "best" test will depend on the objectives of the school, the time available for testing, and the money and personnel available.

GROUP TESTS OF INTELLIGENCE

Pintner-Cunningham Primary Test
California Test of Mental Maturity
Otis Quick-Scoring Mental Ability Tests
Kuhlmann-Anderson Intelligence
Lorge-Thorndike Intelligence Tests
Terman-McNemar Test of Mental Ability
American Council on Education Psychological Examination

### The Pintner-Cunningham Primary Test[1]

**Description.** This test includes seven nonverbal subtests described as follows:

1. Common Observation: Child marks all of the objects in a given set which fit into some category. (See Figure 4–1, row 1.)
2. Aesthetic Differences: The child is told to mark the "prettiest" (that is, the best) of three drawings of the same object. (Figure 4–1, row 2.)
3. Associated Objects: The child marks the two objects that belong together in each row of pictures—for example, the hat and the coat. (Figure 4–1, row 3.)
4. Discrimination of Size: The pupil is instructed to mark

[1] Harcourt, Brace & World, Inc., New York, New York.

the items of clothing which are of the right size for the individual pictured. For each article of clothing—shoes, hat, gloves, and so on—one is too large, one is too small, and one is of the right size.

5. Picture Parts: In this test a series of pictures of increasing complexity is shown. These contain children, toys, animals, and other items. The same items are shown outside the "standard" picture, mixed in with other objects. The child is instructed to

Figure 4–1 *Illustrative Items from the Pintner-Cunningham Primary Test*

Test 1. Mark the things that Mother uses when she sews her apron.

Test 2. Mark the prettiest house.

Test 3. Mark the two things that belong together.

Test 7. Look at each picture. See how it is drawn. Make another one like it in the dots.

Reproduced by permission of Harcourt, Brace & World, Inc.

mark all of the objects in this group which appeared in the picture.

6. Picture Completion: In each incomplete picture, the pupil is asked to locate and mark the correct missing part from among several parts shown.

7. Dot Drawing: The child is to copy drawings which are formed by joining dots. (See Figure 4–1, row 4.)

All the tests are nonverbal, since most of the children for whom the test is intended have not learned to read. Directions are given orally.

**Scope.** The Pintner-Cunningham Primary Test covers kindergarten, Grade 1, and the first half of Grade 2. There are three equivalent forms, A, B, and C.

**Scoring.** Scores from the seven subtests are combined to give a total point score. Mental ages corresponding to point scores may be read from tables in the Manual. Pintner-Cunningham MA's are chronological ages for which the given point scores are typical (see page 34). These MA's are divided by the child's CA to obtain an IQ. An alternative—and better procedure—is to convert the point scores into deviation IQ's, following the method used in the Wechsler tests. The mean IQ is, of course, 100, and the SD is 16, equal to that of the Stanford-Binet. Pintner-Cunningham IQ's are not strictly equivalent to Stanford-Binet IQ's though the same abilities appear to be measured by the two scales. Correlations between the two test batteries run from .70 to .90 for kindergarten and primary school children. This indicates that Pintner-Cunningham is a valid measure of the abstract intelligence measured by Stanford-Binet. The reliability or stability of Pintner-Cunningham scores is high, as shown by the close correspondence of one form with another.

### THE CALIFORNIA TEST OF MENTAL MATURITY (CTMM, LONG FORM, 1963 REVISION)[2]

**Description.** These tests contain both verbal and nonverbal

[2] California Test Bureau, Monterey, California.

or pictorial materials. There are twelve subtests classified under five heads, or "factors": logical reasoning, spatial relationships, numerical reasoning, verbal concepts, and memory. All test items are in multiple-choice form. The five test groupings were verified through a factor analysis of the subtests, which showed that each "factor" measures a fairly discrete ability. Test format is good, and instructions can be followed easily by the examinee.

**Scope.** The CTMM covers the age range from preschool to college. There are six levels:
Level 0: pre-primary, kindergarten through low grade 1
Level 1: primary, high grade 1 through grade 3
Level 2: elementary, grades 4-6
Level 3: junior high, grades 7-9
Level 4: secondary, grades 9-12
Level 5: advanced, grade 12-adult

A battery (one level) takes about one and one-half hours to administer. This includes time for giving out the tests and reading directions and working time. Each level is printed in a different color to aid in ready identification.

**Scoring.** Separate scores can be obtained for each of the five factors, or areas, measured by the battery. Also separate scores may be found for the verbal and nonverbal sections. The profile (Figure 4-2) gives the names and groupings of the subtests. The chart provides for factor scores, language and non-language scores, percentile ranks, standard scores, MA's, and IQ's. The actual grade placement of an examinee can be compared with the grade placement appropriate to his age level. All of the scaled scores are derived from the raw scores by means of appropriate tables. A stanine scale, that is, a scale in which each factor score may be located in one of nine ability groupings, provides for quick interpretation.

The profile in Figure 4-2 is especially useful in analysis and diagnosis. The highs and lows of a pupil's performance can be readily seen from their locations on the chart. Thus it is clear that Robert Allen's *PR* (percentile rank) in Logical Reasoning is 88, which places him in the stanine 7 (9 is the highest, 1 the lowest). His PR in Memory is 54, and this PR places him in the stanine 5. IQ's are "deviation scores" (page 40) and not ratios. This is an improvement over earlier editions. Robert's language IQ is 95, and his non-language IQ is 112. His "full IQ" is 104. Robert did relatively better on the mathematical-spatial items than on the verbal-memory items.

Robert, who was tested in October in the Fifth Grade, has an actual grade placement of 5.1 (see Figure 4–2). This corresponds to a chronological age of 127 months. Since Robert's CA is 129 months, he is two months older than the typical pupil in Grade 5.1.

The validity of the CTMM is quite satisfactory as determined from correlations with Stanford-Binet and other criteria. A complete item-analysis was carried out of the earlier CTMM's with subsequent rearrangement and replacement. This greatly adds to the test's validity. Reliability is high for each level, as reported from the standardization sample of nearly 40,000 children.

## OTIS QUICK-SCORING MENTAL ABILITY TESTS[3]

**Description.** These tests differ from many group tests of intelligence in that the test items are not grouped into separate subtests according to type of item. Instead, the different items—analogies, arithmetic problems, opposites, and the like—are printed in a continuous repetitive pattern, so that items of a certain sort (opposites, for example) follow each other at stated intervals. This arrangement is sometimes called a *scrambled* test, or more precisely a *spiral omnibus* arrangement. Items are progressively more difficult from the start to the finish of the test.

The following items are like those in the Otis Beta Test,[4] an examination prepared for grades 4–9.

[3] Harcourt, Brace & World, Inc., New York, New York.
[4] The first two items are samples from the Beta Test. Other items are like those found in the test.

Figure 4-2 Profile for the California Test of Mental Maturity

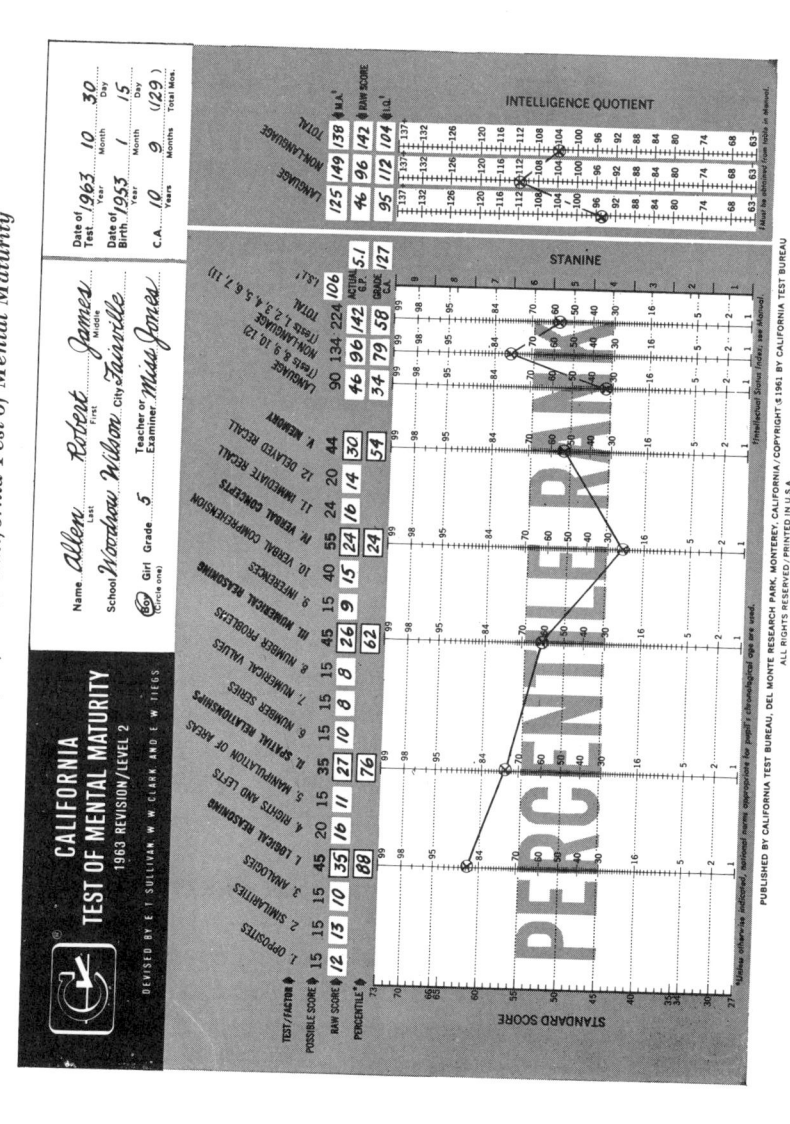

Reproduced by permission of the California Test Bureau.

1. Which of the five things below is soft?  
   1. glass  2. stone  3. *cotton*  4. iron  5. ice

       1  2  3  4  5  
      ( ) ( ) (x) ( ) ( )

2. A robin is a kind of  
   1. plant  2. *bird*  3. worm  4. fish  5. flower

       1  2  3  4  5  
      ( ) (x) ( ) ( ) ( )

3. Hat is to head as shoe is to  
   1. arm  2. leg  3. *foot*  4. fit  5. glove

       1  2  3  4  5  
      ( ) ( ) (x) ( ) ( )

4. North  
   1. hot  2. east  3. west  4. down  5. *south*

       1  2  3  4  5  
      ( ) ( ) ( ) ( ) (x)

5. At five cents each, how many pencils can be bought for 40 cents?  
   1. 45  2. 8  3. 200  4. 5  5. 12

       1  2  3  4  5  
      ( ) (x) ( ) ( ) ( )

**Scope.** The Otis Quick-Scoring Tests cover the age range from Grade 1 through college. There are three batteries:

    Alpha Test (90 items) nonverbal—grades 1–4;

    Beta Test (80 items) verbal, numerical, and spatial—grades 4–9;

    Gamma Test (80 items) primarily verbal—high school and college.

**Scoring.** The Otis tests are easy to administer, and scoring is facilitated by a cutout stencil which can be superimposed on the test booklet. The tests are almost "self-administering." There is a single time limit, which varies from twenty to thirty minutes. Mental age equivalents to total score are read from tables in the Manual. The Otis IQ's are deviation scores and are measures of brightness. These IQ's are only generally comparable to Stanford-Binet IQ's; the two "scores" are not equivalent. The reliability of the Otis tests is high.

## Kuhlmann-Anderson Intelligence Tests[5]

**Description.** This is a series of thirty-nine separate subtests grouped into nine overlapping test batteries. The subtests include verbal and nonverbal materials. The early levels are entirely pictorial, but the tests become more verbal and abstract as we go up the age scale and finally are entirely verbal. Each test battery consists of ten subtests.

**Scope.** Each of the nine batteries is printed in a separate booklet and is designed to cover one or more grade levels, as follows:

| | | |
|---|---|---|
| Kindergarten: | subtests | 1–10 |
| Grade 1 | subtests | 4–13 |
| Grade 2 | subtests | 8–17 |
| Grade 3 | subtests | 12–21 |
| Grade 4 | subtests | 15–24 |
| Grade 5 | subtests | 19–28 |
| Grade 6 | subtests | 22–31 |
| Grade 7–8 | subtests | 25–34 |
| Grade 9–12 | subtests | 30–39 |

Administration of the K-A tests is somewhat more difficult than the Otis, since the tests in the batteries are often separately timed. K-A tests require from thirty to forty-five minutes to administer.

**Scoring.** In setting up a scoring plan, the authors of K-A have employed what is called the "median mental age" method. This may be described briefly as follows. Each of the ten subtests in a battery yields a mental age. These MA's (see page 33) are chronological ages for which a given score is typical or average. Thus if the children who are ten years and two months old earn in general a score of 21 on a given subtest, then the score of 21 corresponds to or is equivalent to a MA of 10–2 on this subtest. MA's are read from tables in the Manual. The *median* MA is the

---
[5] Personnel Press, Inc., Princeton, New Jersey.

median of the ten subtest MA's.[6] This is taken to be the most representative measure of a child's overall ability.

An IQ for the battery is found by dividing the median MA by the child's life age, or CA. This IQ is not equivalent to the Stanford-Binet IQ, though it is related to it. The K-A tests measure primarily verbal or abstract intelligence, especially at the upper age levels. The reliability of the K-A—as shown by the stability of its test scores—is very high. Reliability coefficients have been computed for grades 1 through 9 separately, and these range from .89 to .97.

### THE LORGE-THORNDIKE INTELLIGENCE TESTS[7]

**Description.** This is a comprehensive test, with separate batteries set up on five levels from kindergarten through high school. On the lowest two levels (the Primary Battery) only pictorial items are used. These require understanding and reasoning—that is, logical arrangement. The Primary Battery is suitable for children who do not read well. The three levels for Grades 4–12 contain both verbal and nonverbal sections. Verbal items require word classification, arithmetical reasoning, and vocabulary. Nonverbal items are numerical and pictorial. All of the items are designed to test the ability to solve problems by the use of symbols. The authors state that the IQ's from the verbal and nonverbal parts will differ by as much as 15 points in about 25 percent of the cases, and that such differences may be valuable in studies of reading, school achievement, and vocational prediction.

**Scope.** The Lorge-Thorndike Intelligence Tests cover the elementary- and high-school grades. Sampling in the construction of the test was good, and the test series is well made.

**Scoring.** Raw test scores may be converted by use of tables

---

[6] When ten scores are arranged in order of size, the point (or score) found by counting off five scores from either end of the series is the typical value or median (see page 21).
[7] Houghton Mifflin Company, Boston, Massachusetts.

*Figure 4–3  Sample Items from the Lorge-Thorndike Intelligence Tests, Level 3, Form A, Non-Verbal Battery*

**1.**

0. [drawings]   A   B   C   D   E

Look at sample question 0. The first three drawings in the row are alike in a certain way. Find the drawing at the right that goes with the first three.

The first three drawings are alike in that each has four sides and no lines inside it. The drawing at the right that goes with them is at D. It has four sides and no lines inside it. Make a heavy black pencil mark in the D answer space for question 0. Now look at question 00. Find the drawing at the right that goes with the first three.

00. [drawings]   F   G   H   J   K

The first three drawings are alike in that they have three sides and are getting wider. At the right, the only one that is still wider is at H. Make a heavy black pencil mark in the H answer space for question 00.

**2.**

0.  1   2   3   4   5 →   A 5   B 6   C 7   D 8   E 9

Look at sample question 0. The numbers at the left are in a certain order. Find the number at the right that should come next.

The number that should come next after 1 2 3 4 5 is 6. Make a heavy black pencil mark in the B answer space for question 0. Now look at question 00. Find the number at the right that should come next.

00.  5   5   4   4   3 →   F 1   G 2   H 3   J 4   K 5

The next number should be 3, so you should make a heavy black pencil mark in the H answer space for question 00.

Reproduced by permission of Houghton Mifflin Company.

into deviation IQ's with mean = 100 and SD = 16. Grade percentiles, grade equivalents in raw score, and age equivalents in raw score may be read from appropriate tables.

The reliability coefficients of the Lorge-Thorndike are generally high. Standard errors of IQ's will range from about 4 points (verbal batteries) to about 6 points (nonverbal batteries). The authors believe that the careful selection of items makes for logical or rational validity. Experimental validity has been determined through correlations with other well regarded tests.

### TERMAN-MCNEMAR TEST OF MENTAL ABILITY[8]

**Description.** This test is designed for high school students. It is largely a measure of ability to read and comprehend fairly difficult prose. Two numerical subtests found in an earlier edition of the test were eliminated in order to render the test more unified in content. As it stands, it is a highly verbal battery. There are seven subtests: information, synonyms, logical selection, classification, analogies, opposites, and best answer. Sample items and instructions for each item type are shown in Figure 4–4. These items are easier than are the items found in the test proper and are for illustration. Items in the test are graded in difficulty from easy to hard.

**Scope.** The Terman-McNemar is planned specifically for grades 7 through 12 and for college freshmen.

**Scoring.** Total raw score is converted into a scaled score IQ, which is closely related to Stanford-Binet IQ. Scores may also be expressed as MA's and as percentile ranks. The working time for the test is about fifty minutes. Terman-McNemar comes in two equivalent forms. In the construction of the test, a careful item analysis was made (page 231) in order to weed out unsatisfactory items. This is offered as evidence of the test's validity. The reliability of the Terman-McNemar is reported to be .96 for a single age level.

### AMERICAN COUNCIL ON EDUCATION PSYCHOLOGICAL EXAMINATION[9]

**Description.** This battery of tests was designed to measure scholastic aptitude, or learning ability in school. It comes in two forms, one for high-school students and one for college freshmen. The college test consists of six subtests:

[8] Harcourt, Brace & World, Inc., New York, New York.
[9] Educational Testing Service, Princeton, New Jersey.

Figure 4-4 Sample Items from the Terman-McNemar Test of Mental Ability (Form C)

---

**TEST 1. INFORMATION**

Mark the answer space which has the same number as the word that makes the sentence TRUE.

SAMPLE. Our first President was
 1 Adams  2 Washington  3 Lincoln  4 Jefferson  5 Monroe....

**TEST 2. SYNONYMS**

Mark the answer space which has the same number as the word which has the SAME or most nearly the same meaning as the beginning word of each line.

SAMPLE. correct — 1 neat  2 fair  3 right  4 poor  5 good.....................

**TEST 3. LOGICAL SELECTION**

Mark the answer space which has the same number as the word which tells what the thing ALWAYS has or ALWAYS involves.

SAMPLE. A cat always has
 1 kittens  2 spots  3 milk  4 mouse  5 hair..................

**TEST 4. CLASSIFICATION**

In each line below, four of the words belong together. Pick out the ONE WORD which does not belong with the others, and mark the answer space bearing its number.

SAMPLES.
 1 dog  2 cat  3 horse  4 chicken  5 cow............................
 6 hop  7 run  8 stand  9 skip  10 walk............................

**TEST 5. ANALOGIES**

Study the samples carefully.
 Ear is to hear as eye is to
SAMPLES.  1 cry  2 glasses  3 spy  4 wink  5 see......................
 Hat is to head as shoe is to
 6 arm  7 leg  8 foot  9 fit  10 glove......................
DO THEM ALL LIKE THE SAMPLES.

**TEST 6. OPPOSITES**

Mark the answer space which has the same number as the word which is OPPOSITE, or most nearly opposite, in meaning to the beginning word of each line.

SAMPLE. north — 1 hot  2 east  3 west  4 down  5 south................

**TEST 7. BEST ANSWER**

Read each statement and mark the answer space which has the same number as the answer which you think is BEST.

SAMPLE. We should not put a burning match in the wastebasket because
 1 Matches cost money.  2 We might need a match later.
 3 It might go out.  4 It might start a fire...........................

Reproduced by permission of Harcourt, Brace & World, Inc.

1. *Arithmetic Problems:* twenty problems in multiple-choice form, of the "mental arithmetic" variety.
2. *Completion:* thirty items in multiple-choice form. The test demands word knowledge and definitions.
3. *Figure Analogies:* thirty multiple-choice items. Analogies involve geometric forms, areas, angles, spatial arrangements.

4. *Same-Opposite:* fifty multiple-choice items which demand vocabulary and word knowledge.
5. *Number Series:* thirty items to be completed "logically" with appropriate numbers.
6. *Verbal Analogies:* forty items: relation-finding in verbal terms.

In the ACE, college form, subtests 1, 3, and 5 are combined to give a quantitative, or Q, score; subtests 2, 4, and 6 are combined to give a linguistic, or L, score. Each subtest is separately timed, and each is preceded by a practice exercise. In the high-school form of the ACE, tests 3 and 6 have been dropped, leaving four subtests. Completion and same-opposite were combined to give the L score, and arithmetic and number series to give the Q score.

The ACE has been largely replaced by the SCAT (see page 121) and is no longer published. But many studies in the literature make use of it, and other group tests have been modeled after it.

**Scope.** The ACE is the most difficult of the general intelligence tests described so far. Testing time varies from about forty minutes (high-school form) to sixty minutes (college form).

**Scoring.** The three scores from the ACE—the quantitative, the linguistic, and the total—can be converted into percentile ranks. Extensive norms (in *PR*'s), published annually, cover test results from previous years. Q scores have been found to correlate with achievement (grades) in mathematics and science, but the L score has the higher correlation with general achievement in high school.

The predictive validity (page 32) of the ACE, as determined over several years, is high. ACE correlates from .40 to .60 with college grades; its correlations with Stanford-Binet average about .65. The reliability coefficients of Q, L, and total score are all very high. One feature of the ACE is the publication of norms for different groups. Separate norms are available for boys and girls and for three types of college—four-year, two-year (junior), and teachers colleges. Although the four-year colleges achieve higher mean scores, there is much overlapping of four-year, two-year, and teachers college scores. Differential norms are a distinct aid to educational counselors.

## HOW GROUP INTELLIGENCE TESTS ARE USED IN THE SCHOOL

### Survey Measures

In general, the group test of intelligence is used (1) to give an overall measure of a child's abstract ability (often an IQ), (2) to provide a basis for educational counseling and guidance, and (3) to give a basis for prognosis. The total score on a group test is useful to the school administrator, the classroom teacher, and the parent. Standardized tests supply the school administrator with a systematic record of how different schools, and classes within a given school, compare in general ability to learn. The classroom teacher gets needed information concerning the abilities of individual pupils. Within a given class, the spread of ability is often disturbingly wide. A teacher can tell from his test scores if John and Mary are doing the caliber of work which can reasonably be expected of them, and if he is pitching his instruction at the comprehension level of the class as a whole. Parents can plan the future education of their children more intelligently when they know the level of performance which can be expected of them. Students can set their academic and occupational goals more realistically when they are aware of their strengths and weaknesses as shown by comparison of their scores with norms for their age level.

### Counseling, Guidance, and Prognosis

The total score from a group test—the IQ or other type score—is most useful as a measure of a pupil's overall academic ability. For guidance and counseling the teacher can use the subtests or part scores from the test battery to greater advantage.

The profile of the California Test of Mental Maturity, for instance, has been especially designed for diagnosis. From the language and non-language IQ's, a teacher can judge whether a child is predominantly "verbal-minded" or "object-minded"; and from the five "factor" scores on the profile he can judge how proficient a pupil is in memory, logical reasoning, verbal concepts, spatial-perceptual relations, and numerical reasoning. In Figure 4-2, for example, low scores in reasoning and vocabulary indicate poor academic ability—that is, a lack of the ability to solve problems efficiently by means of symbols (numbers and words). High scores in these factors reveal high academic aptitude and, when combined with other traits, suggest that the pupil is capable of more advanced, perhaps professional, training. Low scores in spatial relations reveal little promise of success in geometry, mechanical drawing, and perhaps manual training. High scores here, plus high scores in the other factors, forecast aptitude for engineering and architecture. The memory factor is based on too meager a sample to provide a reliable measure of a pupil's functional memory. The score might be significant, however, if it is either very high or very low.

Part scores, like those from the CTMM, are helpful in giving the classroom teacher clues about a child's abilities, but these scores must always be interpreted with caution (page 72). The subtests on which such judgments are based are quite short and are often too narrow to permit a broad prediction. Marked differences in part scores should always be substantiated by further investigation; they should jibe with other tests, with grades, and with the teacher's judgment from observation of the pupil's classroom work.

The verbal and nonverbal parts of the Lorge-Thorndike Intelligence Tests provide an overall, comprehensive measure of mental alertness. They also permit separation of pupils who are poor readers, and those whose verbal ability lags behind their non-language abilities.

The Otis Quick-Scoring Mental Ability Tests and the Kuhlmann-Anderson Intelligence tests are primarily useful as overall measures of the general level of mental functioning. The subtests of the Kuhlmann-Anderson are fairly complex. The authors, very wisely, do not recommend that specific scores (mental ages) from subtests be interpreted as measuring definite psychological functions. Wide variations in score from subtest to subtest for a given child may signify gaps in training or in native ability, however.

The Pintner-Cunningham Primary Test is perhaps most useful in helping the teacher and parent decide whether a child is mature enough mentally to do first-grade work. Entrance into first grade should not depend solely on the MA or CA, however. Children who are babyish in their social behavior and poorly developed physically are poor prospects for first grade, no matter how high their IQ's.

Because of its high verbal content, the Terman-McNemar Test of Mental Ability is one of the best predictors of high-school achievement. The homogeneity of the subtests (their high degree of relatedness) renders the test less useful for diagnosis of a student's strengths and weaknesses.

The American Council on Education Psychological Examination is a good predictor of college work. This battery measures initiative in attacking new problems, and mental speed and facility and good work habits, as well as abstract ability. ACE is also useful in guidance, since it provides three scores—a quantitative (Q), a linguistic (L), and a total. The ACE for high-school students is used as a screening test for prospective college freshmen and as a basis for counseling high-school students who plan to continue their education beyond high school. The L score is perhaps most predictive of general college work because of the great importance of reading comprehension in college courses. The Q score has predictive value for science and mathematics, especially when confirmed by other indicators (grades, teachers' judgments, and so on).

The ACE (page 96) provides separate norms for two-year, four-year, and teachers colleges. The four-year colleges have the higher average scores, but variation in score from one type of college to another is very large, as is variation in score within each college type. A student's chances of entering college and staying there will depend to a considerable degree on the college he chooses (see page 124 for discussion of local and nationwide norms) or to which he is admitted. Only superior students should be encouraged to apply to high-standard colleges, and not all of these are good risks unless they have the personal qualities which are required to accompany academic potential. Good personality and a capacity for hard work may not, in themselves, enhance a student's chances of being accepted into a grade-A college, but they will help him stay there once he is in. Students with relatively low scores on ACE have been quite successful in colleges in which the scholastic standards are not too high. In any event, knowledge of his academic strengths and weaknesses will be helpful to a student, whether he plans further school work or not.

Norms for the high-school ACE were based on selected groups and thus may be too high for *all* high-school seniors. In fact, his *PR* on the ACE may be unfair (misleadingly low) for the high-school senior of modest intellectual endowment who does not plan to enter college. Such a youngster may rank well up among eighteen-year-olds in the population but relatively low among those of college caliber.

### Limitations of the Group Intelligence Test

Intelligence tests have definite limitations, and teachers and parents must not expect the impossible from them. For one thing, a group intelligence test cannot increase intelligence, as parents sometimes seem to think it should. A group test IQ is not necessarily a good measure of a pupil's drive to accomplish, or of that dogged determination to stick to an unpleasant task and see it through. A fairly high IQ (even a very high IQ) is not always accompanied by emotional stability, good judgment, and initiative. All these traits are related to good intellect, but the relationship is by no means perfect. Many persons of average intellectual ability succeed in college, while many of those with greater potential fall by the wayside. Intelligence is a necessary, but not a sufficient, attribute for high accomplishment in school or in life.

## WHAT TO LOOK FOR IN A GROUP INTELLIGENCE TEST

The adequacy of a group intelligence test is judged by its validity, reliability, scoring methods, and norms. The object in giving the test, its cost, and such factors as time and personnel must also be considered.

**Validity.** A test is valid, as we have noted, if it measures what it purports to measure (page 31). Group intelligence tests have been validated, in general, against various criteria judged to be indicative of intellect (page 32). Some of these criteria are school grades, ratings of ability, and other intelligence tests. All such criteria are admittedly indirect and fallible; at the same time, they represent measures with which any authentic test of intelligence must correlate. Perhaps the best criterion of the validity of a group test is its success in predicting performance in tasks judged to require intelligence—in school, in business, in the armed forces, or in a profession. Judged by correlation criteria and predictive power, most of the widely used group intelligence tests may be accepted as valid, though never perfectly so.

**Reliability.** We have had occasion to use the term *reliability* with reference to individual intelligence tests. If a child earns an IQ of 108 on one form of a group test and three months later achieves an IQ of 106, or 108, or even 110 on a second form— that is, scores within a few points of the first determination— and if most persons examined show similarly consistent results, the test may be regarded as reliable. Reliability depends essentially on the stability or consistency of a score. When properly given and scored, most standard group intelligence tests are highly reliable.

**Scoring.** Group intelligence tests are first scored in arbitrary points, one or more points being assigned to each correct answer. Point or raw scores are frequently converted into MA's and IQ's. Such IQ's are related but not equivalent to Stanford-Binet IQ's. Although group test IQ's are adequate for screening and often are satisfactory for guidance, the individual intelligence test IQ is a more searching and more nearly constant measure of a child's talents (page 64). In addition to MA's and IQ's, many group tests also provide PR's for raw or obtained scores. These PR's are readily interpreted; they show how high the pupil ranks on a scale of one hundred points. If a high-school senior has a PR of 85 in the (L) part of the ACE and a PR of 80 on the (Q) part, he probably would be a good risk for college work.

A second way of rendering the scores from different subtests in a battery comparable is through the use of standard scores. Point scores may be converted into a standard score scale with a convenient mean and $\sigma$. The subtests of a group intelligence test usually differ in content, in length, and in difficulty. These part scores cannot be compared—or combined—as they stand, but when converted into a common scale, they can be added to give a total in which each subtest has the same weight.

**Norms.** Norms (page 42) are typical measures of achievement. Norms may be nationwide or local (page 43). Local norms are often fairer for a given group in that they take into account the conditions within a given city or state. National norms are most useful for wide comparisons and as standards at which to aim. Norms for college freshmen will generally be much too high for high-school graduates in general. College freshmen are high-school graduates selected according to academic proficiency. Group intelligence test norms are usually given in age-level terms, but they may be in grade-level terms. Figure 4–5 shows the norms for certain occupations on the Army General Classification Test, used in the armed forces in World War II. The higher scores were achieved by men with the most extensive training and were probably the result of both intelligence and training. More intelligent men are able to undertake more exacting training, and this training enables their native talent to express itself. It is interesting to note the large degree of overlapping in score from one occupation to another. It seems evident that many men are functioning at a level below their native capacity.

Figure 4–5   Norms for Various Occupational Groups on the Army General Classification Test

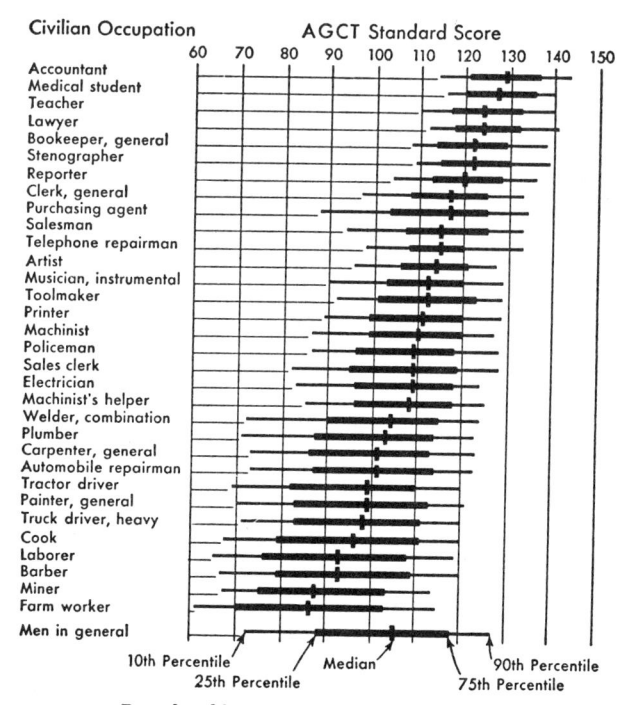

| Civilian Occupation | AGCT Standard Score |
| --- | --- |
| Accountant | |
| Medical student | |
| Teacher | |
| Lawyer | |
| Bookkeeper, general | |
| Stenographer | |
| Reporter | |
| Clerk, general | |
| Purchasing agent | |
| Salesman | |
| Telephone repairman | |
| Artist | |
| Musician, instrumental | |
| Toolmaker | |
| Printer | |
| Machinist | |
| Policeman | |
| Sales clerk | |
| Electrician | |
| Machinist's helper | |
| Welder, combination | |
| Plumber | |
| Carpenter, general | |
| Automobile repairman | |
| Tractor driver | |
| Painter, general | |
| Truck driver, heavy | |
| Cook | |
| Laborer | |
| Barber | |
| Miner | |
| Farm worker | |
| Men in general | |

10th Percentile / 25th Percentile / Median / 75th Percentile / 90th Percentile

Reproduced by permission of Harper & Row.

The educational expectation of a child whose group test IQ is 90, 100, or 115 may be read with sufficient accuracy for most purposes from Table 3–3.

**Other Factors Which May Govern the Choice of a Group Intelligence Test.** In addition to the formal requirements to be met by a group test, there are other considerations which enter into the suitability of a test for a given school system. Among the more important of these are time available for testing, personnel, cost, and acceptability. Catalogues provide data on cost and time allowances—most testing periods are set to fit comfortably into a class period. In most cases, teachers can administer group tests with a minimum of instruction, and scoring can be done with stencils. Acceptability of a test depends on whether the teachers and the community look with favor on standard tests. Much of the disfavor with which parents once regarded mental tests has fortunately disappeared, though one still encounters some skepticism about their value. In initiating a testing program it is always wise to avoid tests which contain what appears to be trick items and those which resemble puzzles. Such tests are likely to be labeled frivolous by teachers and parents. Some parents still think that the object of a mental test is to describe their children as dull or mentally abnormal. When they see that a standardized test can provide a better understanding of a child's capabilities, their objections disappear. From the catalogues listed on page 272, the teacher or administrator should be able to find the test suitable for a given situation.

## SUGGESTIONS FOR FURTHER READING

CRONBACH, L. J. *Essentials of Psychological Testing.* 2nd ed.; New York: Harper, 1960.

FREEMAN, F. S. *Theory and Practice of Psychological Testing.* Rev. ed.; New York: Holt, 1955.

GOODENOUGH, F. L. *Mental Testing.* New York: Rinehart, 1949.

NOLL, V. H. *Introduction to Educational Measurement.* Boston: Houghton Mifflin, 1957.

THORNDIKE, R. L. and HAGEN, E. *Measurement and Evaluation in Psychology and Education.* 2nd ed.; New York: Wiley, 1961.

## SUGGESTIONS FOR LABORATORY WORK

1. Administer three or four standard group tests of intelligence to the class and have the students score their own papers. If the test is for young children, cut the time limits in half.
2. Select one of the tests taken in (1). Examine the Manual for the author's treatment of validity, reliability, scoring methods, and norms. Summarize these data.
3. In another of the tests from (1), count the number of items which, in your opinion, are verbal, numerical, and spatial-perceptual. In which group did you do best? Worst? Does your result jibe with what you know about your abilities?

## QUESTIONS FOR DISCUSSION

1. Is a group test of intelligence anything more than a scholastic aptitude test? What else does it add to your knowledge of a pupil?
2. Why is the score on a reliable intelligence test usually a better estimate of a pupil's ability than is the rating of the teacher?
3. Why do we get different IQ's for the same pupil from different intelligence tests?
4. Is the group test of intelligence more useful in an academic than in a vocational high school?
5. Suppose you are a sixth-grade teacher. You have administered a standard group-intelligence test to your class. What uses do you think you might make from a knowledge of these children's IQ's?
6. A pupil has taken the CTMM (page 88). In counseling this child, what help might you get from a wide difference in his language and nonlanguage IQ's?
7. "Intelligence tests enable us to make a good inference of a child's 'native intelligence.'" Defend or criticize this statement.
8. An author writes that an intelligence test "rather than measuring purely innate ability," actually measures "developed ability." Is this a useful distinction?

## Chapter 5

# EDUCATIONAL ACHIEVEMENT TESTS

The purpose of the educational achievement test—like that of the ordinary school examination—is to discover how much a pupil knows about the subjects he has studied or is studying. Both the general intelligence test and the educational achievement examination measure aptitude for school work ("abstract intelligence"). The difference between the two is one of emphasis rather than of purpose. The intelligence test, as we have seen, tries to gauge mental alertness apart from *specific* school knowledge—that is, it is concerned primarily with the efficiency of mental process as exhibited in problems which demand learning ability, perceptual keenness, memory, reasoning, and the like. The educational achievement test is also concerned with mental processes, but only insofar as they are demonstrated in a student's performance in English composition, arithmetic, history, or science.

The distinction between the two sorts of test is not always clean-cut, and there is much overlap in content and in abilities required. *All* intelligence tests depend in some degree on previous learning, and *all* educational tests depend in some part on native keenness. Educational achievement tests predict future school performance as well as or better than intelligence tests. Achievement in the elementary school, for example, forecasts achievement in high school; and performance in arithmetic predicts later performance in algebra. Prediction is strengthened when an intelligence test is added to the achievement battery. The general intelligence test is perhaps most useful when an estimate of potential aptitude is desired; the achievement test when present school standing and probable success in later school work need to be measured. Both tests provide valuable information and each complements the other.

Educational achievement tests are useful (1) for survey purposes—that is, to determine a class's standing in relation to some norms, and (2) for guidance and evaluation—that is, to provide a clearer understanding of what individual pupils have learned —or failed to learn—in specific school subjects. A better understanding of strengths and weaknesses is a major objective of a testing program. Remedial work can be undertaken more intelligently and teaching improved when we know what errors a pupil is making consistently and what misconceptions and gaps in training led to these errors.

Achievement tests are often used for grouping pupils in order to improve working conditions within the classroom. Thus pupils may be classified into high, average, and low ability groups on the basis of overall educational standing, or within a grade into fast, medium, and slow learners. Prediction of later school success on the basis of educational achievement tests is substantially more accurate than are forecasts based on conventional school marks.

# THE SUPERIORITY OF STANDARDIZED ACHIEVEMENT TESTS OVER ROUTINE EXAMINATIONS

Standardized achievement tests are superior to teacher-made tests in three principal respects.

**1. The Achievement Test Is Better Planned.** The usual teacher-made test in algebra or French is composed of questions and problems covering topics which the teacher believes are worth knowing about his subject. Usually, materials are drawn from a single textbook. Such a test is valuable as a measure of progress in learning, but it is not very broad in coverage and does not permit comparisons with the achievement of students in other schools.

The standard educational achievement examination, on the other hand, is compiled after an analysis of many widely used textbooks and various courses of study and sets of examinations. Thus it represents a consensus—the pooled judgment of many competent teachers and testing specialists. Drawing materials from many sources insures a representative sampling of subject matter. Occasionally a teacher will complain that a general achievement test contains questions about topics (books in English literature, for example) which his class has not studied and that on this account the test is unfair. This is often true, but the criticism is not as damaging as it may seem. Few classes have covered equally well *all* of the topics treated in a comprehensive achievement test. Some teachers will have emphasized one topic, some another, but by and large these inequalities will be evened out in the test as a whole. Rarely will a school have a general and marked advantage (or disadvantage) over another school in educational experience, unless the teaching, the curriculum, and/or the caliber of the students are exceptionally good or poor. When gross inequalities are revealed in test scores of a school or between schools, the reason for such differences should be sought. It seems hardly wise on that account to abandon the test.

2. **The Achievement Test Is More Objective.** The standard achievement test is more objective than the teacher-made examination. In other words, in an achievement test, the grades received by students depend to a minimum degree on the personal opinions, likes, or dislikes of the scorer. In the traditional essay examination, a high degree of subjectivity is almost inevitably present; the mark given to an answer depends on what the teacher regards as important and significant.

3. **The Achievement Test Lays Down More Exact Specifications.** The educational achievement test is more logically planned than the ordinary teacher-made examination because makers of standard tests draw up specifications for an examination. These lists are often lengthy and quite specific, but in general they can be reduced to two—knowledge and application. Thus test items are selected to reveal a pupil's information and understanding of facts, as well as his acquired skills in reading or arithmetic, for example. Items are chosen to reveal a pupil's ability to apply known principles, to interpret, to draw conclusions from given data, and to solve problems. The second of these specifications is the more important, but the first is not to be dismissed lightly as being "mere memory." Students cannot write good English prose, or read difficult passages in history and literature without an adequate vocabulary and knowledge of grammar. Even in so "logical" a subject as geometry, a student cannot solve originals unless he knows the preceding propositions no matter how bright he is. Rote memory, of course, is rarely enough. The old spelling bees found how many detached and isolated words a child could spell though often he had little idea of what the words meant. Modern spelling tests try to discover whether a child can spell a word and also knows its meaning well enough to use it correctly in a sentence—that is, in

context. The newer method provides a better measure of a child's usable vocabulary.

## GENERAL EDUCATIONAL ACHIEVEMENT BATTERIES

The present section will describe five representative achievement test batteries, chosen from many, which are designed to measure general educational achievement in the elementary grades and in the high school.

The Stanford Achievement Test (SAT)[1]
The Metropolitan Achievement Tests (MAT)
The California Achievement Tests (CAT)
Cooperative General Achievement Tests (GAT)
The Sequential Tests of Educational Progress (STEP)
School and College Ability Tests (SCAT)

All these tests make some provision for the analytic study of a student's strong and weak points through a comparison of subtest scores. Part scores are often represented comparatively on a graph or profile.

### THE STANFORD ACHIEVEMENT TEST (SAT)[2]

**Description.** The SAT consists of overlapping subtests grouped at four ability levels from grade 2 through grade 9. All four of the batteries contain three tests of paragraph meaning, word meaning, and spelling (measures of language skills), and two tests of arithmetic reasoning and arithmetic computation (number or quantitative skills). All the tests are multiple-choice in form. In addition to these five subtests, the *Intermediate Battery* (for grades 5 and 6) and the *Advanced Battery* (for grades 7, 8, and 9) include four other tests—language, social

---
[1] These batteries are often referred to in abbreviated form by the capital letters.
[2] Harcourt, Brace & World, Inc., New York, New York.

studies, natural science, and study skills. The language test contains items in capitalization, punctuation, and sentence structure. The social studies test covers fundamentals of history, geography, and civics. The study skills test is an ingenious attempt to discover how well a student reads maps, interprets graphs and tables, and uses references. This information is important to the teacher, since many pupils regularly skip all tables and graphs unless supervised.

There are five forms for each battery. The Primary Battery is printed in a single booklet of eight pages and takes a little more than two hours to administer. Figure 5–1 shows some of the items from the Primary Battery. The Elementary Battery (for grades 3 and 4) contains six subtests: paragraph meaning, word meaning, spelling, arithmetic reasoning, arithmetic computation, and language. The Intermediate Battery requires almost four hours and, of course, has to be spread over several class periods. The authors of the tests have drawn up a convenient testing schedule, with approximate times for each subtest.

**Scope.** The scope of the SAT is as follows:
1. Primary Battery: end of Grade 1, Grade 2, and first half of Grade 3
2. Elementary Battery: Grades 3 and 4
3. Intermediate Battery: Grades 5 and 6
4. Advanced Battery: Grades 7, 8, and 9

These four achievement tests cover the fundamentals taught in most schools during the elementary grades through grade 9.

**Scoring and Norms.** All of the subtests are objective in form, so that scoring can be readily accomplished by stencils or scoring keys. Norms are in grade equivalents to raw scores and also in percentiles for subtest scores.

There are two types of norms. The first, called the *modal-age* grade norm, is recommended for individual diagnosis—that is, for evaluating the scores of individual pupils. From tables in the Manual, a pupil's scores can be compared with those earned by

**Figure 5–1**  *Sample Items from the Stanford Achievement Test, Primary Battery, Form K*

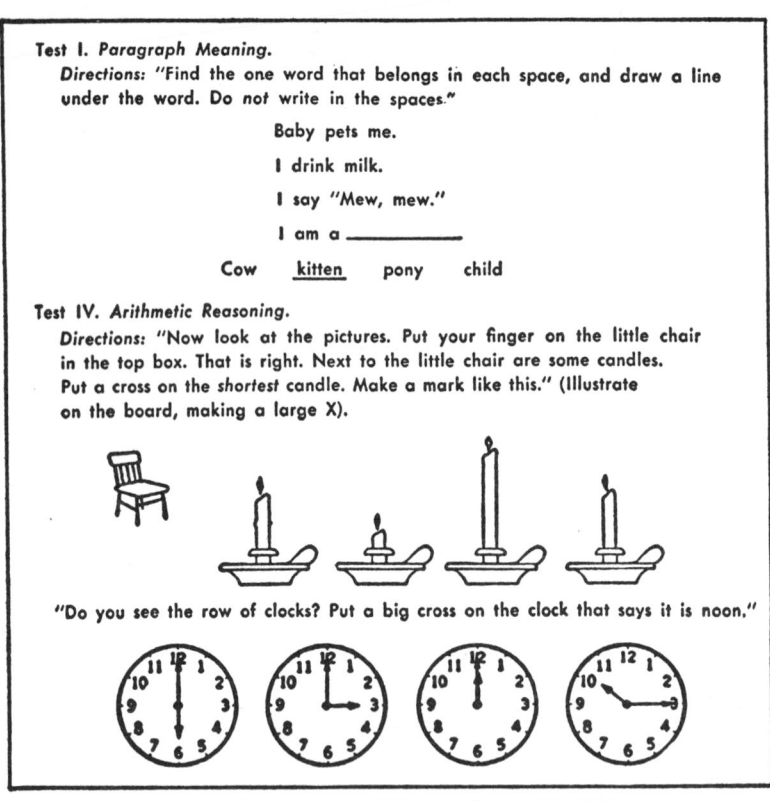

---

**Test I. Paragraph Meaning.**
Directions: "Find the one word that belongs in each space, and draw a line under the word. Do not write in the spaces."

   Baby pets me.
   I drink milk.
   I say "Mew, mew."
   I am a _____
   Cow    kitten    pony    child

**Test IV. Arithmetic Reasoning.**
Directions: "Now look at the pictures. Put your finger on the little chair in the top box. That is right. Next to the little chair are some candles. Put a cross on the *shortest* candle. Make a mark like this." (Illustrate on the board, making a large X).

"Do you see the row of clocks? Put a big cross on the clock that says it is noon."

---

Reproduced by permission of Harcourt, Brace & World, Inc.

children who are *typical* for age and grade. A second norm, the *total-group* grade norm, is based on the performance of all children in a given grade. These norms, given in tables in the Manual, are recommended by the authors if one wishes to evaluate a class average. Raw scores on the subtests are converted into standard score units so that they may be combined and compared (page 37).

The validity of the SAT is high. The tests possess content validity, and the correlations of the batteries with grades and other criteria demonstrate excellent predictive validity. The reliability of the various batteries is also satisfactory.

THE METROPOLITAN ACHIEVEMENT TEST (MAT)[3]

**Description.** The MAT includes five test batteries with a range from grade 1 through the first half of grade 9. All of the test batteries contain subtests of reading and arithmetic; spelling is added after grade 2, and language usage after grade 3. At the intermediate and advanced levels there are ten subtests in all: reading, vocabulary, arithmetic fundamentals, arithmetic problems, English, literature, social studies (history), social studies (geography), science, and spelling. In addition to the complete batteries, partial test batteries are available for use at the intermediate and advanced levels. These include the skill subjects—reading, arithmetic, English, and spelling—plus vocabulary and arithmetic problems. All tests at a given level are printed in a single booklet.

The MAT provides a comprehensive survey of a pupil's educational attainment. Moreover, the profile chart (see Figure 5–2) printed on the last page of the test booklet and the class ability sheet allow the teacher to identify the student's weak points, to correct errors made consistently, to study a pupil's rate of progress from time to time, and to group pupils for instruction or review. Tests in arithmetic and reading are available as separates and may be used when it is not feasible to administer the whole battery.

**Scope.** MAT includes the following batteries:
1. Primary Battery I: Grade 1 and beginning Grade 2
2. Primary Battery II: Grade 2 and beginning Grade 3
3. Elementary Battery: Grades 3 and 4 and beginning Grade 5
4. Intermediate Battery: Grades 5 up to the first half of Grade 7
5. Advanced Battery: Grade 7 up to the first half of Grade 9

[3] Harcourt, Brace & World, Inc., New York, New York.

*Figure 5–2  Profile Chart for the Metropolitan Achievement Tests*

Name George Ferguson   Date Feb. 6   19
Teacher Miss Swift   Grade 6.5   School Twin Oaks
City Richmond   County Henrico   State Va.

### INDIVIDUAL PROFILE CHART
#### METROPOLITAN ACHEIVEMENT TESTS: INTERMEDIATE BATTERY—COMPLETE

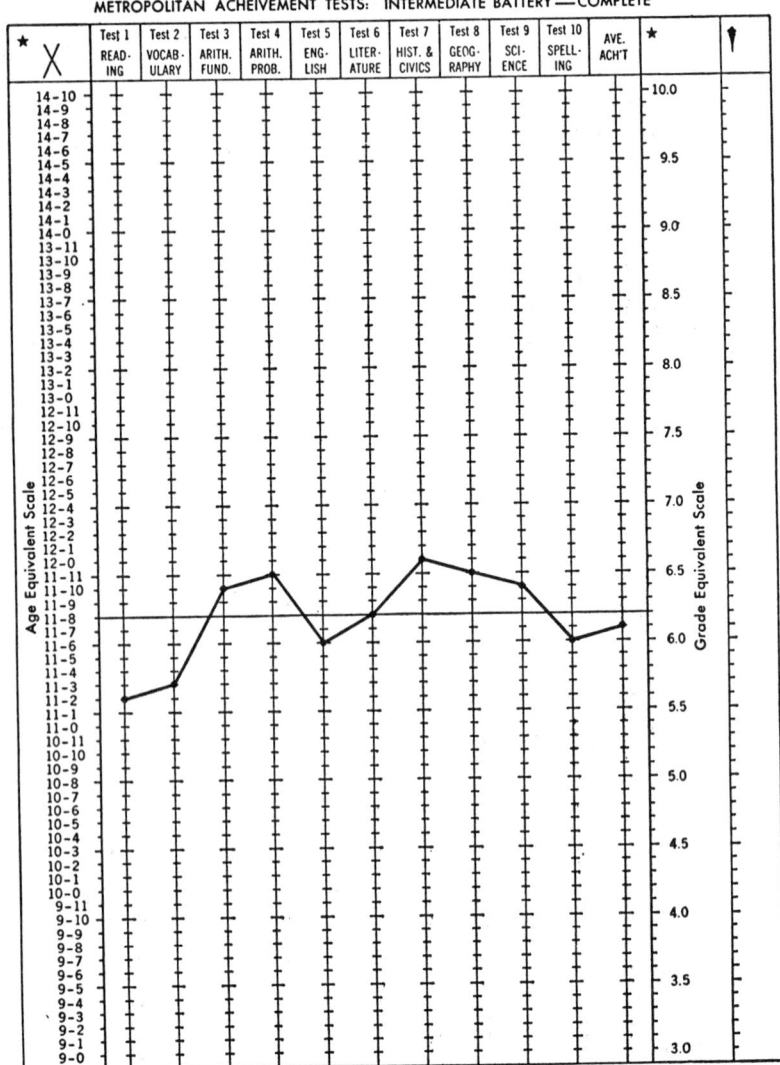

Reproduced by permission of Harcourt, Brace & World, Inc.

MAT covers a wide range of material taught in grades 1–9. Test batteries require from one hour (primary) to about four hours (advanced).

**Scoring and Norms.** The MAT is easy to administer and to score. There are three types of norms: age, grade, and percentile. Norms are given also in a standard score scale which is based on the assumption of a normal distribution of test ability in the sixth grade. Standard or scaled scores are comparable from battery to battery in the same subject but not from test to test within a given battery.

Figure 5–2 shows the profile of George Ferguson, who is 11 years and 8 months old. George is a sixth-grade student, and the MAT was administered on February 6 when he was midway through the grade—that is, at 6.5. George's scores on the ten subtests have been converted into age-equivalents from the appropriate tables in the "Key and Directions for Scoring." His subject ages (also called educational ages or EA's) have been entered on the chart and joined by short straight lines to give the profile of his school achievement. A straight line drawn horizontally across the chart through George's chronological age of 11–8 shows immediately in what subjects he is above or below the scores typical for his age level.

George's raw scores were converted into age- rather than grade-equivalents. These EA's show whether George is accelerated or retarded compared with children of his own age. EA's are useful in guidance. Grade equivalents give the grade levels to which various scores correspond. A profile plotted from grade-equivalents tells us whether a pupil is above or below his present grade level in his various subjects. Both norms are useful. Grade norms are especially useful when comparisons with national or local norms are to be made; age norms are most useful when diagnosis of a pupil's strengths and weaknesses is wanted.

Both the validity and the reliability of the MAT are satisfactory as judged by the usual criteria.

## The California Achievement Tests (CAT)[4]

**Description.** The CAT has been organized into five batteries designed to cover the ability range from Grade 1 to college. The tests are survey in nature and are concerned primarily with skills in six areas: reading vocabulary, reading comprehension, arithmetic reasoning, arithmetic fundamentals, mechanics of English, and spelling. The authors of CAT believe that tests in these areas are more valuable than the tests in such subjects as social studies, where the content varies widely from school to school. The California Tests emphasize power rather than speed. The Elementary Battery requires more than two hours for administration.

CAT stresses the use of the separate tests in diagnosis. Except in spelling, for example, the tests in the six areas are subdivided into sections, each dealing with some important aspect of the subject. For example, in the Elementary Battery, reading comprehension (Test 2) is analyzed into (1) following directions, (2) reference skills, and (3) interpretation of material. Test 3, arithmetic reasoning, is broken down into (1) meanings, (2) signs and symbols, and (3) problems. Scores from each of these subdivisions are plotted on a profile like that of Figure 5–2, usually in grade-equivalent units. The analysis of a pupil's performance is carried still further by a second grouping of items which presumably measure essentially common functions. Thus within the division of punctuation under Test 5, mechanics of English, items are grouped into those which involve commas, periods, question marks, quotation marks. Under the heading of addition in Test 4, arithmetic fundamentals, items are grouped under zeros, carrying, fractions, and decimals. The number of item classifications under a given test varies from 50 to more than 100. A special chart enables the scorer to analyze the pupil's achievement over a wide range.

Careful examination of specific item-groups may reveal why

[4] California Test Bureau, Monterey, California.

a pupil fails consistently to use decimals correctly or to understand fractions, or it may tell us where he is weak in punctuation, or in vocabulary, or in spelling. The CAT attempts to keep an individual pupil from being lost in the "average." At the same time, it must be remembered that individual diagnosis based on a few items is always tentative and may be misleading.

Scope. The CAT consists of the following batteries, which cover the educational levels described.
1. Lower Primary: Grades 1 and 2
2. Upper Primary: Grades 3 and 4
3. Elementary: Grades 4, 5, and 6
4. Junior High: Grades 7, 8, and 9
5. Advanced: Grades 9 to 14

Scoring. Raw scores on the tests may be converted by tables into age, grade, and percentile-within-grade norms. The subtests are objective in form, easy to administer, and easy to score. The six tests of the batteries have satisfactory reliability, but the reliabilities of the various subdivisions are quite low because of the few items included in some groupings (often only one or two). Validity is high for the whole test.

## Cooperative General Achievement Tests (GAT)[5]

Description. These achievement tests deal with three fields or areas—Test I covers social studies, Test II, natural sciences, and Test III, mathematics. Each test battery consists of two divisions: Part I, which deals with fundamental terms, concepts, and definitions, and Part II, which covers applications of knowledge, interpretation, and comprehension. The battery has been planned for grades 10, 11, and 12, but it is probably too difficult for all but superior tenth and eleventh graders. The battery is objective in form throughout.

[5] Educational Testing Service, Princeton, New Jersey.

**Scope.** GAT is a power test designed for the upper school grades and for college freshmen. Each test requires from forty to sixty minutes.

**Scoring.** The tests are all multiple-choice and are easy to administer and to score. Items are graphic, pictorial, and verbal. Norms in scaled scores and percentiles are given for high-school students and college freshmen. GAT is probably most useful in counseling high-school students about the subject fields in which they show the greatest promise.

### THE SEQUENTIAL TEST OF EDUCATIONAL PROGRESS (STEP)[6]

**Description.** As the term "sequential" implies, this battery is designed to measure a student's progress in learning as he goes from the elementary grades through college. The tests deal with critical skills in seven academic areas: *essay* tests, planned to provide standardized tests in writing prose; *listening comprehension* tests, in which the examiner reads a passage and asks questions designed to elicit comprehension, interpretation, and evaluation; *reading* tests, which cover a wide range of content; *writing* tests, planned to measure the student's ability to express ideas; *mathematics* tests, which contain items over a wide range of subject matter and difficulty; *science* tests which deal with the application of scientific knowledge to a variety of situations; and *social studies* tests, designed to show progress in social and civic development.

**Scope.** STEP is designed to measure achievement on the following levels:
  Level 1  freshman and sophomore years of college
  Level 2  grades 10, 11, and 12
  Level 3  grades 7, 8, and 9
  Level 4  grades 4, 5, and 6
Note that Level 1 is the highest level academically, Level 4,

[6] Educational Testing Service, Princeton, New Jersey.

the lowest. STEP attempts to reveal continuity in mental growth and learning from the bottom to the top level.

**Scoring and Norms.** There are two equivalent forms (A and B) for each test in STEP, except for the essay tests, which have four forms. There are grade and percentile norms. Scoring is by stencils. A profile chart allows the examiner to analyze a pupil's performance on the several functions measured by the battery.

## SCHOOL AND COLLEGE ABILITY TESTS (SCAT)[7]

**Description.** A companion battery to STEP is the School and College Ability Tests (SCAT). These tests cover the same range as STEP (grade 4 through the sophomore year in college) and are scaled in the same system of units, so that scores are directly comparable. When the students have had the same educational advantages, SCAT is a good measure of abstract intelligence, though it appears to be a test of educational achievement. To emphasize the necessity for a common educational background, the authors state that SCAT measures "developed abilities," that is, the test measures the proficiencies developed in school when equal opportunities have been provided.

SCAT has superseded the ACE for which it is a good substitute. Its correlations with ACE are in the high .80's for total score, and almost as high for the verbal-linguistic sections. Correlations for quantitative scores are in the mid .70's. SCAT has good predictive value for high school and college achievement. It is a well-made test, relatively easy to give and to score.

**Scoring and Norms.** SCAT furnishes three scores, a verbal, a quantitative, and a total (sum of the two). The first score is largely a measure of skill in and knowledge of language usage; the second deals with arithmetic computation and arithmetic reasoning. There are two verbal and two quantitative subtests: four in all.

[7] Educational Testing Service, Princeton, New Jersey.

An interesting innovation in the scoring of SCAT is the use of *percentile bands* rather than a single *PR* for each raw score. First, a pupil's *PR* is represented as shaded bands or areas on a vertical column (profile) which shows percentile standing from 0 to 100. In Figure 5–3, Richard, a twelfth grade student, was tested in the fall of the year. In the verbal part of SCAT, we read from the appropriate tables that Richard's *PR* band for verbal score extends from 75 to 89; for quantitative score, his percentile band extends from 65 to 82, and for total score from 79 to 86. The medians of these bands are 81, 73, and 83 (dropping decimals). The medians are the best single scores. Percentiles are read from the converted or standard scores, which, in turn, are determined from the raw scores.

Percentile bands give the range within which the chances are good (7 in 10) that a pupil's "true" score falls. They provide "confidence intervals" for a child's score. When the bands overlap—as they do in Figure 5–3—we cannot be sure that a pupil differs significantly in his verbal, quantitative, or total scores. Hence, we are unlikely to make such a statement as that "Richard is better in verbal than in quantitative ability." Percentile bands serve to emphasize the quite often wide range in a pupil's *PR* and to discourage the use of a single score (a $PR = 62$, for example) as if it were an exact measure.

If two pupils in the eighth grade, fall testing, obtain total scores in SCAT that from the table for this grade give percentile bands of 65–76 and 81–90, we may feel reasonably sure that the second child has done better than the first. Here the upper limit of the band for the first pupil (76) falls below the lower limit of the band for the second pupil, 81. There is no overlap and the scores may be taken to differ significantly.

## GENERAL ACHIEVEMENT TESTS IN THE SCHOOLS

We have seen how the general educational achievement test gives the academic level of a pupil or of a class, and how the test

*Figure 5–3* Student Profile To Illustrate the Use of Percentile Bands. The three bands (verbal, quantitative, and total) overlap, and there is no evidence of significant differences among the three measures.

## SCAT STUDENT PROFILE
### SCHOOL AND COLLEGE ABILITY TESTS

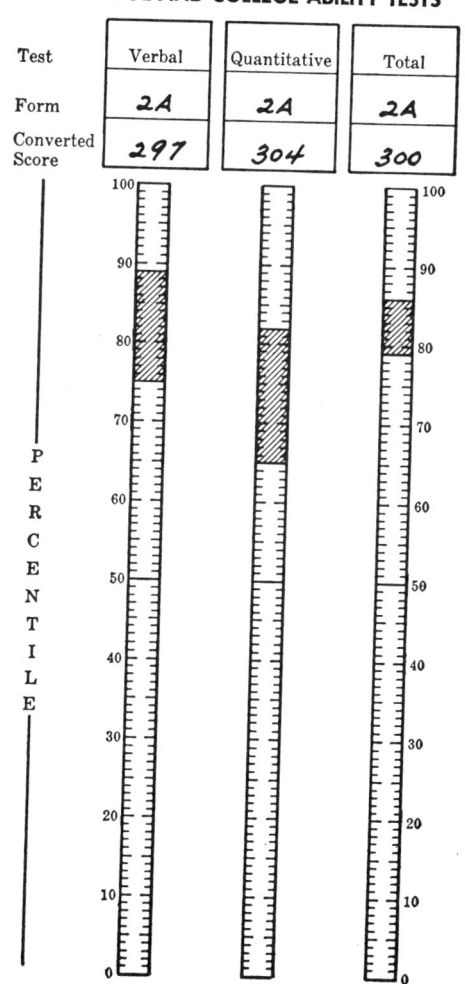

| Test | Verbal | Quantitative | Total |
|---|---|---|---|
| Form | 2A | 2A | 2A |
| Converted Score | 297 | 304 | 300 |

PERCENTILE

Reproduced by permission of the Educational Testing Service.

profile reveals strengths and weaknesses in a variety of subjects and processes. Further illustration of how educational achievement tests may be utilized in evaluation, diagnosis, and prediction will be given in this section.

**Evaluation.** Suppose that Miss Clark has given the SAT to her sixth-grade class of twenty-six pupils. She finds her class mean (average) on the test battery to be about equal to the local norms for the sixth grade, but slightly below the national norm given in the Manual. Does this result mean that Miss Clark is doing a poor job because local norms are less valuable than national? The answer is no, since a number of factors affect achievement in a given school system or a single school, and some of these may cause local norms to be lower or higher than national. Among these factors are the following:

1. Retardation as a result of strict promotional standards and practices. A large percentage of retardation lowers local norms, and the weeding out of poor students, by transfer to special classes, for example, will raise local norms.
2. Promotion by age rather than by achievement. This fairly common practice leads to a progressive lowering of local grade norms.
3. Previous experience of pupils with standardized objective tests. This factor varies widely and often affects local norms.
4. Coaching in the tests themselves. Sometimes teachers coach pupils in materials akin to or identical with those found in the tests. "Teaching for the tests" is bad practice and should be discouraged whenever possible. Coached pupils usually raise the class's performance.
5. Selection. Children from a poor socio-economic background generally score low on standardized tests, while children from good neighborhoods score high, especially on the verbal tests.
6. Motivation. Children do not try hard on tests if the

teacher's attitude is negative, or if the parents think achievement tests are worthless—and say so loudly and often.
7. Transfers, potential dropouts. These children may affect local norms, usually adversely.

In some private schools in which pupils are of generally high caliber because of stringent selection procedures, local norms will often be found to be considerably above national norms based on public-school results. In a large city system we can expect an occasional sixth-grade class to fall below national norms even when the city as a whole is up to national standards. When a number of classes fall below national standards, however, the curriculum, the teaching methods, the promotional standards, and other conditions in the school and the community should be examined.

**Diagnosis.** In looking over the test results for her sixth grade, Miss Clark may find that Harry is below the sixth-grade norm in reading and that Sue is below the norm in arithmetic. At the same time, Mary reads at eighth-grade level, and John (the youngest child in the class) is on the ninth-grade norm in science. Individual differences like these are the rule rather than the exception in most elementary-school classes. It is fairly easy for Miss Clark to prescribe further reading for Mary, and to stimulate John to carry out an individual project in science—for example, classifying the birds in the local community. The below-average children often present real problems and, as a result, are given more of the teacher's time and effort than the bright children. If the extra time which Miss Clark can devote to Harry and Sue is insufficient to bring these children up to the sixth-grade levels in reading and arithmetic, they should be referred to special classes, if such are available. The larger the number of below-average children, the more difficult is Miss Clark's task, and the more likely she is to neglect the bright children.

The printed norm—local or national—does not necessarily establish the optimum level of performance for every pupil in the sixth, or any other, grade. If Norman, whose IQ is 120, is just on the sixth-grade norm in reading and arithmetic, he is not performing up to expectation; his scores should be above the norm for his grade. On the other hand, if Bill, whose IQ is a modest 94, is at or above the norm for the sixth grade in reading and arithmetic, he is actually doing better than we can reasonably expect of him. The intelligence of the child must always be considered in deciding whether his school work is "normal" for the grade.

Sometimes Miss Clark will suspect from a pupil's sullen behavior, or open aggressiveness, or tendency to whimper at the slightest provocation that emotional factors are causing or contributing to his difficulties in school. Such a pupil should be referred to the school psychologist, if there is one, or to the school physician. The clinical psychologist is often able through tests and interviews to get a clearer idea of a pupil's difficulties than can the teacher. The teacher should visit a child's home if she suspects that parents and home environment are involved, as they often are. Corrective measures (when possible) can be more intelligently applied when the causes of undesirable conduct and/or poor school work are known, rather than merely surmised.

**Prediction.** Whether it will be profitable for a student to take science or mathematics in high school or college can be forecast with substantial assurance from his performance on standard tests. Prediction of later success is usually improved when tests given in elementary schools are combined with a good intelligence test. Intelligence and achievement tests are regularly utilized in many schools for the selection and placement of students in courses of study. The combination of achievement tests and special aptitude tests is valuable for predicting a student's success in a professional school—in law or medicine, for example.

## ACHIEVEMENT TESTS IN SPECIAL SUBJECT AREAS

In the preceding section, we described five general achievement batteries designed to assess academic standing in school. Here we shall consider several representative subject-matter achievement tests. These include tests of reading and arithmetic, as well as tests planned to determine mental maturity (readiness) and proficiency in special subjects. Among the various subject-matter tests, those in reading and arithmetic are most often given, since they represent fundamental skills on which school achievement largely depends. Subject-matter tests are found, of course, in the general achievement batteries, as well as in separate form. The tests listed below were selected as being typical of the very large number available.

>Metropolitan Readiness Tests
>Iowa Silent Reading Tests
>Cooperative Mathematical Tests
>Evaluation and Adjustment Series
>Cooperative French Test (elementary)
>Cooperative Science Test

### METROPOLITAN READINESS TESTS[8]

**Description.** The primary objective of these tests is to discover if a child is sufficiently mature to undertake the study of reading, but the tests also are concerned with "readiness" for arithmetic, and with general physical and mental maturity. The six tests in the battery may be described as follows:

1. *Word Meaning:* child selects picture named by the examiner.
2. *Sentences:* same as (1) except that the examiner uses sentences and phrases instead of single words.
3. *Information:* child marks the picture corresponding to the examiner's oral description.

---
[8] Harcourt, Brace & World, Inc., New York, New York.

4. *Matching:* child must recognize similarities and differences in pictures, geometrical forms, numbers, letters, words.
5. *Numbers:* child must demonstrate a knowledge of number concepts and carry out simple operations.
6. *Copying:* child is required to copy simple graphic forms, as well as numbers and letters.

All test items are pictorial—that is, nonverbal. The test has two parallel forms. The battery is essentially a prognostic test: its purpose is to forecast a child's mental, sensory-motor, and muscular readiness for first-grade work. Figure 5–4 shows some sample items.

**Scope.** The test is for the end of kindergarten and the beginning of first grade. The test requires about sixty minutes working time.

**Scoring.** Norms in percentile ranks allow the teacher to estimate a pupil's readiness for reading (based on tests 1–4), readiness for arithmetic (test 5), and general maturity for first-grade work (tests 1–6). In addition, a child's score is given a rating from A to E. An A rating denotes an excellent risk, the other letters a lesser degree of certainty down to E, which implies almost certain failure.

**Prognostic Value of the Metropolitan Readiness Tests.** The test battery as a whole forecasts general maturity for the first grade, but its subtests may be used diagnostically to provide information about individual children. If Ben makes low scores on tests 1, 2, 3, and perhaps 4, for example, he has inadequate maturity in language for first-grade work, or he has had too little experience with and comprehension of language generally. If Louise earns low scores on tests 4 and 6, she is probably too immature to undertake written work. Since these two tests also measure visual perception and hand-eye coordination, an eye

*Figure 5–4    Sample Items from Metropolitan Readiness Tests*

Test 1. Word Meaning. In the first row, the child marks the baby; in the second row, the house.

Test 4. Matching. In each row the child circles the picture identical to the one in the circular frame.

Reproduced by permission of Harcourt, Brace & World, Inc.

examination and training in motor skills may be indicated. Test 5 (numbers) shows readiness for number work, and the child who scores high should be able to use numerical symbols. Test 6 (copying) has proved to be a good measure of physical and mental maturity. From this test, the teacher can pick up tendencies to reversals in drawing and writing, phenomena fairly common at this age level. If a child has not developed reading readiness by age seven and one-half, he should be examined by a physician, an oculist, and perhaps a psychologist.

## Iowa Silent Reading Tests[9]

**Description.** This test consists of two batteries, one for elementary schools and one for high schools and colleges. Both batteries measure reading rate, vocabulary, sentence comprehension, paragraph reading, and skill in locating information. Speed, as well as power, is an element in the battery. The Elementary Test includes a reading comprehension test called "directed reading"; the Advanced Test, a test of poetry comprehension.

**Scope.** The two batteries cover the following range:

Elementary Test (four forms)—Grades 4–8
Advanced Test (four forms)—high school and college freshmen

Working time for each battery is about fifty minutes.

**Scoring.** There are six subtests in the Elementary Test:
1. Rate and comprehension in reading connected prose.
2. Directed reading of prose to get answers.
3. Vocabulary and word meaning.
4. Paragraph reading: selecting the main idea and adding appropriate details.
5. Sentence meaning: understanding brief sentences out of context.
6. Work-study skills: alphabetizing and using an index.

Test 1 yields two scores (rate and comprehension) and Test 6 two scores (alphabetizing and use of index). Tests 2, 3, 4, and 5 yield one score each. These eight subscores are converted into scaled scores by tables appended to each test. Scaled scores may be plotted on a profile to show the variations in performance. Percentile norms are also provided by grade for each subtest and for the total score. There are age and grade equivalents to total score.

[9] Harcourt, Brace & World, Inc., New York, New York.

The Iowa Test can be used to identify (a) the extremely slow reader, (b) the careless reader who fails to follow directions, omits necessary details, and skims over important facts, and (c) the rapid but uncomprehending reader.

### Cooperative Mathematics Test for Grades 7, 8, and 9[10]

**Description.** This test consists of four parts: I, skills; II, facts, terms, and concepts; III, applications; IV, appreciation. Questions and problems cover basic arithmetic as well as simple algebra and geometry. The test may be used for survey purposes, but it is perhaps more valuable in evaluation and guidance. Sample items from the test are shown in Figure 5-5.

### Evaluation and Adjustment Series (High School)[11]

**Description.** This is an extensive battery of subject-matter and other tests (twenty-four now and more to be added) designed for high-school use. The tests cover such traditional areas as algebra, biology, geometry, physics, history, and literature. In addition, there are tests of reading comprehension, "problems in democracy," health knowledge, and study skills. The content of the tests has been drawn from standard textbooks, courses of study, and professional literature. Tests may be administered separately or as a general survey.

**Scope.** For survey and diagnosis in grades 9 through 12. There are two forms for most tests.

**Scoring.** Raw scores are converted into scaled scores for each test, so that comparisons can be made from test to test. Results can also be compared graphically by means of a profile. Many of the tests provide charts showing what score is to be expected

---

[10] Educational Testing Service, Princeton, New Jersey.
[11] Harcourt, Brace & World, Inc., New York, New York.

*Figure 5–5  Sample Multiple-Choice Items from the Cooperative Mathematics Test for Grades 7, 8, and 9*

---

From Part I, *Skills:*

39.  $\sqrt{16}$ equals
    39–1  $\frac{1}{8}$
    39–2  2
    39–3  8
    39–4  4
    39–5  32 . . . . . . . . . . . . . . .39(   )

From Part II, *Facts, Terms, and Concepts:*

7.  Which of the following is a unit in the *metric* system?
    7–1  Ounce
    7–2  Centimeter
    7–3  Yard
    7–4  Bushel
    7–5  Gross . . . . . . . . . . . . . .7(   )

From Part III, *Applications:*

24.  If a man spends 12% of his salary on bonds, and buys a $37.50 bond each month, what is his monthly salary?
    24–1  $312.50
    24–2  $312.60
    24–3  $350
    24–4  $376.20
    24–5  $450 . . . . . . . . . . . . . .24(   )

From Part IV, *Appreciation:*

20.  Which of the following has **no** *volume?*
    20–1  Cylinder
    20–2  Cone
    20–3  Square
    20–4  Cup
    20–5  Rectangular box . . . . . . . .20(   )

---

Reproduced by permission of the Educational Testing Service.

at given IQ levels. IQ's are from the Terman-McNemar Test of Mental Ability. The reliability of the various tests in the battery is satisfactory. The separate tests require from forty-five minutes to an hour of working time.

## Cooperative French Test (Elementary)[12]

**Description.** The specifications for this test call for knowledge of French grammar and vocabulary, plus the ability to use the language in reading and translation. The test has three parts—vocabulary, grammar, and reading. The vocabulary section is a multiple-choice test of fifty words. Grammar (thirty-five items) requires the selection of one of five choices to complete correctly the translation of an English sentence into French. In the reading section, forty incomplete sentences in French must be completed from a list of five options. The reliability of the test is high.

**Scope.** This test is intended for the first two years of high school or for the first year of college French.

**Scoring.** Scaled scores are provided for each of the three parts of the test and for the total. There are percentile norms for high-school and for college classes. Working time for the test is forty minutes.

## Cooperative Science Test (Grades 7, 8, and 9)[13]

**Description.** There are three parts to this test: Part I, information and background; Part II, terms and concepts; Part III, comprehension and interpretation. The test is planned to measure knowledge and application. Part II is in multiple-choice form. Part III consists of readings in science, each reading followed by questions designed to assess the student's understanding, as well as his ability to interpret and apply what he has read (Figure 5-6).

**Scope.** Grade 9 and superior seventh and eighth graders.

**Scoring.** There are scaled scores for the three parts and for the total. Percentile norms are given for Grades 7, 8, and 9. The

[12] Educational Testing Service, Princeton, New Jersey.
[13] Educational Testing Service, Princeton, New Jersey.

Figure 5–6  *Sample Multiple-Choice Items from the Cooperative Science Test for Grades 7, 8, and 9*

---

**From Part I, Informational Background:**

3. It is believed that dinosaurs lost out in their struggle for existence chiefly because
   - 3-1 they were killed by man for food.
   - 3-2 man could not tame them.
   - 3-3 they were not adapted to changes that took place in the earth's surface and climate.
   - 3-4 they were not fitted to eat plant food.
   - 3-5 they had no brains. . . . . . . . . 3( )

**From Part II, Terms and Concepts:**

2. The instrument used to look at and study the surface of the moon and the planets is the
   - 2-1 galvanoscope.
   - 2-2 microscope.
   - 2-3 telescope.
   - 2-4 electroscope.
   - 2-5 radiometer. . . . . . . . . . . . . 2( )

13. If two plants of the same species but of different varieties are mated, the offspring are called
    - 13-1 mongrels.
    - 13-2 sports.
    - 13-3 biennials.
    - 13-4 lentils.
    - 13-5 hybrids. . . . . . . . . . . . . 13( )

**Part III, Comprehension and Interpretation:**

This test consists of multiple-choice items to be answered after reading a paragraph of scientific prose or examining a table. The selection must be understood and interpreted.

---

Reproduced by permission of the Educational Testing Service.

working time for the whole test is about eighty minutes. Reliability of the whole test is high.

## WHAT TO LOOK FOR IN AN EDUCATIONAL ACHIEVEMENT TEST

The suitability of an educational achievement test for a given situation must be determined from an examination of its validity, reliability, scaling techniques, and norms. The cost, time, and personnel needed to administer and score the test also must be considered. These same requirements apply to group tests of intelligence. Each of the main characteristics of a mental test, except perhaps validity, has been commented on at appropriate places throughout this chapter. A summary of the relevant data under each category will now be offered.

**Validity.** An educational achievement test is valid when it measures what it undertakes to measure. Most subject-matter tests possess content validity. An arithmetic test, a geography test, or a reading test, for example, is valid by definition when it contains a sampling of arithmetic problems, geography questions, or paragraphs to be read. The standardized educational test is made up of items taken from a variety of sources: widely used textbooks, courses of study, examination questions, and outlines. The items in tentative form are checked by experienced teachers and are put into objective form by test construction specialists. A broad selection of items ensures a comprehensive sampling of materials.

One validation technique employed in some educational tests is the following: The test is provisionally drawn up and is administered to an experimental group; only those items which show an increasing percentage passing with age or with grade are retained. (Other techniques of item analysis will be described in Chapter 9.) All of these procedures are directed toward selecting questions which will work together as a team, cover a wide range of difficulty, and be related closely in content (homogeneity). The standard test, when finally made, is a compact and closely knit instrument for measuring what it purports to measure. Data on validation procedures will be found in most manuals which accompany standardized achievement tests.

**Reliability.** The reliability of the educational achievement tests described in this chapter has been generally reported as high. This means that parallel forms of the test correlate highly (over .90 in most cases) so that we may have confidence in the stability of a child's score. In most test manuals, reliability is expressed by the "reliability coefficient," also called the self-correlation of the test, or by the standard error of an obtained score. The correlation of a test with itself (by retest) or between alternate forms of the same test tells us how closely the pupil's scores "stay put." The standard error of a score tells us how much fluctuation to expect in a child's score on request. If a standard error is three points, for example, the odds are two to one that Bill's score of 64 will vary up or down from the first determination by not more than three points on a second trial on the test. The smaller the $SE$ of a test score, the greater the stability of the obtained score. The $SE$ of a test score gives us more information concerning reliability than does the reliability coefficient alone (page 30).

Scores obtained on most standard tests are highly stable, but part scores based on a relatively few items are variable and may be quite unreliable. Conclusions about strengths and weaknesses based on unstable scores are always tentative and must be regarded only as suggestive.

**Scaling.** Most educational achievement tests are first scored in arbitrarily assigned points, with a certain number of points being given for a correct answer. These point scores are usually converted into scaled scores by tables printed at the end of the subtest. (The meaning of standard scores and of $T$-scores was discussed in Chapter 2.) Raw or obtained scores (point scores) from the subtests of a battery differ in length, difficulty, and content; they cannot be compared or combined as they stand. When scaled, scores expressed in different units are comparable. Scaled scores—and sometimes raw scores—are usually converted into age and/or grade equivalents—that is, into the age and grade values which correspond on an average to the given scores. If the average child of nine years and four months earns a score of 38 on an Arithmetic Fundamentals Test, then the score of 38 "equals" an educational age (EA) of 9–4. If children who are half way through the seventh grade (that is, at 7.5) earn a mean score of 63 on a Reading Test, the score of 63 has a grade equivalent of 7.5.

The educational age (EA) may be divided by the chronological age (CA) to give an educational quotient (EQ).

$$EQ = \frac{EA}{CA}$$

This EQ is a measure of acceleration and is somewhat analogous to the IQ. The EA and EQ are often useful, provided they are understood to refer *only* to the tests on which they are based and are not thought of as general indices.

**Norms.** Norms are typical measures of performance. In a standardized educational test, the mean score made by a large and representative group of fifth-grade pupils is the norm for fifth-grade children on this test. Norms are expressed in age and grade equivalents, as percentile ranks, and in the form of scaled scores. A child's grade placement is found by computing the tenths of the school year which have passed before the test was given. If the school year begins about September 1 and ends June 15, a sixth-grade class tested in the period between March 16 and April 15 is assigned the grade position of 6.7—the class is 7/10 into the school year. Most standardized educational achievement tests report nationwide norms in their manuals. These typical performances are based on the achievement of large groups of children from all over the country. As we have pointed out, local norms (for city or state or both) are often better measures of pupil achievement. Any pupil's scores relative to those of other pupils should be evaluated on the basis of his effort, his intelligence, and the socio-economic level of his home and community.

**Other Factors in the Selection of a Test.** The cost of a testing program, the personnel required, and the time it will take from other school activities—all must be considered in adopting a given test or tests. Tests which fit easily into a class period, which can be scored objectively by use of stencils by a clerk, and which are acceptable in form and content to teachers and to parents are generally the least disruptive of the school routine.

## SUGGESTIONS FOR FURTHER READING

ANASTASI, A. *Psychological Testing.* 2nd ed.; New York: Macmillan, 1961.

GREENE, H. A., JORGENSEN, A. N., and GERBERICH, J. R. *Measurement and Evaluation in the Elementary School.* 2nd ed.; New York: Longmans, Green, 1953.

JORDAN, A. M. *Measurement in Education.* New York: McGraw-Hill, 1953.

TRAXLER, A. E., et al. *Introduction to Testing and the Use of Test Results in Public Schools.* New York: Harper, 1953.

## SUGGESTIONS FOR LABORATORY WORK

1. Administer two or three standardized achievement tests to the class, cutting the time to one-half if necessary. Have students score their own tests and plot profiles where called for.

2. Analyze a standard reading test, listing the objectives which you think the author had in mind. Do you agree that these objectives were fulfilled?

3. Select a test taken in (1). Consult the Manual for data on validity, reliability, scaling procedures, and norms.

## QUESTIONS FOR DISCUSSION

1. For which of the following purposes would a standardized achievement test be useful:
   (a) To discover which pupils have not mastered multiplication and division of fractions.
   (b) To determine which pupils are reading too slowly.
   (c) To determine for the class which punctuation skills need further work.

(d) To section the class into two groups for teaching arithmetic.
(e) To discover the subjects in which each pupil is strong and in which weak.

2. A teacher lists the following as objectives of a course in history and civics:
   (a) To present facts in the field.
   (b) To prepare the class for the duties of citizenship.
   (c) To further appreciation of democracy.
   (d) To foster criticism of governmental processes.
   (e) To aid pupils in thinking about problems in government.
Which of these objectives is the teacher most likely to fulfill?

3. The Manual of Test ABC states that the test may be used for diagnostic purposes. What do you look for in a test to determine whether it has diagnostic value?

4. A professor of English states that batteries of standardized tests tell the English teacher nothing that cannot be better found out from a theme and an interview. Do you agree?

5. Why is it necessary that subtests in a battery to be used for diagnosis have high reliability?

6. In some schools, teachers prepare for a testing program by having students review older standardized examinations. What effect could this have on the students' morale? On the comparability of test results from school to school? Is it good educational practice?

7. In School A, the pupils in Grades 4 to 7 are given the California Achievement Tests. Scores are recorded in grade equivalents only. What other types of scores would be valuable? Why?

8. The Manual of a reading test reports a correlation of .40 with English marks in the first year of high school. Is this good evidence of validity? Discuss.

9. Suppose that the Metropolitan Achievement Tests have been administered in grade 5 in October. How might you, as the teacher, use the results of the test?

10. For what predictive purposes would it be desirable to have the results from the following tests:
    (a) A test of ability to read difficult scientific prose drawn from various fields.
    (b) A test of skill in grammar: punctuation, capitalization, sentence structure, and so on.

11. How could you use the results from a group intelligence test to supplement scores made by your pupils on an achievement battery?

12. Is it important to have tests of speed, as well as of power?

13. A pupil gets 43 items right in a test of 60 items. What else would you need to know in order to evaluate this score?

14. How does the educational achievement test take into account the "whole child" concept?

15. Sometimes there are fairly large differences between a pupil's scores on an achievement test, and the teacher's judgment of his ability as reflected in his grades. Give some reasons for this disparity.

16. What are some of the announced objectives of high school and/or elementary school education that are not well covered by standard achievement tests? What can a teacher do about this problem? Try to be specific.

## Chapter 6

## APTITUDE TESTS

When a youngster possesses traits and abilities which enable him to speak French readily, acquire mathematics, deal handily with tools, or play a musical instrument well, he is said to have *aptitude* for the given activity. Aptitudes probably are inherited basically, but they cannot appear unless the environment is favorable—that is, unless the opportunity is provided. Frequently some training, often a great deal of it, also is necessary before an aptitude reveals itself in performance.

Aptitude tests are not essentially different in form or in content from intelligence and educational achievement tests, since all mental tests are in reality measures of aptitude. Intelligence tests measure capacity for school work and for vocations requiring school training, and achievement tests measure proficiency in English grammar, mathematics, science, and other subjects. Perhaps the chief difference between these tests and those designed to measure aptitudes is that an aptitude test is concerned almost entirely with the future—with prognosis. Thus an engineering aptitude test is used typically to forecast an examinee's chances of success in engineering. The aptitude test alone, of course, is rarely able to provide a wholly satisfactory estimate of probable performance later on. For an individual's efforts to be maximally effective, aptitude must be supplemented by training. Furthermore, the examinee must possess initiative, interest in the job, and favorable personality characteristics.

We have classified aptitude tests under four heads: (1) general, (2) special, (3) professional, and (4) talent. The two best-known general aptitude batteries are those designed to assess aptitude for (a) mechanical tasks and for (b) clerical work. Many special tests of speed, coordination, and reaction time have been devised to measure aptitudes believed to be crucial in industry. Achievement tests also are employed as aptitude tests to reveal an examinee's performance in languages or mathematics, for example, and hence provide a measure of his promise in more advanced courses. In the field of professional work, aptitude test batteries have been assembled to assess the traits believed necessary for success in medicine, in law, in engineering, and in teaching. Aptitude in music and art generally is called talent, and tests are available to forecast achievement in these areas.

## GENERAL APTITUDE BATTERIES

The general aptitude battery attempts to forecast probable success in a number of related tasks or vocations by sampling a wide range of behaviors believed to be involved in the activity. In this section, two batteries designed to measure aptitude for mechanical work are described, together with two batteries planned to measure aptitude for clerical proficiency.

## Mechanical Aptitude

The term "mechanical aptitude" includes a variety of behaviors. One of the earliest mechanical aptitude tests consisted of a box containing a number of common gadgets in separate compartments. Each of these contrivances (a lock, doorbell, clothespin, and so on) was to be assembled with the aid of simple tools. The score was determined by the speed and accuracy of assembly. This kind of test is often described as a "job sample" or "vocational miniature," since it involves what has to be done on a small scale. Among the subtests in paper-and-pencil batteries devised to measure mechanical aptitude are (1) tests requiring motor speed and dexterity of movement; (2) tests of the ability to visualize or perceive mechanical and spatial relations (important in reading blueprints and in architectural drawings); (3) tests of mechanical information concerning tools, machines, and the construction and use of various contrivances; and (4) tests of mechanical reasoning as demonstrated in the ability to solve problems dealing with tools, pulleys, levers, machine parts, and the like. In addition, in assessing mechanical aptitude, inventories are used which are designed to reveal interest in mechanical things. Such interest may be shown, for example, when a boy reads *Popular Science* avidly, has his own tools, tinkers with radios, or builds space machines. One of the most useful findings to come out of the testing program in World War II was the discovery that paper-and-pencil tests of mechanical aptitude are as predictive of success in many mechanical jobs as are actual job samples covering the work.

The following two test batteries are representative of the best tests in this field:

>MacQuarrie Test of Mechanical Ability
>Bennett Mechanical Comprehension Test

## MacQuarrie Test of Mechanical Ability[1]

**Description.** This battery consists of seven paper-and-pencil tests:
1. Tracing: following a narrow path.
2. Tapping: making dots rapidly.
3. Dotting: placing dots precisely.
4. Copying: making a figure from co-ordinates.
5. Location: locating items by co-ordinates.
6. Block Counting: counting hidden blocks in a stack.
7. Pursuit: tracing a line through a tangled pattern.

Sample items from the MacQuarrie tests are shown in Figure 6–1.

All these tests are relatively simple and all are speeded: testing times are short. The MacQuarrie tests are designed to measure hand-eye coordination, finger movement and speed, manual dexterity, visual acuity, and spatial perception of direction and size. Taken as a whole, the MacQuarrie battery measures *motor dexterity* at a fairly low level of difficulty rather than aptitude for engineering or for architecture. (For the latter, the Bennett Test of mechanical comprehension is recommended.) Some of the MacQuarrie subtests are predictive of special tasks; the tests in tracing, dotting, and pursuit, for example, measure aptitude for typing; and tests of block counting, tracing, pursuit, location, and copying are related to performance in mechanical drawing and the reading of blueprints. The Manual which accompanies the MacQuarrie advises the use of subtest patterns for predicting success in various jobs.

**Scope.** The MacQuarrie test can be administered from Grade 7 on. It has been employed chiefly in the prediction of success in factory and other manual-manipulative work.

**Scoring.** Percentile norms are available for the subtests and for total score. The working time for the whole test is about twenty minutes. Since some of the tests in the battery are al-

---

[1] California Test Bureau, Monterey, California.

*Figure 6-1 Sample Items from the MacQuarrie Test of Mechanical Ability*

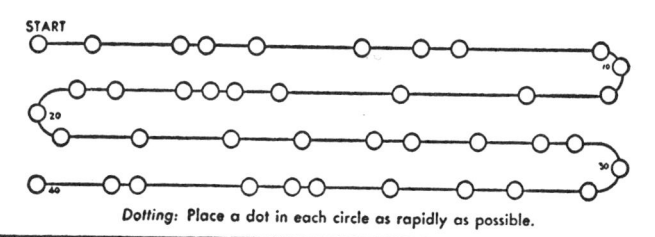

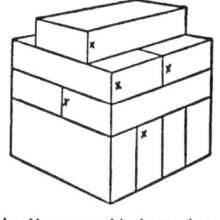

**Dotting:** Place a dot in each circle as rapidly as possible.

**Copying:** Copy figure by joining dots.

**Blocks:** How many blocks touch each block with an X on it?

**Pursuit:** Follow each line by eye and show where it ends, by writing its number in the correct box at the right.

Reproduced by permission of the California Test Bureau.

lotted only ten to twenty seconds, a stop watch is needed in order to time the tests accurately. The reliability of the whole test is high. Reliabilities of the seven subtests are lower, but are fairly satisfactory for such short tests.

BENNETT MECHANICAL COMPREHENSION TEST[2]

**Description.** This is a paper-and-pencil test in which comprehension of mechanical relations is determined by means of pic-

[2] The Psychological Corporation, New York, New York.

tures and sketches. The test is fairly advanced in difficulty. Each picture or drawing has a simply phrased question designed to reveal the examinee's understanding of the mechanical problem presented. Figure 6–2 shows samples from the test battery.

The Bennett test measures the ability to solve problems involving physical relations. Thus it is a measure of abstract intelligence as well as a test of mechanical ingenuity.

**Scope.** There are four forms of the Bennett test. Form AA, the easiest, is suitable for trade and high schools and for less well trained workers. Form BB, more difficult, is for engineering school applicants, technicians, and engineers. Form CC, the most difficult, differentiates among examinees of high ability levels. The fourth form, WI, is for women.

**Scoring.** Percentile norms, which are supplied for each test form, are applicable to a variety of student and occupational groups. The test is valuable in guidance, in selecting applicants with aptitude for mechanical thinking, and in the selection of students wanting to study mechanics and engineering. The MacQuarrie is a useful supplement to the Bennett test when speed and manual dexterity as well as more abstract thinking about mechanical relations are required.

The reliability of the Bennett is satisfactory. Validity is hard to determine, but the test is valid in relation to such criteria as grades in high-school shop courses and occupational and industrial performance.

### Clerical Aptitude

Tests planned to gauge clerical aptitude are concerned mainly with perceptual speed and accuracy in reading, writing, and marking, and with manual dexterity and skill. Office workers are designated in several ways, such as general clerk, sales clerk, shipping clerk, filing clerk, typist, and receptionist. The jobs differ in the kind and variety of their duties, but all demand

CLERICAL APTITUDE    147

*Figure 6–2   Samples from Bennett Mechanical Comprehension Test*

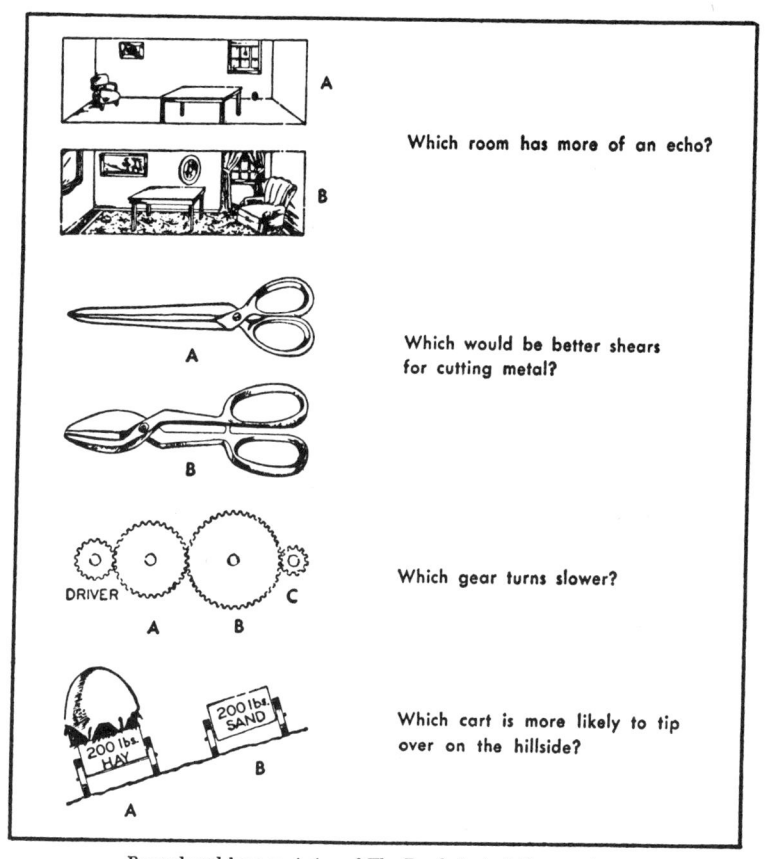

Which room has more of an echo?

Which would be better shears for cutting metal?

Which gear turns slower?

Which cart is more likely to tip over on the hillside?

Reproduced by permission of The Psychological Corporation.

(to a greater or lesser extent) reading, writing, sorting, checking, filing, folding, sealing, and stamping.

The present section will describe two tests of clerical aptitude, the first fairly narrow in functions covered, the second much broader.

> Minnesota Clerical Test
> General Clerical Test

## Minnesota Clerical Test[3]

**Description.** This battery covers speed and accuracy in perceiving clerical detail. There are two parts, number comparison and name comparison. In the first, the examinee is shown two hundred pairs of numbers each containing from three to twelve digits. If the two numbers are alike, the examinee places a check (√) between them; if they are unlike, he leaves the space blank. In the second test, proper names (which match or fail to match) are substituted for number pairs. Samples are shown below:

79542 _____ 79524
5794367 ___√___ 5794367

John C. Linder _____ John C. Lender
Investors' Syndicate ___√___ Investors' Syndicate

The Minnesota Clerical Test is not designed to encompass all the factors which ensure proficiency in office work, but it does attempt to predict ability to handle addresses, bills, accounts, and so on. The Minnesota test has been found to have prognostic value in the selection of clerks, packers, checkers, inspectors (of products), and other factory jobs.

**Scope.** This clerical test may be used with students from junior high school on and for adults.

**Scoring.** The working time of the test is about fifteen minutes, so that both speed and accuracy enter into a score. Individual differences appear in the scores and must be taken into account in interpreting the test. A very careful examinee, for example, may make few errors but earn a relatively low score because of slowness and overcautiousness, and a fast but careless worker may mark more items but tend to make many errors.

[3] The Psychological Corporation, New York, New York.

Percentile norms are available for boys and girls, junior and senior high-school students, and several groups of industrial workers. Among the latter there are norms for women who are machine operators, typists, and clerks and for men who are tellers (bank), accountants, and various sorts of clerks. A high score earned by a student does not necessarily mean that this examinee will make a good clerical worker, though it is a decidedly good omen. But, a high-school counselor is certainly wise to question the vocational promise of a commercial and business student who scores below the twenty-fifth percentile of clerical workers. The reliability of the test is high.

## GENERAL CLERICAL TEST (GCT)[4]

**Description.** This test battery is designed to measure three kinds of aptitude judged to be valuable in office work. There are nine subtests in the battery. Parts I and II test clerical speed and accuracy; Parts III, IV, and V numerical ability; Parts VI, VII, VIII, and IX verbal facility. The first two (checking and alphabetizing) measure perceptual speed and accuracy as expressed in such activities as sorting, coding, and alphabetizing. The next three measure numerical aptitude as shown in computation, error location, and arithmetical reasoning. The last four measure verbal facility by means of spelling, reading comprehension, vocabulary, and grammar. The overall score is a good measure of abstract intelligence, as well as of aptitude for clerical work. The test is to be recommended, therefore, for secretarial jobs which demand a relatively high level of intelligence.

**Scope.** The battery is intended for use with high-school and business-school students. The GCT may also be valuable when testing applicants for more responsible clerical positions. The working time for the test is about fifty minutes.

[4] The Psychological Corporation, New York, New York.

**Scoring.** Percentile norms are available for high schools and for business schools, as well as for various sorts of clerical workers. Norms for each subtest, as well as for total score, are provided. The reliability of the whole test is high—greater than .90. The reliability of the subtests is much lower, and the counselor must be tentative in judgments based only on parts of the test.

## APTITUDE TESTS IN SPECIAL AREAS

In this section five test batteries often useful to the educational counselor and classroom teacher will be described. These specialized examinations are illustrative of many tests in this field:

    Differential Aptitude Tests
    Minnesota Paper Form Board
    Murphy-Durrell Diagnostic Reading Readiness Test
    Orleans Algebra Prognosis Test
    Turse Shorthand Aptitude Test

Sensory-motor tests of visual and auditory keenness and special tests of motor skills, dexterity, and coordination are often classified as aptitude tests. Apparatus tests of this sort are valuable in industry and the military service, but they are not used routinely in the schools and will not be described here. Some of the devices are very complex and require specialized training on the part of the examiner. *Oral Trade Tests* constitute another sort of specialized aptitude test which will not be treated here. These tests are really oral interviews, are administered individually, and are valuable in appraising the vocational training and work experience of an applicant.

### DIFFERENTIAL APTITUDE TEST (DAT)[5]

**Description.** This battery is designed for educational and vocational guidance of high-school students. There are seven subtests, each of which yields a separate score.

[5] The Psychological Corporation, New York, New York.

*Verbal reasoning:* A difficult verbal analogies test, which measures ability to handle verbal relations. Aspirants for professions should earn high scores.

*Numerical ability:* An arithmetic test covering a wide range of operations. This test is an important predictor for science and engineering.

*Abstract reasoning:* A non-language test which demands the solution of problems expressed in diagrams and figures. The test measures a high level of abstract intelligence.

*Space relations:* Ability to distinguish a three-dimensional object from a two-dimensional pattern. Useful in engineering, architecture, and drafting.

*Clerical speed and accuracy:* A test of speed and accuracy in the performance of clerical tasks. Speed is an important factor.

*Mechanical reasoning:* A form of the Bennett Mechanical Comprehension Test. Useful as a predictor of engineering aptitude when combined with the first four tests above.

*Language usage:* Two tests scored separately which measure the ability to spell and to locate errors in sentences. Emphasizes the mechanics of language as compared with test #1, which emphasizes abstract comprehension.

The illustrative items in Figure 6-3 show the nature of the subtests.

A main feature of the DAT is that the total score is broken down into several components, so that from a student's profile there is a record of comparative performance in eight fundamental activities. The Manual gives explicit instructions for administering and scoring the test battery. In addition, a *Casebook* illustrates the use of the profile in diagnosis and is helpful to guidance counselors.

**Scope.** For grade 8 and for grades 9-12.

**Scoring.** Percentile norms are supplied for grades 8 through 12 for total score and for scores on each subtest. Since there are large sex differences, percentile norms are given for boys and girls separately. Scaled scores (with a mean set at 50) are employed in plotting the profiles. Figure 6-4 shows the profile of a

*Figure 6–3  Sample Items from the Differential Aptitude Tests*

**MECHANICAL REASONING**
Which man in this picture has the heavier load?

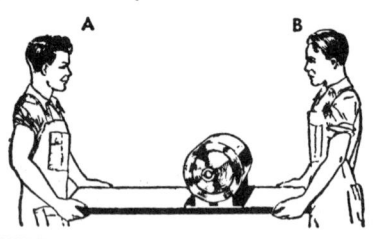

**CLERICAL SPEED AND ACCURACY**

TEST ITEMS

| | | | | | |
|---|---|---|---|---|---|
| V. | AB | AC | AD | AE | AF |
| W. | aA | aB | BA | Ba | Bb |
| X. | A7 | 7A | B7 | 7B | AB |
| Y. | Aa | Ba | bA | BA | bB |
| Z. | 3A | 3B | 33 | B3 | BB |

SAMPLE OF ANSWER SHEET

| | AC | AE | AF | AB | AD |
|---|---|---|---|---|---|
| V | ::::: | ::::: | ::::: | ::::: | ::::: |
| W | BA | Ba | Bb | aA | aB |
| X | 7B | B7 | AB | 7A | A7 |
| Y | Aa | bA | bB | Ba | BA |
| Z | BB | 3B | B3 | 3A | 33 |

In each test item, one of the five combinations is underlined. Find the same combination on the answer sheet and mark it.

**LANGUAGE USAGE: *I Spelling***
Indicate whether each word is spelled right or wrong.

EXAMPLES

W. man

X. gurl

SAMPLE OF ANSWER SHEET

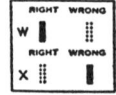

| | RIGHT | WRONG |
|---|---|---|
| W | ▮ | ▯ |
| X | ▯ | ▮ |

**LANGUAGE USAGE: *II Sentences***
Decide which of the lettered parts of each sentence contains errors, if any, mark the corresponding letters on the answer sheet.

Ain't we / going to the / office / next week / at all.
   A        B        C        D        E

| A | B | C | D | E |
|---|---|---|---|---|
| ▮ | ▯ | ▯ | ▯ | ▮ |

Reproduced by permission of The Psychological Corporation.

boy who could profit from educational counseling. Note that James is high in the space and mechanical tests, but mediocre to low in all the others. The boy is certainly not "verbally minded," though he appears to have real talent in mechanics. The teacher will understand James better if he has his profile available.

*Figure 6-4 Sample Items from the Meier Art Judgment Test*

Reproduced by permission of the Bureau of Educational Research and Service, State University of Iowa.

Which of the two presentations is the more pleasing?

The DAT represents the modern practice of substituting a number of analytic scores (for example, on a profile) for a single overall score. We have noted (page 118) that diagnosis of strong and weak points from short subtests is always precarious because of their low reliability. The reliability of the total DAT is very high, and the authors have increased the value of a diagnosis from the subtests by computing the minimal difference between subtest scores which will be significant, that is, nonchance. This makes it possible to say, for instance, that Roy's score in abstract reasoning is significantly higher than his score in clerical speed and accuracy, or that Betty's scores in verbal reasoning and numerical ability do not differ significantly.

Despite its general excellence, the DAT has some practical drawbacks to its use in schools. For one thing, the battery is long (working time approximately three hours) and the cost relatively high. Good norms are available for the high-school grades (boys and girls taken separately), but there are relatively few data on occupational and vocational groups. The battery appears to have content validity, and various experimental studies indicate that it possesses empirical validity. For example, workers in the electrical, mechanical, and building trades score above average on mechanical reasoning, and clerks are about average in numerical ability and in clerical speed and accuracy and language usage. Engineering students score very high on all the subtests except the clerical tests, but are above the mean here. Men in the skilled trades (baker, butcher) are average in mechanical reasoning, and low in numerical ability, abstract reasoning, and space relations. Pre-medical students score high on all subtests, and especially high in verbal reasoning, numerical ability, and sentences. In the high school, verbal reasoning and sentences are predictive of grades in English; numerical ability, verbal reasoning, and abstract reasoning show substantial correlations with mathematics and science. Unfortunately, the data do not reveal *how* successful a man is likely

*Figure 6–5 Profile of a High-School Boy on the Differential Aptitude Tests*

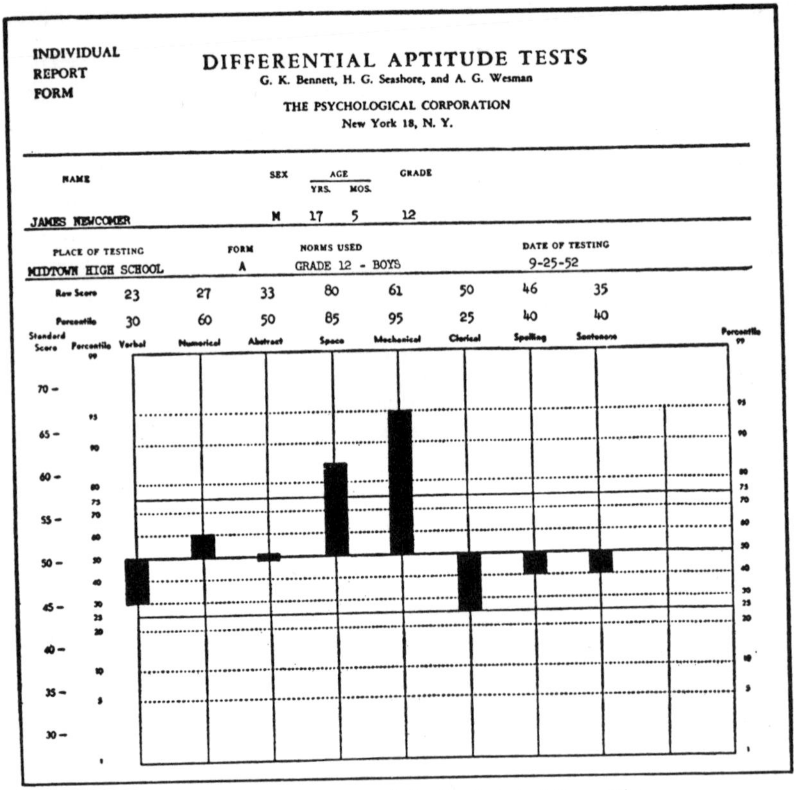
INDIVIDUAL REPORT FORM
DIFFERENTIAL APTITUDE TESTS
G. K. Bennett, H. G. Seashore, and A. G. Wesman
THE PSYCHOLOGICAL CORPORATION
New York 18, N. Y.
NAME
SEX
AGE
YRS. MOS.
GRADE
JAMES NEWCOMER
M 17 5 12
PLACE OF TESTING
FORM
NORMS USED
DATE OF TESTING
MIDTOWN HIGH SCHOOL
A
GRADE 12 - BOYS
9-25-52
Raw Score 23 27 33 80 61 50 46 35
Percentile 30 60 50 85 95 25 40 40
Standard Score
Percentile
Verbal
Numerical
Abstract
Space
Mechanical
Clerical
Spelling
Sentences
Percentile

Reproduced by permission of The Psychological Corporation.

to be over a long period of time in a profession, occupation, or trade. But the tests provide significant clues.

## Minnesota Paper Form Board (MPFB)[6]

**Description.** This is a well-known paper-and-pencil test dealing with spatial relations. It represents an effort to put a form-board on paper. Sample items are shown in Figure 6–5.

[6] The Psychological Corporation, New York, New York.

## MINNESOTA PAPER FORM BOARD 155

Each test item presents a geometrical figure cut into two or more parts. The examinee is to decide how the parts would look if fitted into a complete figure; he does this by selecting the drawing which shows the correct arrangement. Studies have shown the Minnesota Paper Form Board to be a good index of ability to perceive spatial relations and to manipulate figures in two dimensions. The test is useful as an aid in predicting success in shop work, grades in technical courses, in dentistry, art work, and shop and factory output. It does not tap the more intellectual aspects of engineering—for instance, the ability to use symbols in solving problems. But it does test one component in engineering skill. A boy scoring high in the MPFB is not *necessarily* apt in engineering, dentistry, or art, but he has promise and is worth further examination. A boy who scores low had best be encouraged to try some other kind of work. As often happens, we can give negative educational and vocational advice with far greater assurance than we can offer a positive

Figure 6–6  Sample Items from the Minnesota Paper Form Board Test

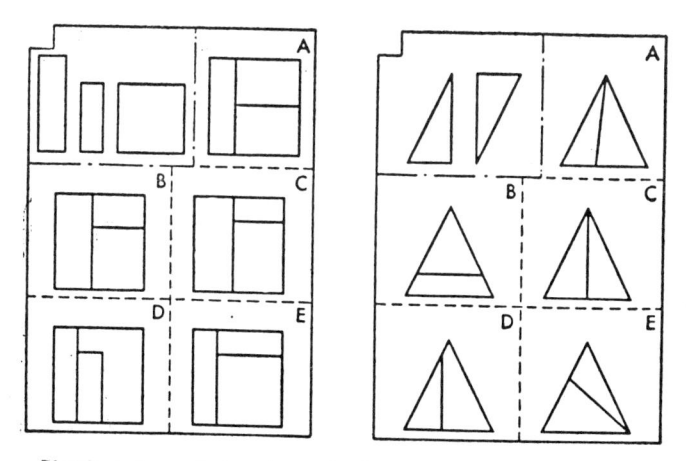

Directions: For each item choose the figure which would result if the pieces in the first section were assembled.

Reproduced by permission of The Psychological Corporation.

course of action. Thus, we can tell a youngster that he had better not attempt engineering, but we cannot always offer him specific advice as to just what he *should* do.

**Scope.** Grade 7 and above.

**Scoring.** Norms are available for school grades and for various occupational groups. There are two forms of the MPFB, and the test is easy to administer and score. Counselors have found the test useful as a supplement to verbal intelligence and achievement tests, especially for students planning to study architecture, engineering, commercial art, and other vocations requiring spatial perception and visualization.

### Murphy-Durrell Diagnostic Reading Readiness Test[7]

**Description.** This test has been designed to measure three characteristics believed to be important in the acquisition of reading skills: auditory discrimination, visual discrimination, and learning rate. Like other readiness tests it is prognostic, in that it forecasts whether or not a child is ready to begin reading. It is also an achievement test and could be so classified since it measures the educational maturity of a youngster. The Metropolitan Readiness Tests (page 127) may be classified as aptitude tests rather than as achievement tests.

The Murphy-Durrell test provides useful information for the first-grade teacher in deciding when to start a formal reading program and what outcomes to expect. At the same time, a good intelligence test will be useful in estimating general mental maturity.

**Scope.** Early in the first grade or before.

**Scoring.** Test 1 and Test 2 (auditory discrimination and visual discrimination) require about an hour each. Test 3 (learning) is both an individual and a group test; there are twenty

[7] Harcourt, Brace & World, Inc., New York, New York.

minutes for group instruction and three brief individual periods. Obtained raw scores are converted into percentile norms for Tests 1 and 2; ratings are used in Test 3.

### ORLEANS ALGEBRA PROGNOSIS TEST (REV.)[8]

**Description.** This is a good illustration of a prognostic test. Its purpose is to determine if a pupil is likely to succeed in (is ready for) algebra. The test is administered before the pupil undertakes the study of algebra. There are nine parts, consisting of simple lessons covering some aspect of algebra—for example, use of symbols, substitution in equations, literal nomenclature, and solving of problems, followed by tests on the material presented. An arithmetic test and a summary test of the material are included. The test has been shown to have good prognostic value, as indicated by its correlations with algebra grades and achievement test scores in algebra.

**Scope.** For students planning to study algebra.

**Scoring.** The test requires about forty-five to fifty minutes. There are percentile norms corresponding to point scores, and there are expectancy charts predicting how well a child making a certain score can be expected to do in algebra. The reliability of the test is satisfactory.

### TURSE SHORTHAND APTITUDE TEST[9]

**Description.** This test is illustrative of aptitude tests developed for use with commercial and vocational subjects. The purpose of the test is to determine whether an examinee is likely to be successful in learning shorthand. There are seven subtests: stroking, spelling, phonetic association, symbol transcription, word discrimination, dictation, and word sense.

[8] Harcourt, Brace & World, Inc., New York, New York.
[9] Harcourt, Brace & World, Inc., New York, New York.

**Scope.** For students planning to study shorthand.

**Scoring.** There are percentile norms for students beginning the study of shorthand. The Turse test is correlated with achievement in shorthand and is valuable in prognosis. The working time of the test is about an hour.

## APTITUDE TESTS FOR THE PROFESSIONS

Tests of aptitude for the professions are primarily achievement tests designed to forecast a student's chances of success in training for medicine, law, or engineering. These tests are specialized in content and are essentially work samples in the designated field. Professional aptitude batteries are validated against grades in courses. It is not known precisely just how predictive these tests are of success in the actual practice of a profession, but there is some evidence that such aptitude tests are related—sometimes highly related—to later success.

The classroom teacher should be familiar with the general content and purpose of the professional aptitude tests, though he will rarely be called on to administer or score them. These batteries are not generally available, are often part of a testing program, are highly specialized, and are usually scored and interpreted in a testing center. Accordingly, we shall give a less detailed description of them.

### MEDICAL COLLEGE ADMISSION TEST[10]

**Description.** This test consists of four parts: verbal, quantitative, general information, and science. The verbal section includes tests of vocabulary, and reading comprehension tests in science, social studies, and the humanities. The quantitative part requires that the examinee solve problems making use of numbers and symbols. The "general information" section is a

---

[10] The Psychological Corporation, New York, New York.

multiple-choice examination covering current social, economic, and political affairs. The science part of the test contains questions drawn from pre-medical courses in biology, chemistry, and physics. Samples from the various sections reveal the character of the examination.

VERBAL ABILITY

*Directions:* Choose the numbered word which means the *same* or most nearly the same as the word in capitals.
1. DIVERT
   (1) postpone   (2) dispossess   (3) share   (4) deflect
2. RIPOSTE
   (1) retort   (2) sleep   (3) meal   (4) vault

QUANTITATIVE ABILITY

*Directions:* Choose the one best answer to each of the following questions.
9. If the sum of two numbers is 60 and their ratio is 3/2, then the larger number is
   (1) 30   (2) 36   (3) 40   (4) 45
10. If the diagonal of a cube is 10, what is the length of an edge?
   (1) 3 1/3   (2) $5\sqrt{2}$   (3) $10/3\sqrt{3}$   (4) $10\sqrt{3}$

GENERAL INFORMATION

*Directions:* In the following questions there is a key term in capital letters. From among the four alternatives following each key term choose the one which is most closely associated with the key term.
13. TRIPLE ALLIANCE
   (1) France-England-Germany
   (2) France-England-Russia
   (3) Germany-Austria-Italy
   (4) France-Spain-Portugal
14. NEOLITHIC
   (1) Ice Age
   (2) Iron Age
   (3) Bronze Age
   (4) Stone Age

## SCIENCE

*Directions:* In each of the following questions choose the one best answer.

22. A mixture of 50 ml of dry hydrogen STP and 50 ml of dry oxygen STP is exploded in a eudiometer. How much and what kind of gas will be found in the eudiometer immediately after the explosion?
    (1) 25 ml of steam only
    (2) 50 ml of steam only
    (3) 25 ml of steam and 25 ml of $O_2$
    (4) 50 ml of steam and 25 ml of $O_2$

The verbal, quantitative, and science parts of the battery are related directly to standing in medical school. The "general information" section is not related to medical knowledge. It is included in an attempt to select candidates for medicine who will be successful in adapting to the needs of the time. In their *Announcement* the authors write: "Special preparation for the test is not necessary. A systematic review of science and elementary mathematics may be of some value, but intensive last-minute cramming probably will not improve scores."[11]

### LAW SCHOOL ADMISSION TEST[12]

**Description.** This battery is designed for use in selecting the best candidates from among those applying for law school. The battery has six parts: principles and cases, data interpretation, reading comprehension, debates (the examinee determines whether a statement supports, refutes, or is irrelevant to a given resolution), best arguments, and paragraph reading. Some of the material is difficult. The test battery has a correlation of about .50 with law school grades. When combined with college marks, it is highly predictive of success in law school.

---

[11] *Medical College Admission Test—1964 Announcement* (New York: The Psychological Corporation, 1964), p. 17.
[12] Educational Testing Service, Princeton, New Jersey.

## Pre-Engineering Ability Test[13]

**Description.** This test consists of two sorts of material: (a) comprehension of scientific materials, and (b) general mathematical problems designed to measure competence in this area. The first part of the test involves reading scientific prose, tables, and graphs, and answering questions based upon these materials. The second part consists of problems in arithmetic, algebra, and geometry. The Pre-Engineering Test correlates about .50 with grades in the first term of engineering school. The reliability of the battery is high.

## National Teacher Examination

**Description.** These examinations are planned for use by school systems as an aid in the selection of teachers, and they are employed also by teacher-training colleges as a means of evaluating their students. The examinations are constructed, administered, and scored by the Educational Testing Service. Their objective is the measurement of professional background, general intelligence, and general culture. There are two parts of the battery, four common examinations, and a series of optional examinations. The first set covers a student's general background for teaching, and the second his mastery of some special field.

The common examinations comprise the following subtests:

Professional information: Child development, educational psychology, guidance, measurement, principles and methods of teaching.
General culture: Sections on science and mathematics and on literature, history, and the fine arts. Examinations cover the development and current state of affairs in these fields.
English expression: Grammatical errors to be detected in sentences.
Nonverbal reasoning: A pattern completion test in which the examinee must fathom the relationships in a given figure and choose the correct figure to complete the pattern.

[13] Educational Testing Service, Princeton, New Jersey.

The optional examinations cover eight areas of specialization: education in elementary schools, early child education, biological sciences, English, industrial arts, mathematics, physical sciences, and social studies. The four common examinations have exhibited substantial relationships with ratings for effectiveness of teachers by supervisors. The tests do not attempt to measure personality factors, interest, or drive.

## TESTS OF ARTISTIC APTITUDE OR TALENT

Tests in this area are concerned with finding whether an examinee possesses some of the factors which appear to be necessary for success in music or in art. So many traits contribute to the success of an artist or a musician that it is impossible for an aptitude test to do more than tap some of the more obvious components. Perhaps the best the aptitude tests can do in many instances is to aid the counselor in steering away from the arts those aspiring students who have no real talent and whose money and time might be better spent in other pursuits.

It is doubtful whether the classroom teacher will have the time, the training, or the equipment needed to administer and interpret the aptitude tests in this area. Teachers engaged in guidance should be familiar with such tests, however—with what they are and what they are trying to do. Two tests of music and one of art will be described in this section. They are representative of aptitude measures in this field.

> Seashore Measures of Musical Talents
> Diagnostic Tests of Achievement in Music
> Meier Art Judgment Test

### SEASHORE MEASURES OF MUSICAL TALENTS[14]

**Description.** This is a test of "ear for music." The test battery consists of six separate tests covering such attributes of tone as pitch discrimination, loudness, rhythm, time, timbre, and tonal

---
[14] The Psychological Corporation, New York, New York.

memory. The tests are given by phonograph records. Each test item or problem presents a pair of tones or a tonal sequence. In the second playing, one of the tones is changed, or the sequence of tones is altered in some way. In the pitch discrimination test, the examinee marks on a test sheet whether the second tone is higher (H) or lower (L) than the first. Comparisons become progressively more difficult as the difference in pitch between the two tones decreases. In the time and loudness tests, the second, or comparison, tone differs in strength or in pattern from the first. The rhythm test requires the examinee to decide whether the second of two patterns is alike or different from the first. The timbre and tonal memory tests differ somewhat from the others. In the first, two tonal patterns are compared for quality (consonance); in the second, a short series of from three to five tones is played, and then played a second time with one note changed. The subject must write down the number of the altered note. The stimuli (tones) presented by the phonograph records are as pure (uncomplicated) as possible.

**Scope.** The Seashore Tests are applicable from the fifth grade on.

**Scoring.** Scores from the six subtests are plotted on a profile to give a graphic representation of performance. Percentile norms are available for fifth and sixth graders, seventh and eighth graders, and adults. The Seashore Tests have been used in schools of music and in music courses in academic schools. Admittedly the tests do not run the gamut of musical talent, but they do measure important aspects of musical aptitude. A child who ranks low on these tests has a poor ear for music and is a doubtful selection for extensive musical training. The reliability of the battery runs about .80.

## DIAGNOSTIC TESTS OF ACHIEVEMENT IN MUSIC[15]

**Description.** As the name implies, this test battery is designed to find how well students have acquired the theory and technical

[15] California Test Bureau, Monterey, California.

knowledge needed to read and understand music. The test consists of ten parts: diatonic syllable names, chromatic syllable names, number names, time signatures, major and minor keys, note and rest values, letter names, signs and symbols, key names, and song recognition. Test content is based on materials recommended by musical authorities as fundamental in musical education. A piano is required for the tests.

**Scope.** For grades 4 through 12. Test items are graded up sharply in difficulty.

**Scoring.** Norms for the test are based on the degree of mastery shown by students for the various sorts of material. Strengths and weaknesses are revealed by comparison of scores upon the ten parts of the test. The reliability of the whole test over the rather wide range for which it is applicable is very high. Reliability for separate grades is lower, but probably satisfactory. Working time for the test is about sixty minutes. The Diagnostic Tests are a useful supplement to "ear" tests like the Seashore. An ear for music is necessary for any musical activity; a knowledge of the technical aspects of music is necessary for one aspiring to be a musician.

## MEIER ART JUDGMENT TEST[16]

**Description.** This test consists of a hundred problems in each of which an artistic judgment is demanded. Each test item is presented in two versions. In the first version, there is a painting or drawing by some well-known artist, or an acknowledged artistic design; in the second, the same theme is presented but in altered form, the change being in symmetry, balance, unity, or rhythm. All pictures are in black and white, so that no complication or clue is introduced by color. The examinee is told that the two versions of the picture differ and is asked to select

---

[16] Bureau of Educational Research and Service, State University of Iowa, Iowa City, Iowa.

the better version. The test is, accordingly, a measure of aesthetic judgment, the criterion being the consensus of experts in art. (See Figure 6–6, facing page 152.)

**Scope.** The Meier test is intended for junior and senior high schools, as well as for colleges and art schools.

**Scoring.** Norms are for students in art courses. High scores do not necessarily mean that the student is destined to be an artist, but a low score should be a warning signal to one planning a career in art. The Meier test has correlations of from about .45 to .50 with grades in art courses, but low correlation with scores on verbal intelligence tests. This does not mean that artists are unintelligent, but that many factors besides abstract ability must enter into artistic appreciation. The reliability of the test is about .75 for fairly homogeneous groups.

## HOW TO JUDGE AN APTITUDE TEST

Like tests of intelligence and of educational achievement, aptitude tests must be judged by the adequacy of their validation, reliability, scaling, and norms. Various comments concerning these aspects of the tests described in this chapter have been made in appropriate places. This and other material will now be summarized.

**Validity.** Aptitude tests generally possess content validity. Tests of speed, dexterity, seeing mechanical relations, solving mechanical problems, and the like seem proper for measuring mechanical aptitude. Moreover, tests of sorting, writing, reading, and alphabetizing appear to be appropriate for assessing clerical ability. In the tests of professional aptitude and in those of talent, the content has been chosen with a view toward forecasting performance in school and (hopefully) in life.

Aptitude tests have been validated against various criteria, including grades in courses and success in vocations or trades. Such measures of practical or working validity have been determined for the Minnesota Paper Form Board, the MacQuarrie, and the DAT.

**Reliability.** The reliability of the standard aptitude tests is generally satisfactory, and we can have confidence in the stability of a score. In some cases, the standard error of a score, as well as the reliability coefficient, is given by the author of a test.

**Scaling.** In most aptitude tests, raw scores are converted into percentile ranks. In some tests (the DAT, for example) scaled scores are used on the profile in making comparisons of a given student's scores.

**Norms.** All aptitude tests have norms either in percentiles or in scaled scores. A few tests give norms for certain occupational groups. One drawback to the use of vocational aptitude tests, however, is the lack of adequate norms in many job areas. There is a need for information regarding the predictive value of professional and vocational tests for persons long out of school. It would be a great advance if we knew how well an aptitude test could forecast the *success* of engineers or lawyers, for example, and not simply grades in courses.

## SUGGESTIONS FOR FURTHER READING

ANASTASI, A. *Psychological Testing.* 2nd ed.; New York: Macmillan, 1961.
CRONBACH, L. J. *Essentials of Psychological Testing.* 2nd ed.; New York: Harper, 1960.
GREENE, E. B. *Measurements of Human Behavior.* Rev. ed.; New York: Odyssey, 1952.
NOLL, V. H. *Introduction to Educational Measurement.* Boston: Houghton Mifflin, 1957.

## SUGGESTIONS FOR LABORATORY WORK

1. Administer several standardized aptitude tests to the class. Cut the time allowance if necessary. Students should score their own tests and plot profiles when called for.

2. Find in the Manual the specifications that the author lays down for his aptitude test. Examine the items of the test. Do you agree that the test has content validity? Are any data given on experimental validity?

3. Make a study of the Differential Aptitude Tests. Analyze the battery for validity, reliability, scaling procedures, and norms.

## QUESTIONS FOR DISCUSSION

1. How do aptitude tests differ from readiness tests in purpose and content?

2. Why does a test battery like the Minnesota Clerical Test vary greatly in the accuracy of its forecasts of office work?

3. Why are aptitude tests used more often in high schools than in elementary schools?

4. Give some reasons that paper-and-pencil tests of mechanical ability are as useful as are work samples in determining aptitude.

5. How would you set up a program for selecting candidates for a nursing school? Outline the procedures you would use.

6. Would you use the Bennett Mechanical Comprehension Test to select workers in an automobile factory?

7. It has been said that the best measure of aptitude for mathematics (or for any subject) is the achievement to date. Do you agree?

8. How could you discover whether the Meier Art Test is measuring native artistic ability and not training in art?

9. A girl of 16 scores very high on the Seashore Music Test. Would you advise her to undertake a career in music? Why or why not? What else might you need to know about her?

10. How can a followup study of graduates of law and medical schools be useful to a counselor using a professional aptitude test?

11. To what extent do you think a civil engineer would need abstract intelligence? An auto mechanic?

12. At what level (elementary, high school, college) is teaching skill more important than native aptitude? Less important?

## Chapter 7

## PERSONALITY TESTS

In previous chapters, we have indicated on several occasions that prediction of success based on measures of intelligence, school achievement, and aptitude must always be qualified by the statement "provided the personality traits are favorable." In the present chapter, we shall attempt to see how well we can determine favorable and unfavorable personality traits.

There are a number of descriptions of personality, and the usefulness of any definition will depend in most cases on the purposes of the author. For the teacher or school counselor, a practical working definition is that personality is a student's characteristic way of doing things. Suppose that two boys, John and Jim, are about the same age, have about the same IQ, and do about the same caliber of school work. But suppose further that John is friendly, highly motivated, and likeable; that Jim is sullen, indifferent in attitude, and not sought out by teachers and classmates. The decided contrast in the behavior of these two boys arises from their distinctive personality traits, not from their differences in mental ability. Failure in school—or in life—is often the result of a person's inability to make good use of his potential personal assets. Obviously, lack of success may arise either from negative (unpleasant) personality traits or from failure to make use of positive (pleasant) personality traits.

The psychologist has attempted to evaluate personality traits in three ways: (1) by rating scales, (2) by questionnaires and inventories, and (3) by what are called "projective tests." The first two approaches are the most readily applicable in the schools. Projective tests should be employed only by clinical psychologists and psychiatrists, since they require special training for administration and interpretation. These "tests" are essentially clinical instruments and are most often used diagnostically in cases of severe personality disorders or in behavior problems where drastic emotional disturbances are suspected. Rating scales and inventories, however, can be administered and interpreted in a useful way by teachers and counselors.

## RATING SCALES

The rating scale is a device for obtaining judgments of the degree to which an individual possesses certain behavior traits and attributes not readily detectable by objective tests. In the school situation, rating scales provide appraisals of a teacher (or of a candidate for a teaching position) in several characteristics. Ratings by teachers or principals are often required for students seeking entrance to college or looking for a job. In making a rating, the judge expresses his opinion by marking along a graduated scale or by checking in the category which he feels best describes the person being rated.

Perhaps the most useful type of rating device is the Graphic Rating Scale or some variation of it. The typical graphic scale consists of a straight line (for example, five inches long) which is taken to represent the range of behavior in the trait. In lieu of a line, several categories representing graduations in the trait may be provided. The illustrations in Figure 7-1 are samples from various rating scales.

Units on the graphic rating scale are represented by the successive scale divisions, but the directions make it clear that the check mark indicating the judgment may be placed anywhere along the scale line. A graphic scale is often scored by separating the scale line into one hundred points. A person's rating is then determined by the distance of the judge's check from the low end of the scale. A more summary method is also used; if there are five main divisions on the scale, the highest division may be designated "1," the next division "2," and so on down. This is probably as much accuracy as one can expect from the scale.

### Requirements of a Good Rating Scale

A good rating scale should satisfy the following requirements.

**Traits Should Be Carefully Defined.** A sentence or a phrase is more informative than a single word. Thus, the meaning of "tact," "initiative," or "dependability" should be pinned down by descriptive phrases or by actual examples. Intelligence, energy level, personal appearance, work habits, and the like are better judged than are character traits (loyalty, courage, unselfishness) because they are more readily observed in social behavior. Character traits must be inferred from a variety of behaviors. It often helps to clarify a rating if the judge is required to record specific instances ("behaviorgrams") of the trait which support his opinion. On the American Council on Education rating scale, for example, space is left in which the judge may provide observations which justify his rating.

A good scale avoids terms which are a hodgepodge of a number of activities—for example, "standing in the community," "social position," or "moral qualities." By the same token, a good

*Figure 7–1   Sample Items from Various Graphic Rating Scales*

1. From a graphic rating scale for clerical workers:
Accuracy—Consider carefully quality of work, freedom from error.

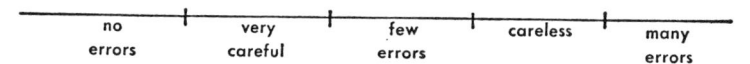

| no errors | very careful | few errors | careless | many errors |
|---|---|---|---|---|

2. From a behavior rating scale for children:
Is his attention sustained?

| Distracted: jumps rapidly from one thing to another. | Difficult to keep at a task until completed. | Attends adequately. | Is absorbed in what he does. | Able to hold attention for long periods. |
|---|---|---|---|---|
| (5) | (4) | (3) | (2) | (1) |

3. From the American Council on Education Rating Scale for prospective college students:
Does he get others to do what he wishes?

| Probably unable to lead his fellows. | Lets others take lead. | Sometimes leads in minor affairs. | Sometimes leads in important affairs. | Displays marked ability to lead his fellows; makes things go. |
|---|---|---|---|---|

4. From a rating device for teacher candidates:
(Put a check under the appropriate heading)

| Tact | Very inferior | Inferior | Average | Superior | Very superior |
|---|---|---|---|---|---|

5. From a rating scale for teachers:
(Circle the number which best indicates the degree or extent to which the qualities are practiced.)
0 = unsatisfactory; 1 = below average; 2 = average;
3 = above average; 4 = superior.
Emotional maturity:
To what extent does the teacher exhibit desirable balance between emotional responsiveness and emotional control? Consider disposition, sense of humor, restraint and thoughtfulness in dealing with others, feelings of security, objectivity of interest, freedom from excessive fears and worries and warmth of feeling and expression.   0  1  2  3  4

6. From a rating scale for officer candidates:
Relations with fellow candidates:

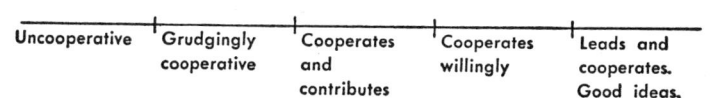

| Uncooperative | Grudgingly cooperative | Cooperates and contributes | Cooperates willingly | Leads and cooperates. Good ideas. |
|---|---|---|---|---|

scale avoids narrow, specific terms. The dean or principal rarely knows intimate details about a teacher—whether he sings in the choir, loves his mother, or plays golf well. Information of this sort is called for, however. School authorities often do not have occasion to observe or to learn about a teacher's personal behavior and, in general, should not be asked to supply such information.

In the adjective-checking form of the rating scale, the judge may be asked to check one of two contrasting adjectives—for example, dependable–undependable, aggressive–timid. Information of this sort is of little value. Behavior is rarely all-or-none in this fashion. Nor is it useful to give the judge a list of highly abstract terms and ask him to check those which apply to the ratee. Behavior occurs in specific situations, not in a general, undefined fashion.

**The Number of Divisions on the Scale Should Be Neither Too Numerous Nor Too Few.** The optimum number of divisions on a graphic scale is perhaps five to seven. Fewer divisions than five causes the groupings to be too coarse; more than seven divisions demands fractionings of the trait which are too fine for most raters, with the result that a large part of the scale may be unused. A five-division scale is popular, since it corresponds to the marking system A, B, C, D, and E. Furthermore, the five categories "high," "above average," "average," "below average," and "poor" seem to mark off fairly natural divisions.

**Directions to the Rater Should Be Explicit.** The adequacy of the directions given the rater will have a substantial effect on the validity and reliability of his ratings. The rater (1) should be given as explicit directions as possible, (2) should be told what is meant by the distribution of a trait, and (3) should be warned against assigning too many "average" ratings. This last is sometimes needed when the persons to be rated are not well known to the rater, when the meaning of the traits is not well understood, and when the rater is overcautious. Raters must be warned against the "halo effect" (see page 173) and the tendency to see logical relations among traits—to assume, for example, that intelligence and moral behavior or intelligence and good work habits of necessity go together.

As for the distribution of traits, the best first hypothesis (in lieu of other information) is to assume that ratings will be distributed in the form of a normal curve. When the baseline of the normal curve is subdivided into five equal parts, the percentages in each division (reading from either end of the curve) are 7, 24, 38, 24, and 7. If there are seven divisions on the scale, the percentages in subdivisions are 4, 10, 22, 28, 22, 10, and 4. The directions should make it clear that the exact proportions in the normal curve should not be followed slavishly. But the point should be stressed that when a group of teachers is rated for "skill in instruction" on a five-division scale, we must expect many more in the middle of the scale than at either end.

The tendency to assign too many "average" ratings (the "caution factor") is to be contrasted with the tendency to assign too many high ratings (the "generosity factor"). Stress on the normal distribution of most traits will help correct this tendency. If the low end of the rating scale is described by such unpleasant terms as "stingy," "stupid," "mean," this part of the rating line may be avoided by many raters. The "halo effect" mentioned above is the tendency to rate a person high on all traits if he is well liked or is regarded as highly intelligent. Conversely, if a person is disliked, there is a tendency to rate him low on all traits. To minimize halo, the rater is usually told to rate *all* candidates on a single trait, then to rate all on a second trait, and so on. This procedure is impractical, of course, when the rater is called on to consider one person at a time and rate him on, say, ten traits. We are often forced, therefore, to resort to warnings against halo and careful definition of traits.

## VALIDITY AND RELIABILITY OF A RATING SCALE

Ratings for intelligence and for special aptitudes made on a graphic rating scale can be validated against objective test scores. But ratings of personality traits cannot be so validated, since we rarely have criterion scores and must perforce fall back on a consensus of judges. In ratings of personality traits, validity and reliability mean virtually the same thing. If three or more raters agree that Brown is a skilled worker or a friendly person, the average of these ratings is reliable (consistent) and valid (worthy of confidence). If two supervisors decide independently that Miss Miller has a pleasing voice and sympathetic manner, our confidence in these judgments is greater than if only one supervisor had so stated. In general, confidence increases with the number of agreements among independent ratings.

Theoretically, there is a distinction between reliability and validity (page 29), but this distinction does not hold for ratings. If competent judges agree that John is a steady worker, and a cooperative, pleasant colleague, then for all practical purposes he is just that. The copybook definition that character is what you are and reputation what people say about you is not true in everyday behavior.

It can be shown that if the estimates of two judges correlate .60, then the average of these ratings will correlate .75 with those of two equally good judges. It is, of course, difficult to decide when two judges are "equally good." We can never guarantee this to be true, but we can (a) select judges who at least know the ratees well, (b) provide careful definitions of the traits to be rated, and (c) allow for individual differences in rating standards.

### SUMMARY ON RATING SCALES

Generally, ratings from graphic scales will deserve confidence when
1. Qualities which can be *observed* in behavior are rated. Energy, appearance, and teaching skill are better rated than are character and moral traits.

2. Characteristics to be rated are illustrated. The use of behaviorgrams (page 170) and specific instances will strengthen the ratings.
3. Raters have actually observed the persons to be rated in situations where personality might be revealed.
4. Independent ratings are pooled.
5. Judges are confident that the ratings are valuable.
6. Different standards are accounted for by explicit directions or by statistical techniques.

The above rules are perhaps most useful when one has the problem of constructing a rating device. They may not seem to be very helpful to the teacher who is faced by a ready-made scale. Teachers and supervisors rarely have the responsibility for devising a rating scale, but teachers are rated by supervisors and supervisors by principals. Moreover, students are rated by teachers and by principals for personality traits judged important by colleges or prospective employers. Hence, the teacher should be familiar with how the rating scale is put together and how it works. Raters can improve a rating device by offering criticisms and recommendations. Eventually, comments of this sort should lead to better ratings or to a better scale.

## QUESTIONNAIRES AND PERSONALITY INVENTORIES

The behavior inventory calls for short answers to a standard set of questions believed to bring out personality characteristics. The inventory or questionnaire is a formal interview or self-report rather than a "mental test"; the examinee is not required to solve problems, but is asked to express opinions, preferences, and feelings. Questionnaires have been developed by psychologists for use in three main areas: (a) personal-social behavior, (b) attitudes, and (c) interests. The personal data sheet or personality inventory deals with motives and needs, as well as with emotional and social factors. Adjustment to life—

or more accurately, perhaps, maladjustment to life—is revealed by a person's self-report of his worries, fears, feelings of insecurity or of depression, frustrations, lack of confidence, and the like. The typical attitude inventory canvasses the examinee's feelings, opinions, and beliefs about various institutions (for example, the church) and about social and political matters (for example, war, freedom of speech, and internationalism). Finally, the interest questionnaire deals with preferences for occupations, people, school subjects (such as physics or history), books, sports, hobbies, and avocations.

A personality inventory may take the *direct* or the *indirect* approach. In the first, the examinee is asked for specific information; in the second, he does not know (though he may guess or suspect) the import of the questions. For example, the examinee may be asked if he is afraid of high places (direct) or he may be asked (among other questions) whether he would rather be a bookkeeper or an airline pilot (indirect). In the indirect form of the question, the assumption made is that an examinee is less likely to fake or rationalize his answers when he is not sure what motive or what personality trait the inventory is trying to uncover.

## THE PERSONALITY INVENTORY

Personality inventories were used by the armed forces in World Wars I and II to screen out the maladjusted and those likely to become mentally ill. These personal data (or PD) sheets consisted of lists of symptoms reported by men who subsequently had suffered from "nervous breakdown" or were classified as psychoneurotic. These adult questionnaires have been revised by deleting the more serious and disturbing items so that they can be used in the schools. Questions which were removed were concerned with the more reprehensible forms of adult behavior such as those involving liquor and sex offenses. In the schools, the questionnaire is used to locate pupils with potentially handicapping personality problems. The acceptability of a PD sheet for pupils, parents, and the community is necessary if the inventory is to be used generally as a group test. A teacher will be well advised to make sure that the inventory he decides to use has the approval of the school authorities. It is important that the reading level demanded by an inventory be carefully scrutinized, since many items may not be understood.

The personality inventory is most valuable in the schools for counseling and guidance—that is, for spotting pupils with existing or potential personality difficulties. When used individually and in face to face contacts, the PD sheet is more flexible and becomes essentially a directed interview. Answers given by the student can be pursued further until their meaning is clear. This cannot be done, of course, when the inventory is administered in group form. Of the personality inventories available (many cover the same ground), the following represent acceptable "tests" for use in the schools:
California Test of Personality
Pintner's Aspects of Personality
Bernreuter's The Personality Inventory
Gordon's Personal Profile and Personal Inventory
Bell's Adjustment Inventory
Thurstone Temperament Schedule
Each of these questionnaires will be considered in this section.

CALIFORNIA TEST OF PERSONALITY[1]

**Description.** This test series covers the elementary grades to adulthood. Each battery is divided into two sections designed to measure (1) personal adjustment and (2) social adjustment. The subtests in section 1 are designed to bring out how a person thinks and feels about himself, his feelings of confidence and adequacy, his tendencies to withdraw within himself and to ex-

[1] California Test Bureau, Monterey, California.

hibit nervous symptoms. In section 2, the six subtests question the examinee on his knowledge of social standards, his social skills, his freedom from antisocial attitudes, and his relations to family, friends, and the community. The questions are Yes-No in form. Figure 7-2 gives samples from the test.

**Scope.** There are five separate test batteries:
>Primary Series, kindergarten to grade 3
>Elementary Series, grades 4-8
>Intermediate Series, grades 7-10
>Secondary Series, grades 9-college
>Adult Series

Overall time for administering a test battery is approximately fifty minutes.

**Scoring.** Answers are recorded in the test booklet itself or on a prepared answer sheet. Scoring is objective and simple. A profile of the different scores and overall adjustment score can

*Figure 7-2   Sample Items from the California Test of Personality, Elementary, Grades 4-5-6-7-8, Form AA*

PERSONAL ADJUSTMENT (Circle YES or NO)
10. Do your parents or teachers usually need to tell you to do your work?   YES   NO
23. Do people often think that you cannot do things well?   YES   NO
25. Do you feel that your folks boss you too much?   YES   NO
38. Are you proud of your school?   YES   NO
50. Would you rather stay away from most parties?   YES   NO
68. Do you often feel tired before noon?   YES   NO

SOCIAL ADJUSTMENT
77. Is it necessary to thank those who have helped you?   YES   NO
87. Do you help new pupils to talk to other children?   YES   NO
101. Do people often act so mean that you have to be nasty to them?   YES   NO
114. Do you like both of your parents about the same?   YES   NO
123. Is it fun to do nice things for some of the other boys or girls?   YES   NO
139. Do you try to get friends to obey the law?   YES   NO

Reproduced by permission of the California Test Bureau.

be constructed. The pupil's earned score (point score) is entered opposite the personality component and the percentile rank corresponding to this score is found in the appropriate table. Percentile ranks for total personal adjustment and for total social adjustment may also be entered.

The reliability of the five batteries is quite high (.80–.94). Percentile norms are provided for each subtest and for the battery as a whole. This inventory is a useful indication of a pupil's all-around adjustment. Diagnosis from the subtests is suggestive rather than conclusive, but many valuable clues which serve to explain a child's behavior may be obtained.

### Aspects of Personality (Pintner)[2]

**Description.** This inventory consists of three parts: ascendance-submission, extroversion-introversion, and emotionality. It was designed to aid the classroom teacher in locating children who have developed—or are likely to develop—serious behavior problems. Samples of the kinds of items found in the test are as follows:

| | |
|---|---|
| I have a lot of nerve | Same—Different |
| I like to read before the class | Same—Different |
| I feel tired most of the time | Same—Different |
| When a child tries to push into line ahead of me, I am not afraid to tell him to get back | Same—Different |

The pupil indicates his agreement or disagreement with a statement by marking or circling "same" or "different."

**Scope.** Aspects of Personality is intended for use in the elementary grades and junior high school.

**Scoring.** This inventory is easily scored by a stencil. There are separate norms for boys and girls and for two levels of maturity. A low score on the ascendance-submission part indicates a shy

[2] Harcourt, Brace & World, Inc., New York, New York.

child, a high score an aggressive one. High scores on extroversion-introversion suggest good adjustment; low scores suggest withdrawing tendencies and daydreaming. Low scores on emotional stability suggest flightiness and lack of control. The total score is a rough index of personal adjustment, and probably only wide deviations should be investigated. The test often provides useful clues.

### THE PERSONALITY INVENTORY (BERNREUTER)[3]

**Description.** This is one of the best-known personality inventories. It consists of one hundred twenty-five questions to be answered by circling the "Yes," "No," or "?" placed before each item. The questions deal with anxieties, lack of self-confidence, worries, timidities, reclusiveness, and other symptoms believed to be indicative of maladjustment.

The scoring stencils provided allow an individual to be evaluated along four personality dimensions. These are described by Bernreuter as B1–N, *neurotic tendency;* B2–S, *self-sufficiency;* B3–I, *introversion-extroversion;* and B4–D, *dominance-submission*. A high score in B1–N implies overanxiety and emotional instability; a low score, the opposite. A high score in B2–S indicates a strong degree of self-sufficiency and self-confidence; a low score, dependency and need for support. B3–I and B4–D are the well-known dimensions of introversion-extroversion and dominance-submission. The introverted person tends to be imaginative and to live within himself; extroverted persons rarely worry and are outgoing. A dominant person takes the lead or direction in face-to-face situations; submissive persons tend to let others dominate and give them advice. Various combinations of the scales are advised depending on the personality traits desired.

In addition to the four Bernreuter scales, the inventory can be scored for two more general traits, F1–C a measure of *self-confidence,* and F2–S a measure of *sociability*. These last two

[3] Stanford University Press, Stanford, California.

dimensions were defined by Flanagan. F1–C is a combination of B1 and B3; F2–S is a combination of B2 and B4.

The Bernreuter Inventory has been employed in a wide variety of situations. It has proved to be valuable in counseling, in selecting persons for vocations requiring specific qualities (for example, salespeople, nurses, receptionists, technicians), and in the practice of clinical psychology. It is least valid when administered as a group test to persons not prepared for such a personal inquiry. The inventory can be faked in the conforming or "normal" direction by an intelligent candidate who is looking for a job, and in such instances data from it are worth very little. If the examinee is convinced that the information from the inventory will be used in his favor (if it pays to tell the truth), however, the inventory can yield valuable clues.

**Scope.** The Inventory is designed for adults and for high-school boys and girls.

**Scoring.** Percentile norms for various groups (men and women, students) are provided. Reliability is in the high .80's. The items of the Inventory have been analyzed and only items able to separate contrasting groups are included. In addition, validity was checked by correlations of the Inventory with other personality questionnaires. A system of differential weights (small digits), some plus and some minus, give more or less credit to the different items.

## PERSONAL PROFILE AND PERSONAL INVENTORY (GORDON)[4]

**Description.** The Personal Profile is designed to measure four fairly distinct personality traits: *ascendancy, responsibility* (perseverance or reliability), *emotional stability,* and *sociability.* The examinee is asked to indicate which of four statements (there are eighteen sets) is most descriptive of himself and which is least descriptive. A specimen set is:

[4] Harcourt, Brace & World, Inc., New York, New York.

Able to make important decisions without help.
Does not mix easily with new people.
Inclined to be tense or high strung.
Sees a job through despite difficulties.

Each of these phrases is descriptive—positively or negatively—of one of the four traits included in the inventory.

This personality questionnaire uses what has been called the "forced-choice" technique—that is, the examinee is instructed to choose between statements, two of which appear to be equally acceptable and two equally unacceptable. (See the description of the indirect questionnaire on page 176.) This method of presenting items has certain advantages. If the two choices are fairly well equated for social value, it is hard for the examinee to fake his answer, since he does not know clearly what is behind either choice. Again, the use of forced-choices reduces hesitation and indecision, since the examinee is required to make a decision, rather than simply choosing between "Yes" and "No." If the examinee likes none of the choices, he may select the least objectionable. In addition to the four trait scores, the Personal Profile yields a total score, which may be represented graphically along with the four part scores. Very low total scores have been found to be associated with maladjustment and poorly developed personality.

The Personal Inventory also covers four traits: *caution, original thinking, personal relations,* and *vigor*. The total score depicts the student's personal development in these areas.

**Scope.** The Profile and Inventory are designed for high schools, colleges, and adults.

**Scoring.** Percentile norms are available for each scale, for boys and girls separately, for high school, and for college. The four scores and the total may be represented graphically on a profile. These questionnaires have considerable validity, as is shown in followup studies. Together, the two inventories are useful in counseling students and in screening out those with potential behavior problems. Reliabilities of the subtests and of the total are satisfactory.

### ADJUSTMENT INVENTORY (BELL)[5]

**Description.** This well-known inventory consists of questions to be answered "Yes," "No," or "?" It has been designed to estimate personal adjustment in four areas: *home* (satisfactions and dissatisfactions), *health* (illness and general well-being), *social relations* (shyness, aggressiveness, and so on), and *emotional behavior* (self-confidence, depression, and the like). Samples of the kinds of items in the questionnaire are

| | | | |
|---|---|---|---|
| Are you troubled with shyness? | Yes | No | ? |
| Do you daydream frequently? | Yes | No | ? |
| Are you often low in spirits? | Yes | No | ? |

The Bell Inventory has proved useful chiefly in locating students who need counseling. It provides valuable leads to social and personal maladjustment.

**Scope.** The student form of the Bell is for high school and college students. There is a form for adults which may be used in vocational counseling.

**Scoring.** The inventory is not timed, but ordinarily requires about twenty-five to thirty minutes. The overall reliability is high. There are percentile norms for high-school and college students and for men and women.

### THURSTONE TEMPERAMENT SCHEDULE[6]

**Description.** This inventory consists of a set of one hundred and forty questions, twenty items being grouped under each of seven aspects of temperament or emotional expression. Adjectives describing the seven temperamental traits are *active* (de-

---
[5] Stanford University Press, Stanford, California.
[6] Science Research Associates, Chicago, Illinois.

gree of energy), *vigorous* (participation in physical activities sports), *impulsive* (happy-go-lucky), *dominant* (aggressive, forthright), *stable* (emotionally), *sociable,* and *reflective* (thoughtful, meditative). These seven behavior areas, which were identified through a study of the intercorrelations of many personality variables, are believed to constitute certain basic aspects of social behavior. The inventory is well adapted for use with normal people; items obviously bearing on mental disease have been avoided.

**Scope.** Percentile norms are available for the subsections, and the seven scores may be plotted on a profile for a study of idiosyncrasies. The reliability of the whole inventory is high. However, the reliabilities of the subsections are not high. Hence, though the inventory may provide valuable clues to a counselor, diagnosis based on part scores should be tentative.

## ATTITUDE SCALES

When we know that a man is a Socialist or a Christian Scientist, we feel fairly sure that we can predict his answers to questions dealing with politics or religion. An attitude is a consistent point of view, a way of behaving toward an institution, a social group, or toward personal, political, or religious issues or practices. Attitudes may be fairly narrow or quite broad, and they may be strongly or weakly held. In general, an attitude pivots around strong likes or dislikes. A person's attitude toward drinking, professional sports, popular music, or "eggheads," for example, will be exhibited in expressions of opinion which are often emotional.

Scales for measuring the spread and strength of attitudes have often been used by social psychologists in experimental studies, but rarely are employed routinely in the schools. One of the most comprehensive lists of attitude scales (about thirty in all) has been constructed by L. L. Thurstone and his associates at the University of Chicago. These scales estimate the strength of one's attitude (on either the favorable or unfavorable side) toward such diverse matters as war, capital punishment, church, and communism. In this section, we shall describe two scales both of which have been useful in high school and college. These are

Ascendance-Submission Reaction Study (Allport)
Study of Values (Allport-Vernon-Lindzey)

### ASCENDANCE-SUBMISSION REACTION STUDY[7]

**Description.** This questionnaire attempts to determine whether a person characteristically dominates or is dominated in the face-to-face contacts of everyday life. The A-S Reaction Study usually is classified as a personality inventory, but it can just as well (perhaps better) be described as an attitude scale, since it tries to discover an individual's habitual way of behaving in everyday social contacts. There are two forms of the test, one for men and one for women. Each item presents a situation which might be encountered readily in school, on the street, in a store, or on a bus. Thus, one is asked what he does typically when someone pushes ahead of him in line, and if he often crosses the street to avoid speaking to someone. From two to four possible responses are offered. The examinee selects that option which most nearly represents what he would ordinarily do. Choices range from aggressive to submissive and are weighted to differentiate between the two attitudes. Scoring weights for the separate items were determined experimentally, and the total score shows the strength of the examinee's typical behavior on a dominance-submissiveness scale.

**Scope.** The A-S inventory is designed for use in high schools and colleges, and for adults.

**Scoring.** Scoring is by stencil, the answers being weighted +

[7] Houghton Mifflin Company, Boston, Massachusetts.

(plus) for dominance and — (minus) for submissiveness. Percentile norms are provided for high-school and for college students, and for adult men and adult women. The A-S Study is often useful in educational and vocational guidance. In many occupations, such as nursing, teaching, library work, and clerical jobs, a strongly dominant attitude is a liability rather than an asset. On the other hand, in positions requiring leadership, dominant behavior and self-confidence are crucial when decisions are to be made. The A-S Study is especially valuable when combined with aptitude and other tests. The test has satisfactory reliability.

### STUDY OF VALUES (ALLPORT-VERNON-LINDZEY)[8]

**Description.** This questionnaire sets out to gauge the strength of six basic attitudes, described as follows: *theoretical* (marked by dominant interest in the discovery of truth, the rational approach to life); *economic* (interests lie in practical affairs); *aesthetic* (places greatest value on form and beauty); *social* (chief interest in people); *political* (primary interest in power, influence, and renown); and *religious* (committed to mystical values, seeks to comprehend the universe). The Study assumes that a person's philosophy of life is revealed by the strength of his basic attitudes. (See Figure 7–3.)

**Scope.** College students and adults.

**Scoring.** To score, the weights assigned the various items are added. The total score for each of the six Values can be plotted on a profile to show graphically the relative strengths of the individual's attitudes. Norms are for college students, for men and women separately, and for some occupational groups. The Values inventory has shown expected differences between medical and theological students and characteristic differences among other occupational groups. The inventory is useful in

---

* Houghton Mifflin Company, Boston, Massachusetts.

Figure 7–3  *Specimen Items from a Study of Values (Answers are indicated by checking or marking.)*

> (Answers are indicated by checking or marking.)
> 
> *Theoretical v. Economic:*
> 1. The main object of scientific research should be the discovery of truth rather than its practical applications. (a) Yes; (b) No.
> 
> *Religious v. Social:*
> 9. Which of these character traits do you consider the more desirable: (a) high ideals and reverence; (b) unselfishness and sympathy?
> 
> *Aesthetic v. theoretical v. political v. economic:*
> 10. Which of the following would you prefer to do during part of your next summer vacation (if your ability and other conditions permit)—
>    a. write and publish an original biological essay or article
>    b. stay in some secluded part of the country where you can appreciate fine scenery
>    c. enter a local tennis or other athletic tournament
>    d. get experience in some new line of business

From Allport-Vernon-Lindzey, "Study of Values." Reproduced by permission of Houghton Mifflin Company.

vocational counseling and in personnel selection. It is also valuable in forecasting the direction of a student's interests.

## INTEREST INVENTORIES

The interest inventory is essentially a self-report or survey covering a person's own interests, values, preferences, and feelings over a wide range of activities. The importance of interests early became apparent in industry when studies of worker efficiency made it clear that job success depends as much on motivation as on aptitude and training. In the school, knowledge of a student's dominant interests is of real significance for the counselor or teacher. The printed interest inventory supplies systematic information about a student's attitudes, feelings, and personality trends which otherwise could be revealed only in a long personal interview, if at all. Students often report patterns of interest which differ widely from their stated educational and vocational goals. The astute counselor may be able from study of the inventory to suggest occupational areas which the student hitherto had not even thought of.

The interest inventory is generally more acceptable in school than is the attitude scale or the personal data (adjustment) blank. Many students resent the personal questions of the adjustment blank and sometimes find them emotionally disturbing. For this reason, they conceal their true feelings, especially if they are not conventional or socially acceptable. An interest inventory is not likely to be faked or responded to adversely. Examinees find it impersonal, less prying, and often interesting in itself. Hence their appraisals are usually honest. From an interest inventory, a counselor gets a clearer idea of a student's occupational aspirations. He also may get valuable clues about a student's personality trends—for example, his desire for security rather than for adventure, for active rather than passive roles, for people rather than books.

The best-known interest inventories are vocational and were intended for adults. As a result, they are not very useful below the eighth grade. This is not a serious disadvantage, however, since the interests of elementary children are often uncrystallized and may be superficial, unreliable, and unrealistic. The moving pictures, TV, and romantic stories invest certain activities (that of the actor, the game hunter, space adventurer, and detective, to cite a few) with artificial glamor. Moreover, a pupil's information concerning many occupations—time required, aptitudes needed, financial returns to be expected—is often meager and distorted. Even in high school and college, when choice of vocation becomes crucial, information on many occupations is not available. A number of pamphlets describing the requirements for various occupations will be helpful to counselors and students (see page 272).

This section will describe three interest inventories, one suitable for pupils whose reading level is up to the sixth-grade standards, and two for high-school and college students and for adults.

> Occupational Interest Inventory
> Kuder Preference Record
> Strong Vocational Interest Blank

OCCUPATIONAL INTEREST INVENTORY[9]

**Description.** This inventory provides scores in three interest areas. First, there are scores in six basic fields of occupational interest: *personal-social* (personal contacts, service fields); *natural* (outdoor activities, farming); *mechanical* (machinery design, building, constructing things); *business* (activities of the business world, the "profit motive"); *arts* (music, literature, drama); *sciences* (chemistry, engineering, biology). Second, certain items are designated *verbal, manipulative,* or *computational,* and scores in these areas provide information about the direction of one's interests. Finally, an attempt is made to gauge the *level* of an examinee's interests—whether his interests identify him with simple routine aspects of a job or with the more expert performances and skills.

The six basic fields of occupational interest show considerable overlap, and their identity as strictly separate compartments of interest is doubtful. At the same time, the Occupational Inventory does give the counselor a better notion of the intensity and range of a person's dominant interests than could be obtained from casual conversation, and it furnishes many clues to type and level of commitment. Vocational or other advice based on interest scores should always be tentative, however, and subject to confirmation from other sources. The items of the Inventory are forced-choice in form. The Manual gives many suggestions about the ways in which results may be interpreted. A few samples from the intermediate form of the Inventory will show

[9] California Test Bureau, Monterey, California.

the kinds of question asked. The large letter before a question gives the interest *field*, the small letter the interest *level*, and the symbol the interest *type* (whether verbal, manipulative or computational).

*Part* I

Directions: Draw a circle around the letter of the activity you prefer. For example, if you prefer to drive an ice-cream truck and sell ice cream, draw a circle around A 1 as shown below:

(A 1) Drive an ice-cream truck and sell ice cream.
☐ F 1 Wrap articles in the shipping department of a store.
However, if you prefer the second activity, draw a circle around F 1. A second item, to be marked according to the same directions is

△ K 14 Conduct visitors through art galleries and museums
E 14 Help build automobiles, ships, or airplanes

*Part* II

Directions: Below you will find three activities under each number. You are to choose the one you prefer to do of the three in each group. Indicate your choice by marking the letter preceding the activity.

f 11 Design or construct stained glass, metal ornaments or plastic figures
b 11 Make pottery, statues or book ends
b 11 Carve wood or stone or make metal ornamental figures

**Scope.** The Intermediate Inventory begins with grade 7 but may be used with bright sixth graders. The Advanced Inventory is for grade 9 and for adults.

**Scoring.** Percentile ranks for the six basic interest fields may be read from the appropriate tables. Standard scores from converted raw scores also are provided. Part scores may be represented graphically by profiles for a clearer comparison of interest-strength. The working time for the test is thirty to forty minutes. Scoring is simple: the items designated by letters and symbols are counted.

## Kuder Preference Record[10]

**Description.** The Kuder Preference Record (Form B1) is a widely used vocational interest blank. There are three hundred and sixty items in all, arranged in groups of three. In each set of three, the examinee is asked to indicate which activity he would like *most* and which he would like *least*. Response is made by punching a small hole with a pin, and the answer is recorded on a specially prepared answer sheet placed under the test blank. The samples below (given as examples in the Record) are for illustration:

Directions: You will find a number of activities listed in groups of three on the following pages. Read over the three activities in each group. Decide which of the three activities you like *most*. Note the letter in front of it and punch a hole beneath the 1 beside this letter in the column at the right, using the pin with which you have been provided. Then decide which activity you like *least* and punch a hole beneath the 3 beside the corresponding letter in the column at the right.

Example #1

P.  Visit an art gallery

Q.  Browse in a library          ← least

R.  Visit a museum       most →

[10] Copyright 1942, G. Frederic Kuder. Reprinted by permission of Science Research Associates, Inc., Chicago, Illinois. (There are three forms: two vocational and one personal.)

(The punch in the hole beneath 1 beside R shows that the examinee would most like to visit a museum. The punch in the hole beneath 3 beside Q means that he would least like to browse in a library.)

Example #2

|   | | 1 | | 3 |   |
|---|---|---|---|---|---|
| S. Collect autographs | | ○ | S | ○ | |
| | | 1 | | 3 | |
| T. Collect coins | most → | ● | T | ○ | |
| | | 1 | | 3 | |
| U. Collect butterflies | | ○ | U | ● | ← least |

(The punch beneath 1 beside T means that the examinee would most like to collect coins. The punch beneath 3 beside U means that he would least like to collect butterflies.)

All items are of the forced-choice type in that the examinee has to make a selection among limited options, but the stipulation of two choices (most and least) allows some latitude. The test provides for ten interest-areas: *outdoor* (agriculture, nature), *mechanical, computational, scientific, persuasive, artistic, literary, musical, social service,* and *clerical.* The student or young adult may be asked to express interest preferences required in many vocations unfamiliar to him. In most cases, this is a help to the counselor, who can then describe these vocations to his client. The Manual provides valuable information about the interest patterns typical of persons successful in various lines of work. The purpose of the Kuder Record is to reveal interest trends over several broad areas rather than in fairly specific occupations. There are, for example, fifty-three occupations grouped under scientific interests. Items in the Record were first organized on a logical basis in the light of everyday experience and common sense. Later, items were analyzed statistically in order to isolate clusters of items highly correlated. These clusters were taken to reveal a core of interest.

The Kuder Record relies for its validity primarily on content analysis and logical relations. The number of choices offered and their nature sometimes confuse students; and the inability to find clear-cut preferences may lead to dissatisfaction with the forced-choice aspect of the test. Below the eighth grade the reading level of the Record is probably too high, and it should not be used. The fact that the scoring plan does not weight sharply strong versus weak interest has been another criticism of the test. At the same time, the Kuder Record is an excellent measure of the range of *expressed* interest and, as such, is valuable in educational and vocational guidance. It is often possible to point out to a student that he has expressed many interests not in line with his vocational goals. The median reliability coefficient for the nine interest-areas is .91.

STRONG VOCATIONAL INTEREST BLANK[11]

**Description.** This was the first vocational interest blank and is still the best-known. There are forms for men and women. The Blank has gone through several revisions and in its latest form comprises four hundred items grouped in eight categories. These are *occupations* (likes and dislikes), *school subjects, amusements, outdoor* and *indoor activities,* responses to *peculiarities of people,* choice of *activities, comparison of interests,* and evaluation of *personal abilities.* The examinee indicates his choices by circling or marking. Answers to the items are given numerical weights, obtained by comparing the replies of a defined occupational group (lawyers, for example) with the replies of people in general. In all, forty-five occupations or areas of interest are covered by the Blank.

**Scope.** For men and women.

**Scoring.** A person's score on a given scale (his interest in teaching, for example) is found by totaling the plus (+) and minus (−) credits obtained from the options he has marked.

[11] Stanford University Press, Stanford, California.

A separate key is used for each vocation. Thus an examinee's blank may be scored for the interests of an engineer, a physician, and a sales manager. Point scores are converted into standard scores to afford a direct comparison. A useful scale of letter grades is also available: A represents close identification of interests with the given vocation, B+, B, and B— somewhat lesser agreement, and C+ and C a very different interest pattern from that of the occupation under study. For example, a college student may have A and B scores in the interests of a minister and social worker, and C+ and C scores in the interests of a mathematician or physicist.

Somewhat less time-consuming and often more valuable than specific vocational scores are the scales for interest clusters. There are eleven of these clusters, for example, *personal-social* ("uplift," interest in social science, interest in becoming a teacher, preacher, or school superintendent), *mathematics-science* (chemist, engineer), and *business-commercial* (salesmen, various business interests, making money). The use of clusters or occupational families provides greater flexibility in the use of the Strong Blank.

The Vocational Blank is in reality a systematic interview. By its aid, the counselor becomes better acquainted with the strengths and directions of a student's interests. It may happen that a young man's interests differ sharply from the vocational plans which his parents have for him. The counselor must then point out discrepancies and try to resolve them to the satisfaction of all concerned.

## SUMMARY OF PERSONALITY INVENTORIES

**Validity.** Insofar as an inventory includes questions which experts agree are relevant to the area being tested, the questionnaire has content validity. The adjustment inventories (PD Sheets) are made up of items drawn from texts on abnormal psychology and cover conditions which have been found to be symptomatic of mental illness. The interest inventories have been validated experimentally against a number of criteria: expressed interest of successful professional and businessmen, successful completion of training courses, ratings for work success, staying in an occupation versus leaving it, and degree of job satisfaction. Correlational analysis has been used to locate clusters of items which embrace a common core of interest or a community of interest patterns. Followup studies of the Strong Vocational Interest Blank show that men tend to stay in occupations for which they expressed strong interests as students and to change occupations for which their expressed interests were weak.

In using interest inventories, several precautions should be taken. It is well to remember that interest and aptitude are not the same thing, and that many youngsters express interest in vocations for which they have little capacity. Again, the interests of young people—especially those below the age of twenty-five—often change markedly. Adolescents may express unrealistic interests which change drastically later. More than one determination of interests, therefore, should be made. Finally, it must be remembered that advice about occupational families is much safer than advice about specific jobs. Any inventory, personality or interest, should be supplemented by school and intelligence records and ratings for health, appearance, motivation, and socio-economic status.

**Reliability.** The reliability coefficients of most inventories is high—.80 or more. Since interests change over a period of time, reliability determinations can be relied on only for short periods.

**Scoring.** Inventories usually are scored by assigning weights to the various options presented. These points are converted into percentile norms, standard scores, and sometimes letter grades. Norms for the adjustment inventories are most often for students, less often for occupational groups. The interest inventories report norms for occupational families (Kuder) and for specific occupations (Strong). Test manuals provide many useful suggestions for the interpretation of the inventories.

## SUGGESTIONS FOR FURTHER READING

ANASTASI, A. *Psychological Testing.* 2nd ed.; New York: Macmillan, 1961.
FREEMAN, F. S. *Theory and Practice of Psychological Testing.* Rev. ed.; New York: Holt, 1955.
JORDAN, A. M. *Measurement in Education.* New York: McGraw-Hill, 1953.
TRAVERS, R. M. *Educational Measurement.* New York: Macmillan, 1955.

## SUGGESTIONS FOR LABORATORY WORK

1. One of the best ways to become acquainted with a personality inventory is to take it yourself. Members of the class should take as many of the questionnaires as are available, score them, and draw up profiles where called for.
2. Examine the Manual for the Kuder Preference Record (Vocational). What is said about validity, reliability, scaling techniques, and norms?
3. Study the Manual for the Allport A-S Reaction Study and/or the Manual for the Bernreuter Personality Inventory. How are these inventories constructed?

## QUESTIONS FOR DISCUSSION

1. In an adjustment inventory, the number of positive symptoms becomes the score. What is meant by saying that Stanley is on the median for a personal data sheet?
2. Which interest blank, the Kuder or the Strong, is more appropriate for high-school students?
3. How might an interest inventory be used in studying a child's personality trends?
4. How closely related are interests and aptitude? Does the relationship change with age?
5. Why are personal data blanks of little value when administered as "group tests"?
6. Under what circumstances do you think the interest inventory would be most helpful? At what age levels? Give reasons for your answers.
7. What factors limit the usefulness of paper-and-pencil adjustment inventories?

8. A high-school senior expresses a strong interest in engineering, but his interest inventory score does not confirm this interest. What would you as counselor suggest to him?

9. The Strong Vocational Interest Blank has a key for various specific occupational interests—dentist, banker, carpenter, for example. What difficulties do you see in such restricted interest patterns?

10. Why is a personal data sheet easier to fake than an interest blank, even when the items are not forced-choice?

11. Given as group tests, personality inventories are often misleading. Why is this?

12. What pattern of personality traits do you consider most useful for (a) a high-school teacher, (b) a laboratory assistant, (c) a supervisor?

13. Can strong interest in a vocation (for example, medicine) compensate for lack of aptitude?

Chapter 8

# OBJECTIVE-TEST ITEMS AND SHORT-ANSWER TECHNIQUES

There are at least two reasons for the teacher interested in guidance to be familiar with the main types of objective test items. In the first place, the most widely used standard group tests are made up of items of the objective sort. (See Chapters 4 and 5.) Hence, a knowledge of the strengths and weaknesses of objective questions will enable a teacher to make a more discriminating choice among several tests of intelligence, educational achievement, or aptitude proposed for use in a school. Second, a teacher-made test is greatly improved when the teacher knows the principles which govern the writing of objective-type items and the assembling of such items in an examination.

This chapter will describe some of the better-known—and

widely used—verbal objective-type items. These include the true-false, multiple-choice (best-answer), matching, completion, and short-answer essay questions. The advantages and disadvantages of each of these item types are listed and examples given to illustrate errors to be avoided in writing items of each type. Objective tests employ numbers, geometric forms, pictures, and diagrams, as well as words. (Figure 8–1 provides a number of illustrations.) Some of the varieties of nonverbal items frequently encountered in standardized tests fall under the following heads:

1. *Number Series Completion.*[1] The examinee is asked to complete a series of numbers—which are related in some way—by the addition of one or more appropriate numbers.
2. *Figure Completion.* The examinee must complete a figure by the addition of a line or other detail.
3. *Likenesses and Differences.* From a list of pictures showing objects or activities, the examinee is required to select several which belong together or to select an item which does not belong with the others.
4. *Picture Completion.* The examinee is to complete a picture from which one or more items have been omitted.
5. *Errors in a Drawing.* The examinee must locate and correct errors in a drawing.
6. *Arranging Pictures.* The examinee is to arrange a set of pictures in orderly fashion which tells a story.

## COMPARISON OF OBJECTIVE ITEMS AND ESSAY QUESTIONS

The traditional essay question often covers too much ground, and is open to large errors in scoring and interpretation. Consider the question "Discuss the causes of the War of 1812" as an example of a common form of essay question. Answers to this question will almost certainly include material that is true

---

[1] This test is also classified as verbal.

*Figure 8–1  Objective-Test Items*

*Directions:* The examiner reads several statements about each set of pictures. The student is told to put a + in the ( ) after the number if the statement is true, a O if it is false.

1. ( )1
2. ( )2
3. ( )3
4. ( )4
5. ( )5
6. ( )6
7. ( )7
8. ( )8
9. ( )9
10. ( )10
11. ( )11
12. ( )12
13. ( )13
14. ( )14

Example: The examiner reads, "Un cheval vient de s'abbattre sur la route." The student puts a + or O in the ( ) after the number of the statement.

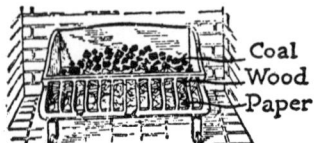

*Directions:* What chemical property determines which of the materials will be placed nearest the ash pit?

Coal
Wood
Paper

(1) heaviest residue   (4) kindling temperature
(2) reduction of coal  (5) paper
(3) ashes given off    (6) combustion

Answer ( ). Student puts in the number of the answer.

*Directions:* Each of the following incomplete statements or questions is followed by 5 possible answers. For each item, select the answer that best completes the question and write its number or letter on the line to the right.

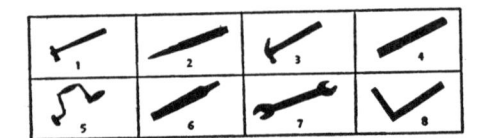

31. A claw hammer is shown in picture 1 3 6 7 8 _____
32. A chisel is shown in picture 2 4 5 6 7 _____
33. A ball peen hammer is shown in picture 1 3 5 6 8 _____
39. Tool #1 can be used to (a) file metal, (b) polish metal, (c) drill holes, (d) take dents out of metal, (e) caulk metal. _____
40. Tool #2 can be used to (a) mark metal, (b) file metal, (c) drive a screw, (d) fasten a bolt, (e) lock a bolt. _____

*Represented by Picture, Drawing, or Diagram*

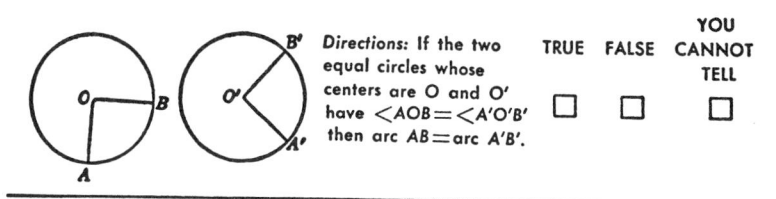

**Directions:** If the two equal circles whose centers are O and O' have $\angle AOB = \angle A'O'B'$ then arc $AB$ = arc $A'B'$.

TRUE ☐   FALSE ☐   YOU CANNOT TELL ☐

**Directions:** Mark two things good to eat.

**Directions:** Which of the five figures can be made from the pattern in Example X? More than one may be correct.

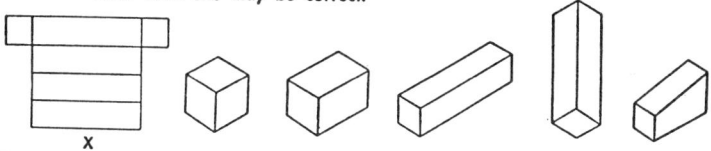

**Directions:** The first three pictures in each row are alike in some way. Decide how they are alike, and then find the *one* picture among the *four* to the right of the dotted line that is most like them and mark its number.

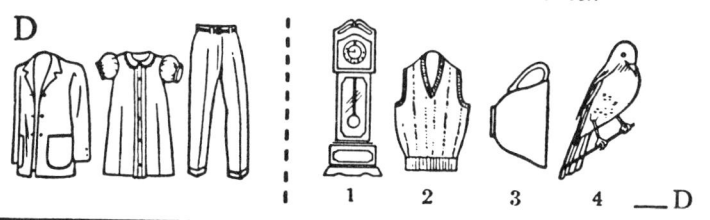

D

1   2   3   4   ___ D

**Directions:** Mark the one thing not like the others.

and relevant, material that is ambiguous, material that is clearly erroneous, and material that is mostly padding. It becomes almost impossible for two or more readers to evaluate the answers to such a question in the same way. However, when choices in objective test questions are recorded by checking one of several possible answers, circling a number, or underlining a word or phrase, the grade on the test will be the same whether the scoring is done by a clerk or by an expert. And the answer will be right or wrong.

Examinations composed of objective items possess several other advantages over questions of the essay type. The objective item not only eliminates unreliability due to personal opinion but it is more easily scored, is economical of time, and allows for a wider sampling of material. Furthermore, the objective test item forces the student to answer a question directly, gives him little opportunity to equivocate or dodge, and for that reason is a more dependable measure of what a student knows. On the negative side, the objective item may provide little opportunity for the examinee to display his understanding and organizing ability. When poorly made, the objective item may lay too much stress on rote memory and unrelated bits of information.

## TRUE-FALSE ITEMS

The true-false test presents a series of statements or questions each of which is to be marked "T" (true) or "F" (false). Instead of circling one of the letters "T" or "F," the examinee may be asked to circle "Yes" or "No," or to write + (plus) or − (minus), or in some other way to designate a positive or negative answer. One of the earliest objective forms, the T-F test is still widely used in group intelligence as well as in educational achievement and aptitude tests. It has been criticized as being a measure of rote memory, a test of detached and unrelated facts and as often being ambiguous and equivocal. Such strictures are justified when the test is poorly or carelessly made. There is a large element of guessing in T-F tests, too, and good items are not easy to construct, however simple the process may seem to be. But when well made, T-F items have valuable possibilities arising from their scope and flexibility. The chief advantages and disadvantages of the T-F item may be summarized as follows:

*Advantages:*

1. It may be used with a wide variety of materials.
2. It may be scored easily and objectively.
3. It is the easiest objective type to construct.
4. It makes possible an extensive sampling of material in a relatively short space.
5. It is a time-saver, thus allowing for frequent testing.
6. The directions are readily understood and followed.

*Disadvantages:*

1. It is often ambiguous and confusing.
2. It is open to guessing and to chance effects.
3. Much subject matter cannot be stated as unequivocally true or false.
4. It may become a test of detached and unrelated bits of information.
5. It may overstress rote memory at the expense of understanding.

Some of the rules useful in constructing teacher-made tests are given below. In judging the adequacy of printed T-F items, it will help to note whether these rules have been observed.

1. Putting the symbols "T" and "F" before each question is preferable to having the examinee write the letters at the end of a statement, thus scattering his answers over the page. Circling or marking saves time in scoring test papers and leads to fewer

errors, since the letters written by an examinee are not always legible. See examples.

<table>
<tr><td>On the test paper:</td><td>On the answer sheet:</td></tr>
<tr><td>Ⓣ F  1. ......</td><td>1. Ⓣ F</td></tr>
<tr><td>T Ⓕ  2. ......</td><td>2. T Ⓕ</td></tr>
</table>

2. Make the number of true statements equal to the number of false statements. The scoring formula for T-F items is

$$\text{Score} = \text{Right} - \text{Wrong}$$

or $\quad$ Score = Total $- 2 \times$ Wrong

Either of these formulas corrects for guessing, and both give the same result provided the pupil has tried *all* of the items. Suppose, for example, that there are sixty items in the test, and a pupil gets forty right and twenty wrong. Then his score is $40 - 20$ or 20, or $60 - 2 \times 20$ or 20. If the child does not try all of the items, the two versions of the formula will not give the same result and the first $(R - W)$ should be used.

If an examinee guesses at every item, he should have one-half of the items right and one-half wrong, and his score $(R - W)$ is properly zero. If an examinee attempts only thirty out of forty items in a given examination, his score may be corrected to a total of 40 by adding one-half of the untried items, that is, half of 10, to his number right. (Presumably he would get one-half of the untried items right by guessing.) It is not necessary to correct every paper to the number of items in the test. But test scores for a class are the more fairly compared when all are based upon the total number of items in the test.

The correlation between number right and $(R - W)$ is perfect when *all* of the items of the test have been tried. Hence, when a child's score has been corrected to the total, number right may be taken as the score instead of $(R - W)$. The question of whether to tell an examinee to guess has excited much controversy, partly because of the opprobrium attached to the term guessing as related to school examinations. A good general rule is to instruct the student to omit only those items which he is sure he doesn't know, to try an item even when not entirely certain of the answer, but never to guess wildly. Since the examinee has been exposed, at least, to the subject matter of the test, the chances are better than even that his answer will be based on some information, even if it is vague and uncertain. Hence, a T-F answer is more likely to be right than wrong.

3. Avoid opinionated and trivial (or trick) items.

*Examples:* T F Character is more important than intelligence.
T F The ABC Test of Mental Maturity contains 75 items arranged into 6 subtests.
T F William Collins Bryant is the author of *Thanatopsis*.
T F One-half of a perfect correlation is .50.

The first of these items calls for a value judgment, which may be true or false; the second and third ask for trivial information; and the fourth is a trick question which happens to be false.

4. Avoid ambiguous statements, those partly true and partly false, and those containing negatives, especially double negatives.

*Examples:* T F Socio-economic factors are often the cause of war.
T F William Jennings Bryan, the great Commoner, was twice elected president of the U.S.
T F Not every teacher is careful to avoid having a student dislike his subject.
T F Not all instincts are maladaptive.

The first item is ambiguous; the second is partly true and partly false; and the 3rd and 4th are confusing because of the negative form in which they are stated. Double negatives are especially hard to decipher.

5. Avoid textbook language and verbatim quotations. Such items encourage rote memory and are often ambiguous when taken out of context.

*Examples:* T F The role of the teacher is to help the pupil establish satisfying goals.

T F Heredity determines what a man can do, environment what he does do.

Textbook verbiage aids in making a correct guess.

6. Avoid specific determiners, such as *all, none, always, never, every.* Broad generalizations introduced by these words are usually false.

*Examples:* T F Feeblemindedness is always present in delinquency.
T F Corporal punishment is never justified.
T F All ministers lead lazy lives.

These items are all too general.

The T-F item is not so popular among teachers as it was formerly, and it is not found so often in standard tests. It is still ranked high, however, and is perhaps the quickest way of surveying a wide range of material. When supplemented by other test forms, T-F is a valuable objective item.

## MULTIPLE-CHOICE OR BEST-ANSWER ITEMS

The multiple-choice item consists of a statement, question, phrase, or word followed by several responses only one of which is correct. Multiple-choice is one of the most flexible of the objective-recognition-type forms. It is a favorite with teachers making their own examinations and is most widely employed in the standard printed forms. Multiple-choice items can be constructed to measure information, comprehension, understanding of principles, and ability to interpret data. The test form is applicable to most subjects and to most materials.

Some of the strengths and weaknesses of the multiple-choice item can be summarized as follows:

*Advantages:*

1. Answers are objective and are rapidly scored.
2. Items may be written to measure inference, discrimination, and judgment.

3. Guessing is minimized when four or five choices are allowed.
4. Items may be constructed to measure recall as well as recognition.

*Disadvantages:*

1. Items are often too factual, stressing memory unduly.
2. More than one response may be correct or very nearly correct.
3. It is difficult to exclude clues.
4. Distractors—that is, incorrect but plausible answers—are often hard to find.

Rules for constructing multiple-choice items for teacher-made tests and for judging the adequacy of such items in printed tests are as follows:

1. Vary the position of the correct response: put the right answer in the first, second, third, fourth positions equally often. A scoring formula for multiple-choice items is

$$\text{Score} = \text{Right} - \frac{(\text{Wrong})}{(n-1)}$$

in which $n =$ the number of choices, usually four or five. This formula is used to correct for guessing on the assumption that each response is equally likely. This conjecture is correct when the examinee has no idea of the right answer, but in educational achievement examinations as well as in other tests, it is a questionable hypothesis. Distractors differ greatly in plausibility and likelihood, and since the student presumably has some knowledge of the question, he is more likely to mark the right than the wrong answer. In most educational achievement tests, taking the number right as score saves time and is accurate enough for most purposes. It must be remembered that in a given test the number of options must be the *same* for each item if the above correction formula is to be used.

2. Do not include responses which are so unlikely or im-

plausible or so unrelated to the question that they give the answer away. Distracting responses should distract, not confuse.

*Examples:* The function of a flower is to
    _____give pleasure to mankind
    _____attract insects
    _____illustrate the modification of leaves
    _____produce seed

The capital of the United States is
    _____Washington
    _____Rome
    _____Tokyo
    _____London
    _____Honolulu

The principal crop of Iowa is
    _____pineapples
    _____corn
    _____oranges
    _____bananas

In the first example, assuming the fourth choice to be the correct one, the distractors are all rather silly. In examples two and three, an examinee would have to be almost totally ignorant of geography to be taken in by the distractors.

3. Do not provide wrong answers which are plausible enough to mislead the good student because they are close to the right answer. The good student is often led astray by knowing a good deal—but not quite enough—about a question, whereas the poor student does not know enough to be misled by a plausible but wrong answer.

*Example:* What was one of the important immediate results of the War of 1812?
    _____the introduction of a period of intense sectionalism
    _____destruction of the U.S. bank

_____defeat of the Jeffersonian party
_____final collapse of the Federalist party

The fourth response is keyed as the correct one. But 39 percent of eight hundred high-school pupils, all of them superior students, checked the first option as correct. Apparently the first answer is plausible to students who know a good deal about the War of 1812.

4. Do not give away the correct answer by providing clues such as (a) familiar textbook phrases, (b) having the right option consistently longer or shorter than the wrong options, (c) repeating the words of the question, (d) asking questions to which the answer must be singular or plural, with only the correct response being in the right number.

*Examples:* In what major labor group have unions been organized on an industrial basis? (Circle one letter.)
  A. Congress of Industrial Organizations
  B. Railway Brotherhoods
  C. American Federation of Labor
  D. Knights of Labor
  E. Workers of the World

The meaning of the German word *Gestalten* is (Check one)
_____a response
_____a just-noticeable-difference
_____a stimulus
_____configurations
_____a perception

A man hears a loud noise and runs to the window. This is an example of
_____motivation
_____memory image
_____stimulus-response
_____posthypnotic suggestion
_____purposive behavior

In the first of these examples, the adjective "industrial" in the question gives the answer away. In the second, if the student knows that *Gestalten* is the plural of the German word *Gestalt*, he has the answer as "configurations." In the third, the textbook phrase "stimulus-response" is a clear clue.

5. In a multiple-choice vocabulary test, none of the response choices should be as difficult as the test word. The difficulty of response words can be determined from their frequency in Thorndike's *Teachers' Word Book*. Response words should be of the same part of speech as the test word, and only one should be correct.

*Good example:* An irksome task is (a) pleasant, (b) engrossing, (c) instructive, (d) wearisome
*Poor example:* Do not despise him means do not (a) hate, (b) malign, (c) deprecate, (d) dessicate him

In the second example, some of the response words are more difficult than the test word. This is not true of the first example.

6. Direct questions or statements followed by a series of options are usually clearer than questions in which the answers are imbedded in the statement. In the latter form, the examinee must read through the statement for each option.

*Good example:* A 10-year-old receives a percentile rank of 40 on a test of arithmetic. This means that
_____he is above the mean of 10-year-olds on the test.
_____he exceeds 60 percent of 10-year-olds.
_____40 percent of 10-year-olds did worse than he.
_____61 percent of 10-year-olds exceeded his score.
*Poor example:* Percentile rank shows the percent (a) at or above, (b) above, (c) at, (d) below, (e) at or below the given score.

The second example is more difficult to decipher than the first.

A test made up of multiple-choice items takes more time to construct than a test of T-F items. Furthermore, good multiple-choice items are harder to prepare than T-F items, since it is often difficult to find acceptable distractors. The advantage of the T-F item is largely offset, however, by the fact that multiple-choice items are more searching and demand a more organized knowledge of the subject-matter. Multiple choice is regarded by most test experts as the best of the short-answer forms.

## MULTIPLE-RESPONSE ITEMS

The multiple-response item is a variation of the multiple-choice type of question. Essentially it presents a statement or topic followed by a number of possible answers, several of which may be checked as correct. The multiple-response examination tests several aspects of a subject, and is useful in obtaining information from tables and charts. This examination form is often called a *check list*. The advantages and disadvantages, as well as rules for construction given above for multiple-choice, apply to multiple-response items as well.

Two examples follow:

*Example:* Under each of the following psychological doctrines, viewpoints, or systems, indicate by a cross (x) those implications or consequences which are characteristic of that doctrine.
1. English Associationism
   _____a persisting self
   _____summation and integration of mental states
   _____universal categories of reason
   _____mental faculties
   _____persisting motor-response systems
2. Purposive Psychology (McDougall)
   _____imageless thought
   _____introspection as the primary method
   _____S-R units

_____motivation in terms of instincts
_____doctrine of the unconscious
_____conative tendencies

Each of these items can be described by more than one choice.

## MATCHING ITEMS

In a matching test, one list of words, names, phrases, formulas, or statements is matched against another list. The test may consist of (a) a list of names in one column to be matched against a list of achievements in a second column; (b) a list of terms to be matched against a list of definitions; (c) labels to be matched against charts and diagrams; (d) authors to be matched against books, dates, or events.

The matching item possesses the advantages of interest and variety as well as ease of scoring. It is, furthermore, somewhat easier to construct than the multiple-choice item. Matching has been frequently used to test the relationship between dates, events, and various facts. On the negative side, the matching item often measures recognition memory rather than understanding, and is especially open to clues. Nor do matching items ordinarily test ability to organize facts or to apply principles.

Rules for making up matching test items may be set down as follows:

1. Do not include too many items in the lists: ten or twelve is the maximum, five or seven often enough. When lists are long, examinees must spend too much time hunting through them. Have the number of items in the column from which selections are to be made larger than the number in the list to be matched. This lessens the chances that an examinee will match an item correctly by a process of elimination.

*Example:* The following statements are representative of different schools of psychology. In the blank spaces before the statements, write the number of the psychologist for whom the statement is typical.

## MATCHING ITEMS

(1) Adler
(2) Angell
(3) Calkins
(4) Freud
(5) Jung
(6) Koehler
(7) McDougall
(8) James Mill
(9) Pavlov
(10) Titchener
(11) Watson
(12) Woodworth

_____Sensory processes have the attribute of clearness, just as they have quality and intensity.

_____There is evidence for the existence of three types of native and unlearned emotional reactions—fear, rage, and love.

_____The inadequacy, the relative futility, of all attempts to ignore the purposive, the goal-seeking nature of behavior renders behaviorism untenable.

_____Any mechanism, except perhaps some of the most rudimentary that give the simple reflexes, once it is aroused, is capable of furnishing its own drive and also lending drive to other connecting mechanisms.

_____The will-to-power is the great motive in mental conflict.

_____The superego represents the repressions of instinct and dominates the ego.

_____Mind is primarily engaged in mediating between environment and the needs of the organism.

_____Sensations are one of the primary states of consciousness; ideas are the other.

2. Select materials from one subject-field only, so that a given item in column 1 has several plausible matches in column 2. Explain clearly the basis of the matching.

*Example:* In column 1 are words which illustrate a number of parts of speech; in column 2 is a list of various parts of speech. Determine what part of speech a word is and then identify it by putting its number before the proper item in column 2. For example, "boy" is a noun, and if "boy" were numbered 5, a 5 would be placed before the word "noun" in column 2. Arrange the choices in alphabetical order.

(1) and   _____adjective
(2) cat   _____adverb
(3) rapidly  _____noun
(4) jump   _____preposition
(5) from   _____verb
(6) rich
(7) either

*Example:* Match the items in column 1 with the appropriate items in column 2.

A. Harvey   _____contagious disease
B. stomach   _____digests food
C. poison    _____discovered circulation of the blood
D. Galen
E. lungs    _____early Greek physician
F. heart    _____supplies oxygen to the blood
G. measles

The first example is quite easy, and it should enable a teacher to spot grammatical confusions. All of the material is from the field of grammar. The second item is poor owing to heterogeneity in the list of choices (names and body organs).

3. Arrange names in alphabetical order and dates and numbers in sequence in order to save the examinee's time.

*Example:* Select the inventor from the first list and put his number opposite his invention in the second list.

(1) Colt    _____Atlantic cable
(2) Edison  _____cotton gin
(3) Field   _____electric starter
(4) Franklin  _____sewing machine

(5) Howe     _____steam engine
(6) Kettering   _____wireless telegraphy
(7) Marconi
(8) Watt
(9) Whitney

4. Avoid clues, for instance, one singular item in both lists, and others plural; or one item in the list of a different part of speech from the others. Watch for irrelevant (but revealing) associations, such as nationality, which give away the matching —for example, if the examinee knows that a certain discovery was made by a Frenchman, he will look for a French name.

A matching item question is compact and usually interesting to students. It enables a teacher to cover a wide territory in fairly short time. Matching is well suited to rapid surveys of specific aspects of a field when persons, events, or definitions are wanted, or when these constitute necessary knowledge for further work in the subject.

## COMPLETION ITEMS

In this test form, sentences are presented from which certain words or phrases have been omitted. Instructions are to fill in the blanks to complete the meaning. Completion requires recall primarily, but it also demands thought and the ability to perceive overall relationships. Little opportunity for guessing is afforded. The chief disadvantage of this test form lies in the scoring, which is not entirely objective and is often time-consuming, and in the fact that too many blanks confuse the examinee and make a puzzle out of the test. Completion has been a favorite of teachers in their own examination-making, though it is not so widely used today as multiple-choice and T-F items.

Rules for writing completion items and errors to be avoided in such items are:

1. Do not copy sentences and paragraphs directly from the textbook, since this puts too much emphasis on rote memory and

parrot-like learning. Rephrase the language of the text, if that is used.

*Example:* Human behavior, more than that of any other animal, is a product of ............

*Example:* Much learning is by trial and ............
The first is a poor item. It is out of the textbook and will be known by those who recall the textbook language. The second is also a poor item—the pat expression "trial-and-error" gives it away.

2. Too many blanks make it impossible for the examinee to get the meaning, especially if the sentence is short.

*Example:* Civilized man ........; uncivilized man ........
This item actually appeared on a printed test. It is impossible to complete it, or else it can be completed in a wide variety of ways, most of which are not indicative of much knowledge.

3. Scoring is more objective if words rather than phrases are deleted. Blank out key words—those which carry the meaning of the sentence or paragraph—not unnecessary elements or the articles *a, an, the.*

*Examples:* Democracy is that form of ................ in which all of the ................ exercise the ............ power through ............ elected by ................
Democracy is that .................... of government in which .................... of the people .................... governing power, ............ representatives elected ............ themselves.

The first form of the item is the better, since the blanks contain key words. The second version deletes connecting words which do not carry the meaning of the sentence.

*Example:* ................ established the first laboratory for the ................ study of psychology in ........................

This is a satisfactory item, if we want to know who established the first laboratory in experimental psychology and when it was founded.

4. Make the blanks long enough to permit legible answers. Have all blanks of standard length to avoid clues about the length of the completing word.

5. When there are several correct answers, provide for these in a scoring key. Alternate answers may be weighted for goodness of completion, but a simple right or wrong scoring is adequate in most cases. A good plan is to allow one point for each correct answer, none for an incorrect one.

6. Guard against clues by taking care that completions do not depend on (a) grammatical form, (b) pat or textbook expressions.

*Examples:* Johnny wears his space suit, even when he ........ to bed.

A much discussed question is the relative importance of heredity and .....................

In the first item, the first singular verb is a clue to the number of the second verb. The second item tests rote memory, and the "pat" expression "heredity and environment" gives it away.

## THE ESSAY QUESTION

The essay question has been a standby of teachers over the years. It is widely used in the "literary" subjects, such as history and English, and in the natural and social sciences as well. The purpose of the essay question is to elicit understanding, organization, and interpretation, rather than to test for detached tidbits of knowledge. The form of the essay question is important. Questions beginning with "who," "what," "when," and "where" are usually to be avoided when they simply ask for a name (for example, Napoleon), a date (1492), an event (Battle of Hastings), or a location (New York City). But such questions are valuable when the information asked for is relevant to the solution of a problem, the making of an inference, or the interpretation of some event. Questions beginning with "why," "how," "with what consequences," or "with what significance" are to be preferred to simple fact questions. Questions beginning with such words as "discuss," "evaluate," "outline," and "explain" invite—and usually get—a mass of details, some not relevant. Such questions are useful, of course, when we wish to know how well an advanced student can select, reject, and organize. But they are hard to score and are virtually useless in a broad survey or for the diagnosis of specific blindspots.

### Restricting the Essay Question

The essay question becomes objective when cast into short-answer form and restricted in coverage. Two methods of controlling the essay question and rendering it more specific may be mentioned.

**Recall Questions.** Recall items are essay questions reduced to the simplest terms. Usually a question is followed by a blank space varying in length. Answers are restricted to short paragraphs, the account of some event, an algebraic equation and its application, and the like. Recall items resemble the completion type, but they provide for fairly free answers and are less restricted.

*Examples:* (1) Define an invertebrate ....................
........................................
        (2) Name three scientists who contributed (a) to atomic theory, and (b) list the major contribution of each.
           (a) 1 .......... 2 .......... 3 ..........
           (b) 1 .......... 2 .......... 3 ..........

(3) List three conditions which must hold true if an intelligence test is to yield a constant IQ.
1. ...................................
2. ...................................
3. ...................................

The first item calls for a one-line answer. Items (2) and (3) ask for specific but basic knowledge. Compare (3) with the essay question, "Discuss the construction of the Stanford-Binet."

**Problem Situations.** A problem is stated, and two, three, or four specific questions are asked, each focused on some important aspect of the situation.

*Example:* A skillful teacher has been characterized as one who
  (a) maintains a permissive atmosphere.
  (b) avoids negative discipline.
  (c) conforms to the wishes of parents.
  (d) does not use repetitive drill.
Write *one* paragraph defending or attacking each of these propositions—that is, four paragraphs in all.

*Example:* A recurring problem in child development is that of maturation. Cite the evidence bearing on the problem from the following points of view:
  (a) neurological
  (b) co-twin control
  (c) parallel groups

## Scoring the Essay Question Objectively

Perhaps the major weakness of the essay examination lies in the unreliability of its scoring. Scoring can be made more objective by the use of the following techniques:
1. When essay examinations are marked anonymously, there is usually better agreement between different scorers.

2. Options should not be permitted, so that all students take the same examination and are graded on the same material.

3. There is less opportunity for preferences, attitudes, and biases to appear when all papers are read for one question at a time rather than each paper straight through. Obviously, comparisons can be sharper with this method.

4. Before reading a question, the teacher can list the basic facts which the question is intended to bring out. Points may then be assigned to these aspects of the answer. For example, if the question deals with a chemical process, the answer list may include (a) the necessary equations of the process, (b) the chemical elements needed, (c) a diagram of the apparatus, and (d) any by-products of the chemical reaction. If the question deals with English literature, the answer may include (a) the author's chief contribution, (b) the cultural setting of the time, (c) the influence of the author's work. A check list of key points, with credits assigned to each, is a useful technique. Thus, from one to three points may be assigned to each part-answer.

5. If the teacher marks the papers for spelling, writing quality, and grammatical expression, as well as for content and organization, credits should be allotted to these aspects of the answer.

The essay question is a valuable examination form when held to one or more defined themes, so that it is scorable. Many teachers are so impressed by the general use of objective-type items in the standard tests that they are inclined to drop the essay entirely. This is a mistake. Many courses, especially advanced courses, in literature and in science employ objective-test items as a first approach to an examination of the subject. But the essay question is the best (perhaps the only) way in which a teacher can determine whether a student can organize his knowledge and arrange his arguments in logical fashion. Short-answer forms should be regarded not as substitutes for the essay, but rather as supplements to it.

## SUGGESTIONS FOR FURTHER READING

GERBERICH, J. R. *Specimen Objective Test Items: A Guide to Achievement Test Construction.* New York: Longmans, Green, 1956.

REMMERS, H. H., RYDEN, E. R., MORGAN, C. L. *Introduction to Educational Psychology.* New York: Harper, 1954.

ROSS, C. C. and STANLEY, J. C. *Measurement in Today's Schools.* New York: Prentice-Hall, 1954.

TRAVERS, R. M. *How To Make Achievement Tests.* New York: Odyssey, 1950.

WOOD, DOROTHY ADKINS. *Test Construction.* Columbus, Ohio: Merrill, 1960.

WRIGHTSTONE, J. W., JUSTMAN, J., ROBBINS, I. *Evaluation in Modern Education.* New York: American Book, 1956.

*Note:* Most textbooks on educational psychology and in measurement and evaluation contain chapters dealing with objective items.

## QUESTIONS FOR DISCUSSION

1. Write five true-false items in some subject field familiar to you.
2. Rewrite the five items in number 1 in multiple-choice form.
3. Construct five matching items in which great scientists, poets, and authors are matched against outstanding contributions to science or literature.
4. If possible, put the items in number 3 in completion form.
5. Rewrite the following essay questions to make them more objective in answering and in scoring.
    a. Discuss some of the proposals for aiding the gifted child. (Hint: break down into specific proposals, such as special classes, accelerated promotions, extra assignments, and the like.)
    b. Evaluate three of the modern learning theories. (Hint: This topic may be subdivided under descriptive labels—behaviorism, for example—or under names of well-known theorists.)
    c. Discuss the causes of the industrial revolution.
6. Point out any construction errors in the following items:
    a. The Frenchman who developed the first successful intelligence test was (1) Kuhlmann (2) Terman (3) Binet (4) Wundt
    b. An efficient man is one who is (1) strong (2) handsome (3) angry (4) pusillanimous (5) capable
    c. T F Edgar Anderson Poe wrote the poem "The Raven."

d. T F  Lack of emphasis on the three R's is not a serious defect in modern educational practice.
e. T F  Strict application of the Golden Rule will make for better living.
f. T F  The median of a distribution of scores is the midpoint, which is influenced markedly by very high or very low scores.
g. The technical name for nearsightedness is ................................
h. Nothing ...................... the classroom teacher so .................. as .....................
i. Overlearning is ................. as ................... a ................. to an arbitrarily ................. criterion of .................
j. The best way to spend one's leisure time is to (1) read good books, (2) look at TV, (3) dig in the garden, (4) play solitaire, (5) relax in an easy chair.
k. The expansion of the binomial $(a + b)^2$ is .................
    1. off
l. I borrowed a book  2. off of my roommate   (Answer) ......
    3. from
m. We get the most calories per pound from
    (1) candy            (4) potatoes
    (2) carbohydrates    (5) proteins
    (3) vitamins
n. When there is a fire drill, the teacher must make sure that her ..................... observe ...................... ................... and ....................
o. T F  The work of Freud has done much to demonstrate that associative connections once formed are never lost, even though under conditions of everyday life they cannot usually be recalled.

## Chapter 9

# CONSTRUCTING THE OBJECTIVE TEST

The classroom teacher needs to know how objective mental tests are constructed for much the same reason that he needs to know what constitutes a good test item (page 224). Standardized tests are now employed routinely in many schools. Teachers who give and score these tests will be better able to interpret results and to appraise what an author says about his test when they understand how the test items are selected and organized. Even more important, perhaps, the teacher who knows a few essential procedures will be able to improve greatly the quality of the day-to-day tests which he makes for his own use.

The construction of a comprehensive battery of educational achievement tests is not a task appropriate for most teachers or for most schools. Standardized printed tests in wide use today are made by testing bureaus. These agencies have a staff of experts in item writing and construction techniques, technically trained assistants, and access to large and representative samples and to laboratory and scoring equipment. The classroom teacher can hardly hope to match this, and fortunately he need not since his test-making is properly on a much more modest scale.

This chapter will outline the basic techniques in test construction. These methods apply to tests designed to measure intelligence, educational achievement, or aptitude.

## PLANNING THE TEACHER-MADE TEST

### WRITING SPECIFICATIONS FOR THE TEST

Before he constructs an examination, the teacher must decide what he wants his test to do. This means that he must lay down *specifications* for the test (page 236). Usually a teacher wants to test his pupils' knowledge of the fundamentals of the subject and also to discover how well they can use this knowledge in solving problems. These requirements may be made less general. Ordinarily, a teacher wants to measure knowledge and understanding in a specific course in which one or more textbooks are used. The examination should not be thought of simply as a means of evaluating pupils for a final grade, for passing or failing them on the term's work. When tests are relatively short and are given fairly often, they are essentially teaching devices. The pupil checks on his own knowledge, and the teacher discovers how much his students know and what topics need further attention.

The importance of definite specifications may be illustrated in several subject areas. In a test of American history, for example, the following topics might be listed as categories under which test items can be placed:

1. Historical facts, events, names, dates
2. Knowledge of geographical areas, maps, locations where events occurred

3. Chronological periods, how related
4. Causal relationships, reasons for trends or movements
5. Social, political, and economic factors in important events

The number of items under any given heading will depend, of course, on the purpose of the examination and the judgment of the teacher.

In a course in biology, one might ask questions covering technical vocabulary, concepts and principles, information regarding structures and activities (foodgetting, reproduction, and so on), broader relations and classifications—for example, the place of the animal in the evolutionary process—problems of adjustment, development, experimental data.

In algebra or geometry, a teacher wants to know how well a student knows the new terms, understands the propositions in the text, and knows the fundamental formulas. Furthermore, he wants to know how well the student can solve problems making use of the knowledge he has gained in the course.

Three standard educational achievement tests in different subject fields may be cited as illustrations of what objectives the authors of these tests had in mind and how they went about accomplishing them.

## COLUMBIA RESEARCH BUREAU SPANISH TEST[1]

This test is designed for high schools and colleges. Part I calls for basic knowledge of the language; Parts II and III require understanding of language structure and application of rules of grammar. In more detail, Part I is a vocabulary test of one hundred words in multiple-choice form. The student is instructed to mark that one of four or five English words which best defines the given Spanish word. Part II is a language comprehension test. There are seventy-five sentences in Spanish arranged in order of difficulty; each is to be read and marked "True" or "False." Part III is concerned with grammar and syntax. This

[1] Harcourt, Brace & World, Inc., New York, New York.

test consists of one hundred English sentences, each followed by an incomplete translation in Spanish, which the examinee is told to complete.

### California Arithmetic Test (Upper Primary, Grades 3 and 4)[2]

This test is part of a comprehensive educational achievement battery, but it may be given as a separate examination. Its objective is to test skill in fundamental operations, to identify consistent errors, and to test the ability to apply what is known to the solution of problems. The eight subtests cover the four fundamental processes (addition, subtraction, multiplication, and division), facility and skill in following directions involving numbers, and simple "mental arithmetic" problems.

### The Nelson-Denny Reading Test[3]

The authors state the objectives of this test as follows: "to predict success in college, to enable a sectioning of college and high-school classes on the basis of reading skills, to aid in the diagnosis of scholastic difficulties." The examination consists of two parts, a test of vocabulary and a test of the ability to read and understand fairly difficult prose. There are one hundred words in the vocabulary test, each word followed by five choices, one of which is to be marked as correct. The paragraph-reading test is made up of nine selections of approximately two hundred words each. Four questions are asked on each paragraph. There are five optional answers for each question, one of which is to be selected by the examinee. It seems clear that the test measures basic knowledge of language as well as the ability to use this knowledge intelligently.

### Deciding on the Type of Objective-Test Item

The teacher must first decide what type of objective-test item is suitable for his test. True-False and multiple-choice are favor-

---

[2] California Test Bureau, Monterey, California.
[3] Houghton Mifflin Company, Boston, Massachusetts.

ites for measuring basic knowledge, and multiple-choice, matching, completion, and essay-recall are all used to assess understanding, interpretation, and application. It is probably least confusing for younger pupils if a subtest or section contains only items of one type and does not switch from one kind to another. The number of items in a test will vary with the academic level of the class and with the time available. How long to make a test can be determined only by a tryout. It is often wise to begin with True-False items; these are easy to make and pupils answer them quickly. In a test of thirty items, for example, the first twenty might be True-False and the remainder multiple-choice or short essay. The first items cover the factual material, the second set (multiple-choice), the "thought questions" or problems. All of the questions proposed for inclusion in the tryout test should be read by other teachers of the subject and criticized for form and content. Items judged to be inappropriate, ambiguous, or too narrow in scope should be revised or discarded. The items which survive this preliminary inspection should still number considerably more than the number planned for the final test. An excess of items is necessary, since some items will always have to be discarded as a result of the item-analysis which follows the tryout.

#### Objectives for Factual and for Thought Questions

The teacher should always select items with certain objectives in mind. He cannot, it is true, always be sure exactly what a given item is measuring, but he can sharpen his aim by knowing what he wants to accomplish. In general, items should
1. Elicit information (sometimes fairly specific) which reveals knowledge of a process, principle, situation, or movement. Multiple-choice and often T-F items will do this.
2. Require the examinee to demonstrate ability to use technical terms and concepts. Again, T-F and multiple-choice are useful.

3. Give the examinee a chance to demonstrate ability to apply a principle, draw a conclusion, arrive at a generalization. Here the essay—either recall or recognition—will serve. Short paragraphs answering fairly specific questions are also valuable.

Not every item, of course, can be fitted neatly into one of these categories. Some items (many we hope) will cut across several. Nevertheless, each item should be written to achieve a definite purpose, to call out some important bit of knowledge, to show understanding or application.

Rules for constructing T-F items, and the advantages and disadvantages of this item form have been given on pages 202–206. In addition to these rules, various common clues must be avoided. Items beginning with *all, none, every,* or containing the words *always* or *never* generally are false (page 206); items containing the words *should, some, usually* are nearly always true (page 206). Long statements are generally true because of the qualifications (page 205). The number of true statements should equal the number of false because this keeps the guessing factor constant and prevents the examinee from detecting answer trends.

For thought questions, multiple-choice, matching, and short essay are preferred. These test forms are described with their respective advantages and disadvantages on pages 206–220. There should be at least four–five alternate answers for each multiple-choice item. The value of a good multiple-choice item lies in the list of distractors—which must distract but not confuse. When alternate answers are too similar or too dissimilar to the right answer they are equally ineffective. Consider the following item:

_____Direct evidence of evolutionary change in the life of the past is offered by
    1. domestication    4. the fossil record
    2. experimental breeding    5. natural selection
    3. isolation

If "bones of prehistoric animals" is substituted for (5) it will be confused with (4); if "modern civilization" is substituted for (2) or (1) it is obviously too irrelevant to be a good distractor.

When multiple-choice questions require much reading, the young pupil is confused before he reaches the alternate answers. If a knowledge of words is wanted, the item may be short. For example,

> The word that means the same as "disappeared" is
> 1. narrowed 4. vanished
> 2. lengthened 5. changed
> 3. decreased

If we want to test reasoning or ability to reach a logical conclusion, the item must be longer. For example,

> _____In a certain area in a large metropolitan city the delinquency rate has remained high for forty years, although during this time Irish, German, Italian, and Negro peoples have succeeded each other in the area. This probably means that
> 1. The tendencies toward delinquency have not changed in forty years.
> 2. For this area, the accepted definitions of delinquency have not changed in forty years.
> 3. During these forty years this area has continued to be a transition area of the city.
> 4. Each delinquent, as he grows up, has many associates to whom he teaches delinquent habits.

Only a few items as long as this can be included in a test, even for older students, because they require a long reading time.

## Arranging Items in Order of Difficulty

For the first experimental tryout of a test, the items must be arranged in order of difficulty from easy to hard. For the preliminary administration of the test, the difficulty of each item as judged by several teachers is sufficient. As tentatively drawn up, the test is administered to a sample of pupils like those for whom the final test is intended, for example, fifth graders or high-school sophomores. When several teachers cooperate and thus increase the size of the experimental group, the final test will be a better examination than if it is administered only to a single small class. It is advisable to get as much information as possible on each item. Hence, those children who take the try-out examination should be urged to attempt every item, even when they are uncertain of the answer. The time allowance for the experimental tryout should be generous, so that every pupil will have time to try every item. This requirement may make it necessary to have a second testing period.

If items are written on separate cards they can be easily shifted around to fit the required order.

### PREPARING DIRECTIONS FOR THE TEST

Directions to the examinees are always important and this is especially true when the children are young or are inexperienced in taking objective tests. If more than one objective form is used, directions should come at the beginning of each part. For a T-F test, for example, the following directions may be read silently by the pupils while the teacher reads them aloud:

*Directions:* These questions are either *true* or *false.* Read each one carefully. If you think it is *true,* circle the letter T in front of the question; if you think it is *false,* circle the F in front of the question.

The following is optional: If you are not sure, make an intelligent guess. You are more likely to be right than wrong. Try every question.

Some teachers prefer to omit the directions about "guessing trys" when the test is for young children and put it in for older pupils. Sample items, written on the board or printed on a test sheet, may be solved by the teacher for the benefit of the whole class. This procedure often prevents disturbing questions once the examination is under way.

For correcting test papers, a scoring stencil is useful for T-F items (page 204), or a test blank may be marked correctly by the scorer and laid alongside the pupil's test sheet. The use of separate scoring sheets makes it unnecessary to duplicate the test blanks over and over should the test be used again. (For correction for guessing see pages 204-205.)

SETTING THE TIME LIMIT

The length of the time interval set for the test when it is in final form will depend on the time available for testing—most often one period of about fifty minutes. Time allowances must always take into consideration the age of the pupils, type of item (amount of computation or reading needed in answering it), whether the test is primarily for survey purposes or for diagnosis, and whether speed and/or power are deemed important. In examinations which are strictly power tests, the time limits should be long enough for all but the very slowest examinee to finish. Sometimes, of course, an examination has to be cut in length in order to have it fit into the available time.

## ITEM ANALYSIS

The two characteristics of an item which we can discover from our experimental tryout are its difficulty and its validity, or discriminative power. These two determinants of an item's value are computed from the same tabulation of the test data. Computation of the difficulty and validity of an item is called item analysis.

DIFFICULTY AND VALIDITY IN ITEM ANALYSIS

The difficulty of an item depends on how many of the examinees in the tryout group answer it correctly. An item answered correctly by 90 percent of the group is obviously easier than one answered correctly by 50 percent or by 10 percent. (The last is a difficult item.) Very difficult and very easy items are ordinarily less useful than items of intermediate difficulty (page 233). The validity or discriminative power of an item depends on how well it distinguishes between the brightest and dullest pupils in the group. If all of the members of the experimental group answer an item correctly—or if none does—the item has no validity, since it does not separate the good from the poor members of the class.

### BISERIAL $r$ IN ITEM VALIDITY[4]

The authors of most standard mental tests have used the biserial $r$ method (or some approximation) in determining the validity of the items in their tests. By means of biserial $r$, we can compute the correlation between success and failure on a *single item* and size of total score on the test, or with some other measure of performance taken as a criterion. The size of the correlation between item and test score shows how well the item is working together with other items, as a member of a team. Items unrelated to total score are discarded.

Steps in the determination of item validity by use of biserial $r$ are:

1. Arrange the test papers in order for total score from highest to lowest.

2. Count off the highest and lowest 27 percent of the papers —if not exactly, as nearly so as possible.[5] If there are one hundred twenty children in the "standardizing group," for example, put thirty-two in the top and thirty-two in the bottom groups.

---

[4] For the computation of biserial $r$, see references at the end of Chapter 2.

[5] There are good reasons for choosing 27 percent. When the distribution of ability is normal, the sharpest discrimination between extreme groups is obtained when item analysis is based on the highest and lowest 27 percent in each case. When larger percents are in the high and low groups, the reliability of the determination is higher, but the difference between the two groups decreases. On the other hand, when percents in the high and low groups are smaller, reliability falls off but the difference between the two groups increases.

3. Count off the number in the high group and the number in the low group who pass each item, and express these figures as percentages. Suppose, for example, that item 18 is passed by 60 percent of the high group and by 30 percent of the low group. From tables prepared for the purpose,[6] we read that the biserial correlation between this item and the whole test is .31. For an item passed by 24 percent of the high group and by only 3 percent of the low group, the biserial $r$ is .44. In general, any item with a biserial $r$ of .20 or more can be taken to be valid if the test is fairly long. In a short test, items of higher validity are needed. Both hard items and easy items are valid (that is, have discriminative power) if they separate the high and low groups. An item passed by 15 percent of the high group and only 1 percent of the low group (a very hard item), for example, has a biserial $r$ of .47, while an item passed by 92 percent of the high group and 65 percent of the low group (an easy item) has a biserial $r$ of .39. Both are good items, though they differ greatly in difficulty.

4. Determine the difficulty of each item by averaging the percentages that pass it in the high and low groups. An item passed by 60 percent of the high group and by 30 percent of the low group, for example, has a difficulty index of .45—that is, $\left(\frac{.60 + .30}{2}\right)$ and an item passed by 15 percent of the high and 1 percent of the low groups has a difficulty index of .08. This summary method of obtaining difficulties of items is not as accurate as the practice of using the whole group, but it saves time and is precise enough for most tests.

5. It can be shown mathematically that items with difficulty indices of .50 or thereabouts are the best items, in the sense of being able to differentiate among the largest number of good and poor students. Not many items, of course, will be found with difficulty indices of exactly .50; the range of difficulties

---
[6] See, for example, Chung-Teh Fan, *Item Analysis Table* (Princeton: Educational Testing Service, 1952).

usually runs from above .90 to below .10. If the test is to cover a wide range of talent (and that is what is wanted in most school examinations), a good plan to follow in selecting items is as follows:

Of items passed by 85–100 percent (very easy) take about — 15 percent
Of items passed by 50– 85 percent (fairly easy) take about — 35 percent
Of items passed by 15– 50 percent (fairly hard) take about — 35 percent
Of items passed by 0– 15 percent (hard to very hard) take about — 15 percent

All of the items, of course, should have satisfactory discriminative power. Note that different proportions at the difficulty levels are selected in accord with the normal distribution.

Items passed by 100 percent or by nobody have no validity in either case, but sometimes an author will place several very easy items at the beginning of the test for psychological effect, and a few very hard items at the end to test the very bright pupils.

6. In using multiple-choice items, it is important for the improvement of the examination to know to what extent good and poor students have chosen the various distractors. If the wrong answers are illogical, obviously absurd, or otherwise not very misleading, the examinee will have little difficulty selecting the right option. The item is easier than it would have been had the misleads been more attractive. Information concerning the efficacy of misleads can be obtained by tallying the responses of the high and low groups to each mislead, as shown below. The group considered is the one hundred twenty children referred to in the illustration above, and there are thirty-two (27 percent) in the high and thirty-two in the low groups. The item is of the multiple-choice type with four options, and the correct answer is keyed as (b).

| Item 26 | a | ⓑ | c | d | Omissions | Total |
|---|---|---|---|---|---|---|
| High Group | 1 | 16 | 8 | 7 | 0 | 32 |
| Low Group | 3 | 7 | 10 | 12 | 0 | 32 |

It is clear that distractor (a) needs to be rewritten, since only four in sixty-four chose it. Otherwise, item twenty-six differentiates between the good and poor students rather well.

A second example shows a slightly different situation. Here (c) is keyed as the correct answer.

| Item 10 | a | b | ⓒ | d | Omissions | Total |
|---|---|---|---|---|---|---|
| High Group | 0 | 15 | 11 | 5 | 1 | 32 |
| Low Group | 5 | 10 | 9 | 8 | 0 | 32 |

Mislead (b) is chosen by more of the good students than is the correct answer (c); and this is true, too, of the poor students. Obviously, mislead (b) must be made less attractive or otherwise changed so that it doesn't compete so strongly with (c). Furthermore, (c) might be strengthened and (a) examined further to see why it failed to attract any answers in the high group.

7. Many teachers find it profitable to keep a file of items for future use. A good plan is to write the item on one side of a card and to list on the back of the card (1) the size and character of the experimental group on which the data are based, (2) the validity of the item (its biserial r with the test score), (3) the difficulty of the item, and (4) data on misleads. Figure 9–1 shows these data on an item taken from a test in contemporary history.

When a teacher has accumulated a large file of items, tests of approximately the same range and validity may be made up as needed.

## A SHORT METHOD OF ITEM ANALYSIS

It is wise for a teacher to understand what the biserial coefficient of correlation means and what it does, since the device is utilized in many standard tests and is frequently mentioned

## Figure 9–1 Item Analysis Data for Test File

### FRONT OF CARD

Item 36: What marked change took place in the political status of India in the year 1947?
    1. She received a mandate from the United Nations.
    2. She won her independence from Britain.
    3. Her people were united under Mohammedan rule.
    4. She joined the Arab League.

### BACK OF CARD

| Item 36: | 1 | 2 | 3 | 4 | Omissions | Total |
|---|---|---|---|---|---|---|
| High group: | 10 | 32 | 6 | 6 | 0 | 54 |
| Low group: | 19 | 11 | 13 | 9 | 2 | 54 |

Sample: 200 high school seniors, tested in June, 1953
Validity: biserial $r = .41$
Difficulty: $= 39$ per cent

in the literature of testing. At the same time, it is not necessary for the teacher to employ the method in order to construct good classroom examinations. The difference between a simple count of "rights" in selected fractions of the best and poorest pupils will suffice as a measure of the validity or discriminative power of an item. First, the items should be gone over by several teachers, the unsatisfactory items discarded, and the remaining items arranged in order of difficulty on the basis of the judgment of the teachers reviewing the items. Next, the test, as tentatively drawn up, should be administered to a sample of children drawn from the classes or age levels to be tested. The additional steps are:

1. Arrange the test papers in order for size of total score, from the highest to the lowest.

## A SHORT METHOD OF ITEM ANALYSIS

2. Count off the 25 percent[7] of the best papers and the 25 percent of the poorest papers. If the total group is small (for example, under fifty) take some larger proportion, say the upper half and the lower half. Suppose there are eighty pupils in the experimental sample (tryout group), so that twenty, or 25 percent, fall in the high group and twenty in the low group. Each item may now be examined to see whether it is able to separate these two criterion groups.

3. Determine the number in each of the two criterion groups who answer each item correctly. If fifteen in the high group answer an item correctly, and five in the low group get the item right, the validity is 15 − 5, or 10, and the *validity index* is 10/20 or .50.[8] If all twenty in the high group answer an item correctly, and none of the low group gets it right, the validity of the item is maximal: 20 − 0 = 20, and the *validity index* is 20/20 or 1.00. The lowest *validity index* of an item by this method is, of course, 0/20 or .00. Validity indices run, therefore, from 0 to 1. There may be a few items of negative validity—more rights in the low than in the high group—but such items are rare. Items having zero or negative validity must be rewritten before they are used or discarded if salvage is impossible.

4. If $R_H$ = number right in the high group and $R_L$ = number right in the low group, the discriminative power of an item is simply $(R_H - R_L)$ or $(R_H - R_L)/N_H$ when written as a *validity index*. Using the same nomenclature, we may write the *difficulty index* of an item as $(R_H + R_L)/(N_H + N_L)$ in which $N_H$ and $N_L$ are the numbers in the high and low groups, respectively. In our example above wherein $R_H = 15$ and $R_L = 5$, the validity index is 10/20, or .50, and the difficulty index is $(15 + 5)/(20 + 20)$, or .50. If $R_H = 18$ and $R_L = 12$, the validity in-

---

[7] Unless the biserial *r* method is used in determining validities, there is no need to observe the somewhat unwieldy 27 percent rule; 25 percent or any convenient larger percentage will serve.

[8] Validities can be left simply as the difference between the number right in the two extreme groups. The chief advantage of a validity index is to put validities in a percentage scale, as are the difficulties.

dex is 6/20, or .30, and the difficulty index is 30/40, or .75. Again, if $R_H = 10$ and $R_L = 2$, the validity index is 8/20, or .40, and the difficulty index is 12/40, or .30.

5. Select the items having the highest validity indices for the final test. Then follow the table on page 234 in apportioning items to the various levels of difficulty, if the test is to cover a fairly wide range of talent.

6. It is advisable to examine the misleads when multiple-choice items are to be used. The method outline on page 235 will aid in locating distractors which are too plausible or not plausible enough. The first kind are too often accepted, and the second are taken by only a few.

7. A card file of acceptable items will prove useful when a teacher wants to lengthen a test or to replace nonfunctioning items. When there are a number of items, a parallel form of the test can be drawn up.

Table 9–1 shows the sort of data which we can expect to get in an item analysis of questions administered to a sample of eighty, as described above. The full table, of course, would contain data on all the items and on all the members of the two criterion groups. Half of the scores in the high and in the low groups are not shown in order to shorten the table, but these omitted scores are included in the totals on which the item analysis is based. Each of the two criterion groups (the high and the low) consists of twenty examinees.

Examination of Table 9–1 shows that item 4 is highly valid and that items 1, 2, and 5 are acceptable. Item 3 has no validity and must be dropped or changed drastically. An item with a validity index of .20 or more may be considered satisfactory—at least tentatively. This figure is arbitrary, however. If the test is shortened, the acceptable point for a validity index should be raised; if the test is lengthened, it should be lowered. Any item with an index larger than 0 has some validity and hence some value. Note that in Table 9–1 the difficulty indices range from .70 (a fairly easy item) to .30 (a fairly hard item).

## TABLE 9–1

### Item Analysis of the First Five Items of a Test Made on Two Criterion Groups, the Highest and the Lowest 25 Percent in Total Score. $N_H = N_L = 20$, and $N = 80$

| Highest Group (Best 25 percent) in Order of Merit | Total test score in order of size | 1 | 2 | ITEMS 3 | 4 | 5 |
|---|---|---|---|---|---|---|
| 1  | 72 | √ | √ | √ | √ | √ |
| 2  | 70 | 0 | √ | 0 | √ | 0 |
| 3  | 68 | √ | √ | √ | √ | √ |
| 4  | 65 | √ | 0 | 0 | √ | 0 |
| 5  | 65 | √ | √ | √ | √ | √ |
| 6  | 65 | √ | √ | √ | √ | √ |
| 7  | 63 | √ | 0 | 0 | √ | 0 |
| 8  | 61 | √ | √ | √ | √ | √ |
| 9  | 60 | √ | √ | 0 | √ | 0 |
| 10 | 60 | √ | √ | √ | √ | √ |
| ⋮ | | | | | | |
| 20 | 54 | 0 | √ | 0 | √ | √ |
| $R_H =$ | | 15 | 16 | 10 | 20 | 8 |
| Lowest Group (Poorest 25 percent) | | | | | | |
| 1  | 35 | √ | √ | √ | √ | 0 |
| 2  | 34 | 0 | √ | √ | 0 | 0 |
| 3  | 30 | √ | √ | √ | √ | 0 |
| 4  | 30 | √ | 0 | 0 | 0 | 0 |
| 5  | 27 | 0 | 0 | √ | 0 | 0 |
| 6  | 25 | √ | 0 | √ | √ | √ |
| 7  | 25 | 0 | 0 | 0 | √ | √ |
| 8  | 24 | √ | 0 | √ | √ | 0 |
| 9  | 23 | √ | √ | 0 | 0 | √ |
| 10 | 23 | 0 | 0 | 0 | √ | √ |
| ⋮ | | | | | | |
| 20 | 12 | 0 | √ | √ | 0 | 0 |
| $R_L =$ | | 8 | 10 | 10 | 8 | 4 |
| $R_H - R_L =$ | | 7 | 6 | 0 | 12 | 4 |
| $(R_H - R_L) / N_H =$ | | .35 | .30 | 0 | .60 | .20 |
| $(R_H + R_L) / (N_H + N_L) =$ | | .58 | .65 | .50 | .70 | .30 |

## SCORING THE FINAL TEST

If the completed test is cast in T-F form, the point scores will be simply numbered right, or R–W if we wish to correct for guessing (page 204). In multiple-choice tests, the correction for guessing is

$$\text{Score} = R - \frac{W}{(n-1)}$$

where $n =$ the number of choices or options. It is sometimes advisable to use the correction for guessing with T-F items, but number right without correction is satisfactory in multiple-choice when four or five options are provided (page 206).

In most cases, it is sufficient for the teacher to express standing on the test in point scores or totals. If several classes have been tested and it is desirable to compare their performance, percentile ranks will be useful. Scaling of teacher-made tests in standard scores or normalized scores is not recommended unless the test is to be used throughout a school system.

Directions for the final test should be explicit, and time limits should be given. Manuals for standardized tests may be consulted with profit for pointers on directions and time limits. A test should not be so long that most students cannot finish in the time allowed.

The use of scoring stencils will speed up marking when many papers are to be examined. In T-F tests, a strip containing the answers (a key) may be laid alongside the left-hand margin and the answers checked as right or wrong, or simply the right answers checked. Separate scoring sheets are useful in dealing with multiple-choice and matching items. Spaces are numbered on the answer sheet for recording answers to the questions on the test. Then the test blank itself is not marked and may be used more than once.

## THE RELIABILITY OF THE FINAL TEST

Perhaps the easiest method of estimating the reliability of a teacher-made test, since there is rarely more than one form, is

## RELIABILITY OF THE FINAL TEST

by what is called the "split-half" technique. In this procedure, the test is administered only once to a sample of examinees, and is then divided into two half-tests. The first half-test contains the odd-numbered items (1, 3, 5, and so on) and the second half-test the even-numbered items (2, 4, 6, and so on).[9] The correlation between scores on the two half-tests is now found and from this $r$ the correlation of the whole test with itself (its self-correlation) is predicted by the well-known "prophecy formula."[10] To illustrate, suppose that in a class of ten seventh graders, an English literature test in multiple-choice form has an odd-even correlation of .50. What is the probable self-correlation of the whole test? The prophecy formula is

$$r\text{ (whole test)} = \frac{2 \times r\text{ (half-test)}}{1 + r\text{ (half-test)}}$$

Substituting $r = .50$ for the self-correlation of the half-test, we have

$$r\text{ (whole test)} = \frac{2 \times .50}{1 + .50} \text{ or } .67$$

This is a satisfactory reliability coefficient (.67) for a single class. For standardized tests administered to very large groups of a wide range of talent, reliability coefficients will ordinarily be higher—.90 or more. For teacher-made tests, however, the reliability coefficients will rarely be more than .60 to .70. Reliability is higher over several grades—that is, when the test is given to more than one grade. The standard error of a test score can be computed by the formula given on page 30, but for the teacher-made test this is often a needless refinement.

Reliability coefficients for a teacher-made test should always be computed from a *new* class, never from the sample used in determining the validities of the test items. Self-correlation in

---

[9] Note that when a test is split into odd and even items, the range of difficulty in the two half-tests is the same and the split is unique. Not just any split into two half-tests is satisfactory.
[10] The Spearman-Brown prophecy formula is treated in all standard texts dealing with statistical method in psychology and education.

the standardization group will always be spuriously high, because the selection of items was based on the scores of the high and low members of the sample.

## VALIDITY OF THE FINAL TEST

A teacher-made test in physics or French, for example, will always have content validity, even when the sampling is quite narrow. Teacher-made tests rarely cover as much material as do standardized printed tests. An approximate measure of validity for a test can be found by correlating test scores against school grades in the same subject. This method is not entirely satisfactory, since school marks are rarely more dependable measures of the subject matter than the tests. When experimental validity is attempted by correlating scores on a teacher-made test with grades or with other test scores, a new group must always be utilized. Such validation, called *cross validation*, is necessary because the group used in item analysis is a special group which has served to select the items in the first place. Cross validation is necessary also when the two criterion groups (the upper and lower extreme groups) are selected on the basis of school grades. A teacher-made test of necessity will correlate with grades achieved by this group, since the group selected the items.

Perhaps the best way to judge the value of a teacher-made test is by its predictive validity. If the test aids the teacher in getting a better notion of the individual differences within the class, and leads to better understanding of the difficulties of the students (meager knowledge, errors in information, and so on), it has fulfilled its purpose.

### SUGGESTIONS FOR FURTHER READING

BEAN, K. L. *Construction of Educational and Personnel Tests.* New York: McGraw-Hill, 1953.

NOLL, V. H. *Introduction to Educational Measurement.* Boston: Houghton Mifflin, 1957.

ROSS, C. C. and STANLEY, J. C. *Measurement in Today's Schools.* 3rd ed.; New York: Prentice-Hall, 1954.

TRAVERS, R. M. *How To Make Achievement Tests.* New York: Odyssey, 1950.

WOOD, D. A. *Test Construction.* Columbus: Merrill, 1960.

## SUGGESTIONS FOR LABORATORY WORK

1. Assume that you have tried out fifty T-F items on a class of forty pupils. Draw up a table like Table 9-1 showing how you would carry out an item analysis.

2. If time allows, construct a test using your class as standardizing sample. Multiple-choice items in arithmetic and vocabulary taken from E. L. Thorndike's *The Measurement of Intelligence* may be used conveniently. Thorndike's book gives items by levels over a wide range of difficulty. Administer a test of about fifty items and item-analyze the results by the method given on pages 235-239.

3. Take a test which has been given to this class or to some other class. Analyze the questions for validity, following the method on page 235.

## QUESTIONS FOR DISCUSSION

1. A sixth-grade teacher has administered a test in fundamentals of arithmetic. What analyses of the test data could this teacher make which would (a) help his future teaching, (b) be of value to individual pupils?

2. Under what conditions would it be profitable to correct scores on a multiple-choice test for guessing?

3. In some schools, one teacher makes all the examinations in a given subject. What are the advantages and disadvantages of this procedure?

4. What might an item of negative validity mean? Of zero validity?

5. Why is it important that the teacher read aloud the directions for a test, and illustrate the marking of an item?

6. In some tests, items are printed in cycles. For example, a T-F item is followed by multiple-choice, matching, and short essay items, and this order is repeated. What advantages and disadvantages can you see in this procedure compared with that of putting all items of one sort together?

## Chapter 10

## SOME PROBLEMS IN THE EVALUATION OF TEST SCORES

INTERPRETING MULTIPLE APTITUDE TEST SCORES

Table 10–1 gives the scores achieved by ten ninth graders on the Differential Aptitude Tests (DAT). Scores on any mental test are more meaningful when supplemented by the pupils' school grades and by a knowledge of personality traits, interests, and ambitions. With this proviso in mind, answer the questions below with reference only to the percentile ranks in Table 10–1.

QUESTIONS ON TABLE 10–1

1. Which two students show the poorest scholastic ability? In what jobs might they do best?
2. Which student exhibits the most consistently high level of ability?

## TABLE 10–1
### Differential Aptitude Scores (Ninth-Grade Class)*
### Scores are PR's

| Students' Names | Verbal Reasoning | Numerical Ability | Abstract Reasoning | Space Relations | Mechanical Reasoning | Clerical Speed and Accuracy | Language Spelling | Usage Sentences |
|---|---|---|---|---|---|---|---|---|
| Mary Cumming | 17 | 10 | 24 | 27 | 19 | 61 | 43 | 30 |
| Larry Edwards | 95 | 96 | 92 | 90 | 91 | 18 | 26 | 22 |
| Jane Goodrich | 32 | 64 | 48 | 73 | 66 | 27 | 30 | 31 |
| Sue Grant | 53 | 43 | 64 | 52 | 23 | 95 | 70 | 90 |
| Laura Hill | 85 | 70 | 80 | 55 | 24 | 64 | 34 | 46 |
| Joe Kramer | 96 | 92 | 90 | 92 | 95 | 85 | 80 | 86 |
| Frank Merry | 90 | 88 | 84 | 67 | 80 | 26 | 50 | 60 |
| Louise Rich | 87 | 86 | 80 | 60 | 42 | 82 | 95 | 90 |
| Frank Seay | 34 | 38 | 31 | 54 | 91 | 33 | 26 | 34 |
| William Thomas | 18 | 22 | 30 | 35 | 20 | 46 | 50 | 44 |

* Separate norms for boys and girls.

3. Which students are likely to have reading difficulties?
4. Which girl should do well in secretarial work?
5. If Joe Kramer wants to go to college, would you encourage him to plan to go into engineering?
6. Would you encourage Larry Edwards to go into his father's accountancy firm after graduation from high school?
7. Jane Goodrich plans to become a medical technician. Would you recommend this vocational goal?
8. Which students will probably find it hard to graduate from high school?
9. Frank Seay's father is an auto mechanic and Frank is interested in this work. Do you think it a wise vocational choice?
10. Is it likely that several students are handicapped by poor spelling and language usage? Why?

CASE STUDIES IN EVALUATION OF ABILITIES

The five case studies which follow provide a great deal of data about five pupils, three in high school and two in elementary school. Questions are planned to focus on things to look for in evaluating the promise of the pupils being considered.

1. Case Study of Robert T.

Robert is 16–2, a sophomore in high school. He is well grown and makes a good appearance. He is well behaved, quiet, interested, though not as a participant, in sports, and does not read much. Robert's father is a house painter; both parents are high-school graduates. Robert wants to go to college, and is encouraged to do so by his parents. He wants to be an engineer.

*School Data*

| *Ninth Grade* | | *Tenth Grade* (First term) | |
|---|---|---|---|
| English | C | English | C |
| Social Studies | B | Social Studies | D |
| Mathematics | B | Physics | B |
| General Science | B | French | D |
| Physical Education | C | Physical Education | C |

## Test Data

| | |
|---|---|
| Otis Quick Scoring (Form Gamma) | IQ 112 |
| California Mental Maturity (Language) | IQ 110 |
| California Mental Maturity (Non-language) | IQ 121 |
| Cooperative General Achievement Test: | Percentile Ranks |
|     I. Social Studies | 38 |
|     II. Natural Science | 52 |
|     III. Mathematics | 36 |
| Kuder Preference Record (Vocational) | Percentile Ranks |
|     Mechanical | 63 |
|     Computational | 51 |
|     Persuasive | 15 |
|     Artistic | 12 |
|     Literary | 46 |
|     Musical | 51 |
|     Social Service | 20 |
|     Clerical | 50 |
|     Scientific | 72 |

1. What do you think of Robert's chances of succeeding in college?
2. Robert's interests are in the mathematics-science area. Are they strong enough for him to plan engineering as a vocation?
3. Robert's school record is weak in English and social studies, and his interests do not lie in persuasive and artistic fields. What occupations would you encourage him not to enter?
4. Is the variation in Robert's IQ's too great to arise from chance?
5. How do you interpret the difference between Robert's language and non-language IQ's?
6. Would you say that Robert's school grades are not in keeping with his IQ?
7. Do you think Robert might be more successful as a technician than as an engineer?
8. Would you recommend that Robert become a salesman?

9. Do Robert's interests jibe with his achievement test records? With his school marks?
10. Might Robert do well as an airplane pilot?

2. Case Study of William S.

William is 18–1, a senior in high school. He makes a good appearance, is husky and muscular. William is easy-going and affable; he likes to hunt and is interested in, and good at, sports. His father is a successful lawyer and his mother is a college graduate interested in club activities. The parents have planned that William will study medicine: his grandfather was a well-known physician in the community. William has accepted these vocational plans but says he is more interested in business and sales work.

*School Data*

| *Tenth Grade* | | *Eleventh Grade* | |
|---|---|---|---|
| English | B | English | C |
| Social Studies | B | Social Studies | B |
| Mathematics | D | Mathematics | D |
| Physics | C | Spanish | B |
| Physical Education | B | Physical Education | B |

*Test Data*

Terman-McNemar Test of Mental Ability   IQ 118
California Achievement Tests (Advanced)

| | Percentile Ranks |
|---|---|
| Reading | 65 |
| Mathematics | 40 |
| Language | 60 |

Differential Aptitude Test (Tenth Grade)

| | Percentile Ranks |
|---|---|
| Verbal Reasoning | 86 |
| Numerical Ability | 42 |
| Abstract Reasoning | 38 |
| Space Relations | 40 |
| Mechanical Reasoning | 32 |

|  |  |
|---|---|
| Clerical Speed and Accuracy | 55 |
| Language Usage—Spelling | 75 |
| Language Usage—Sentences | 93 |

Kuder Preference Record (Vocational)

|  | Percentile Ranks |
|---|---|
| Outdoor | 96 |
| Computational | 32 |
| Persuasive | 90 |
| Artistic | 40 |
| Literary | 86 |
| Musical | 54 |
| Social Service | 36 |
| Clerical | 40 |
| Scientific | 26 |

1. Do you think that William is college material?
2. Would you encourage him to plan on medicine as a career?
3. Do William's grades verify his DAT scores?
4. Is language a strong area for William? Would you, on the strength of this, suggest some vocation other than medicine for William? If so, what?
5. What are William's strong interests, as revealed by the Kuder Record?
6. Are William's achievement test scores in line with his school grades?
7. Do you think William might be happier and more successful in business? In the study of law? Give reasons for your answers.
8. William's IQ does not jibe with his DAT scores. Can you given any reasons why this is so?
9. The Kuder scores are more helpful than the DAT in counseling William. Do you agree with this judgment?
10. How would you explain to William's father his considerable variability in scores? And how would you explain the apparent contradictions?

## 3. Case Study of Mary S.

Mary is 11–8, in the second half of the sixth grade. She is pleasant and well mannered, but is judged by her teachers to be "nervous" and overanxious. Mary wants to be a teacher. Her father is an auto salesman and has a high-school education; her mother is a housewife with junior-college training. There are three other children in the family.

School Data

| Fifth Grade | | Sixth Grade | |
|---|---|---|---|
| Reading | C | Reading | B |
| Social Studies | C | Social Studies | C |
| Arithmetic | B | Arithmetic | C |
| Science | C | Science | C |
| Language | C | Language | B |

Test Data

Kuhlmann-Anderson Intelligence Tests      IQ 110
Metropolitan Achievement Tests      Grade Equivalents

| Reading | 6.1 |
|---|---|
| Vocabulary | 6.8 |
| Arithmetic Reasoning | 5.4 |
| Arithmetic Comprehension | 5.2 |
| English | 6.2 |
| Spelling | 6.6 |
| History | 5.6 |
| Science | 4.6 |

1. In what subjects is Mary weakest?
2. Would you encourage her to plan for teaching as a career?
3. Is Mary college material? Give reasons for your opinion.
4. Could Mary do office and clerical work successfully?
5. Would it help to have a Stanford-Binet IQ for Mary? Give reasons for your answer.

## 4. Case Study of Louise M.

Louise is 12–4, in the first half of the seventh grade. A good student, she is meticulous in her written work and is anxious to

CASE STUDIES IN EVALUATION OF ABILITIES 251

please. Louise's older sister is a secretary, and Louise, who greatly admires her sister, wants to be a secretary too. Louise's father is a successful store manager without much formal education; her mother is a housewife with a high-school education. Both parents approve Louise's choice of vocation. There are three children in the family, a younger brother and the older sister.

*School Data*

        *Sixth Grade*

| Reading | B |
|---|---|
| Social Studies | C |
| Arithmetic | B |
| Science | C |
| English | B+ |

*Test Data*

| California Mental Maturity (Language) | | | IQ 118 |
|---|---|---|---|
| California Mental Maturity (Non-Language) | | | IQ 110 |

SCAT (Sixth-Grade Fall Testing)

| | | | Mdn PR |
|---|---|---|---|
| Verbal | PR band | 70–86 | 78 |
| Quantitative | PR band | 63–87 | 75 |
| Full Scale | PR band | 72–83 | 78 |

1. Would you advise Louise to plan for further training in secretarial school?
2. Is this girl college material?
3. Do Louise's grades correspond with her SCAT scores?
4. How would you interpret the gap between Louise's language and non-language IQ's?
5. Would an inventory like the Bernreuter be useful here?

5. Case Study of John H.

John is 17–6, in the second half of the twelfth grade. He is a superior student, well mannered and poised. John wants to study medicine, but his father, a mail carrier, does not favor this vocation because of the time required. He wants John to go to work and help out at home. John's mother is a college graduate and is enthusiastic about John's plans. There are six children in the family, four younger than John. The high-school principal has offered to get John a tuition scholarship to a local college.

*School Data*

| Eleventh Grade | | Twelfth Grade | |
|---|---|---|---|
| English | B+ | English | A |
| Physics | A | Physics | A− |
| Biology | B+ | Biology | A |
| Mathematics | A | Mathematics | B+ |
| French | B | French | B |

*Test Data*

| Wechsler Adult Intelligence Scale | | | IQ 132 |
|---|---|---|---|
| SCAT (Eleventh-Grade Fall Testing) | | | Mdn PR |
| Verbal | PR band | 85–95 | 90 |
| Quantitative | PR band | 78–93 | 86 |
| Full Scale | PR band | 90–95 | 93 |
| Strong Vocational Interest Blank | | | Interest Level |
| Physician | | | A |
| Dentist | | | B |
| Social Worker | | | C+ |
| Minister | | | C+ |

1. Do John's interests and ambition jibe?
2. Is John a good prospect for the study of medicine?
3. What vocations might be alternative choices?
4. What personal traits would you look for in John?
5. What counsel would you give John's father?

### Sociometric Testing

From observations in school and out, most teachers get a fairly good idea of the social and personal relations within their classrooms. They soon come to know which children are leaders, which are well liked and popular, which are disliked or ignored, and which are picked on and teased. It is sometimes valuable for a teacher to have, in addition to his own opinion, some measure of the attitudes and feelings of the pupils regarding each other. When data of this sort are collected systematically, they may be put into a table or expressed in the form of a *sociogram*, which is a pictorial or graphic representation of the interpersonal relations within some specified group, often a class.

The usual procedure in the construction of a sociogram is to ask the pupils to designate the classmate by whom they would rather sit, or the child (or children) with whom they would prefer to play ball at recess, or to make some other choice of a companion in a real-life situation. Table 10–2 shows the re-

*TABLE 10–2*

*Sociometric Tabulation*

|  | David | Anita | Sally | Gary | Karl | Janet | Jack | Helen | Laura | Ruth |
|---|---|---|---|---|---|---|---|---|---|---|
| David |  |  |  | 1* |  |  |  | 2 |  |  |
| Anita |  |  |  |  |  | 1* |  |  |  | 2 |
| Sally |  |  |  |  |  | 1 |  | 2 |  |  |
| Gary | 1* |  |  |  | 2 |  |  |  |  |  |
| Karl | 1 |  |  |  |  |  | 2 |  |  |  |
| Janet |  | 1* |  |  |  |  | 2 |  |  |  |
| Jack | 2 |  |  |  | 1 |  |  |  |  |  |
| Helen |  | 1 |  |  |  |  |  |  |  | 2 |
| Laura | 1 |  |  |  |  |  |  | 2 |  |  |
| Ruth |  |  |  | 2 | 1 |  |  |  |  |  |
| 1st Choices | 3 | 2 | 0 | 1 | 1 | 3 | 0 | 0 | 0 | 0 |
| 2nd Choices | 1 | 0 | 0 | 1 | 1 | 0 | 2 | 2 | 1 | 2 |

sponses made by ten fifth-grade pupils who were asked to nominate their first and second choices of a child to work with on a class project. (The table reproduces only part of the data for the class.)

A first choice is shown by a 1 under the name of the child chosen, a second choice by a 2. An asterisk (\*) denotes that the choice for first place was mutual. Thus, David chose Gary and was chosen by Gary, and Anita and Janet each named the other as first choice. The summary at the bottom of the table shows David to be the most chosen child, with three firsts and one second. Janet is the next most popular, with three firsts. Sally is chosen by no one, and three of the girls (Helen, Laura, and Ruth) and one boy (Jack) receive no first choices. Tabulation of the responses given by the children will provide the "choice" information that the teacher wants.

A more striking method of representing the social relations within the group is afforded by the pictorial sociogram shown in Figure 10-1. The responses were those of twenty-one kindergarten children—thirteen boys and eight girls. The stars (popular, often-chosen children) are quickly located as are the isolates, whom no one chooses. The two-headed arrows indicate mutual choices.

When used wisely, a sociometric test can be helpful to a teacher, especially when his class is too large for close personal observation. Some of the things which a sociogram may reveal are the following:

1. Good and bad personal relations, free interchange of choices, or the existence of cliques.

2. Clusters and cleavages resulting from differences in race, religion, sex, or economic conditions of families.

3. Differences between in-school and out-of-school social groupings.

The sociometric method has some disadvantages and may do more harm than good if the morale of the class is low because of poor discipline, frequent change of teachers, or other dis-

*Figure 10-1* Sociogram for Twenty-One Kindergartners, Thirteen Boys and Eight Girls

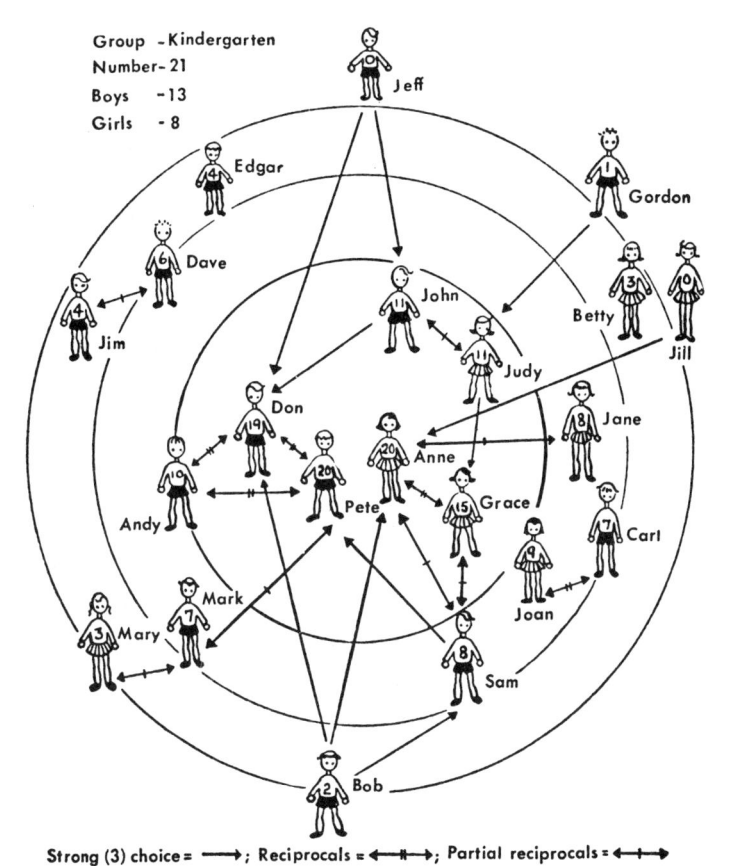

Group - Kindergarten
Number - 21
Boys - 13
Girls - 8

Strong (3) choice = ⟶ ; Reciprocals = ⟵─╫─⟶ ; Partial reciprocals = ⟵─┼─⟶

From Northway, Mary L., and Weld, Lindsay, *Sociometric Testing*. Reproduced by permission of the University of Toronto Press.

rupting influences. For example, choices may be trivial or deliberately false, or some pupils may take the "test" as an occasion to express hostility and resentment against other pupils or against the teacher. Moreover, the choices of young children are often fleeting, vary from time to time, and are quite unreliable. The sociogram, therefore, is not foolproof. At the same time, in the hands of a skillful teacher, sociometric testing will often provide new insights into the personality traits of pupils and thus aid in discipline and in remedial work.

## SUGGESTIONS FOR FURTHER READING

CROW, LESTER D. and CROW, ALICE. *An Introduction to Guidance: Basic Principles and Practices.* 2nd ed.; New York: American Book, 1960.
NOLL, VICTOR H. *Introduction to Educational Measurement.* Boston: Houghton Mifflin, 1957.
SUPER, D. E. *Appraising Vocational Fitness by Means of Psychological Tests.* New York: Harper, 1949.
ZERAN, FRANKLIN N., LALLAS, JOHN E., and WEGNER, KENNETH W. *Guidance: Theory and Practice.* New York: American Book, 1964.

# Appendix A

# STATISTICAL SUPPLEMENT

In order to understand and use test results wisely, a teacher should be familiar with those statistical concepts most often employed in mental testing. One of the best ways to accomplish this is to work through the computation of the basic statistics. In Chapter 2 a number of statistical terms were defined and their application illustrated. In subsequent chapters these statistics have been frequently employed. If, when a statistic is first mentioned, the student will work through its derivation—for example, the tabulation of a frequency distribution or the computation of an $r$—the value of the statistic to mental testing will be clarified. A second or even a third review is often helpful. A good analogy here is the habit of looking up unfamiliar words in a dictionary. Sometimes a word must be looked up more than once before its meaning is clearly grasped.

This *Appendix* deals with the following topics:
  The Frequency Distribution
  The Frequency Polygon and the Histogram
  Averages: Mean, Median, and Mode
  Measures of Variability: Range, $Q$, and $SD$ ($\sigma$)
  The Coefficient of Correlation

### DRAWING UP A FREQUENCY DISTRIBUTION

Test scores are more readily dealt with when they have first been organized into a frequency distribution. Suppose that Miss Norton has administered a standard test to her class of forty pupils in social studies, and that scores are as follows:

37, 38, 36, 31, 28, 33, 24, 19, 25, 34
16, 43, 22, 20, 26, 44, 27, 19, 25, 34
33, 24, 22, 20, 44, 27, 31, 28, 38, 17
31, 26, 34, 17, 19, 20, 22, 24, 26, 29

Table A–1 shows these forty scores tabulated into a frequency distribution in which the interval is five score units. Steps in setting up a frequency distribution follow:

*TABLE A–1*
*Frequency Distribution of Forty Scores on a Social Studies Test*

| Intervals | Midpoints | Tallies | f |
|---|---|---|---|
| 40 – 44 | 42 | ||| | 3 |
| 35 – 39 | 37 | |||| | 4 |
| 30 – 34 | 32 | 𝍷𝍷 ||| | 8 |
| 25 – 29 | 27 | 𝍷𝍷 𝍷𝍷 | 10 |
| 20 – 24 | 22 | 𝍷𝍷 |||| | 9 |
| 15 – 19 | 17 | 𝍷𝍷 | | 6 |
|  |  | $N = \overline{40}$ |  |

(1) Determine the *range*, or the gap between the highest and lowest scores. Examining our set of forty scores, we find the range to be from 44 to 16, or 28.

(2) Select an interval which will be convenient for tabulation. A good working rule is to take a grouping unit which will yield from five to fifteen intervals. This rule may have to be broken when the sample is very large (200 or 300, say) or very small (less than 25).

(3) Divide the range by the interval size tentatively chosen. This gives the approximate (within one) number of intervals. In Table A–1 the range of 28 divided by five gives 5.6, and the number of intervals is six. Five is a better choice than is a larger or smaller unit. For example, an interval of three will spread the data out too thin (into ten intervals), whereas an interval of ten crowds all forty scores into three intervals.

(4) Write the beginning and end of each interval as a score: for example, 15–19. Actually a score of 15 represents the interval from 14.5 to 15.5—that is, a *distance* along an ability scale; and 19 represents the interval 18.5 to 19.5. Hence, the lowest interval begins at 14.5 and ends at 19.5; the second interval begins at 19.5 and ends at 24.5, and so on. Writing score limits instead of actual limits saves time and avoids the confusion which often arises when one interval ends and the next begins with the same figure.

(5) Tally each score under its proper interval as shown in Table A–1. Then write the sum of the tallies opposite each interval under $f$ (frequency). Sum the $f$'s to give $N$.

Note that the midpoint of the topmost interval is 42—that is, 2.5 from 39.5 and 2.5 from 44.5. The midpoints have been entered in the second column. When scores have been arranged into a frequency distribution, *all* of the $f$'s within a given interval are represented by the midpoint of that interval.

### The Frequency Polygon

Figure A–1 shows the frequency polygon of the forty scores tabulated into a frequency distribution in Table A–1. Two axes, a horizontal or $X$-axis and a vertical or $Y$-axis, are drawn at right angles. Score intervals are laid off at regular distances along the

*Figure A-1* *Frequency Distribution of the Forty Scores in Table A-1*

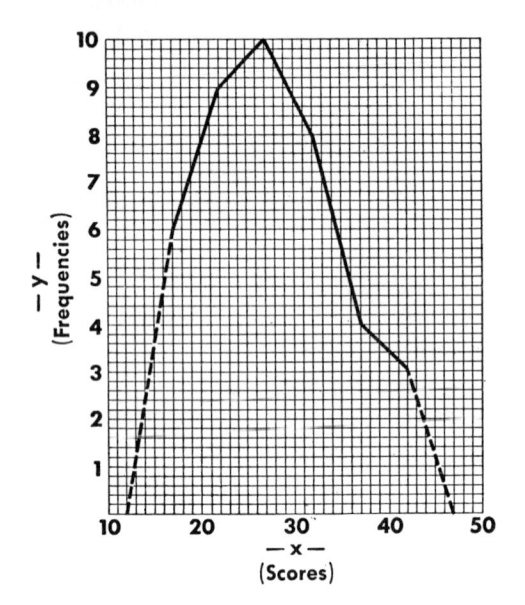

X-axis, or baseline, beginning with 15, the lower limit of the first interval. The six scores on the lowest interval are represented by a point six units up on the Y-axis and just above 17, the midpoint of interval 15-19. The nine scores on the next interval are represented by a point nine units up on Y and just above 22, midpoint of the interval 20-24. The other $f$'s are drawn in in the same manner.

When all of the points are joined by short straight lines, we have the outline of the frequency polygon. To complete the figure—that is, to bring it down to the baseline at each end—two intervals are added, one (10-14) at the low end and the other (45-49) at the high end. The $f$ on each of these intervals may be taken as 0, and hence the frequency polygon reaches the X-axis at 12 and 47.

In order to provide a symmetrical figure—one which is neither too squat nor too thin—units in $X$ and $Y$ must be carefully chosen. A good rule is to select units which will make the height of the figure about 2/3 of its length. In Figure A–1 the maximum $f$ (10) is about 2/3 the baseline length of the polygon.

## The Histogram

The frequency distribution of Table A–1 is again represented in Figure A–2, this time by a histogram, or column diagram. The main difference between the frequency polygon and the histogram is that in the histogram the $f$'s are represented by small rectangles whose height equals the $f$'s of the intervals. In Figure A–2, for example, the height of the first rectangle is 6, its width being the length of the interval 14.5 to 19.5. Each frequency rectangle begins at the actual lower limit of the interval and ends at the actual upper limit. The histogram presents the same facts as the frequency polygon and there is often little to choose between them. When two or more frequency distributions are represented on the same axes, however (as for example, the scores of two classes or two sections of the same class), the frequency polygon is to be preferred to the histogram, because the vertical and horizontal lines in a histogram coincide and are often difficult to disentangle.

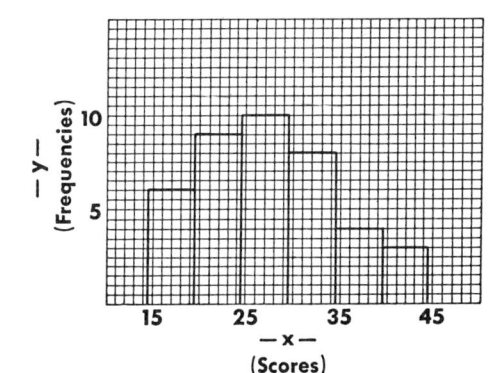

*Figure A–2   Histogram of the Forty Scores in Table A–1*

## COMPUTATION OF AVERAGES

There are three averages in common use: the mean, the median, and the mode.

### The Mean (M)

We have defined the $M$ on page 20 as the statistic found by dividing the sum of the scores by their number. When scores are put into a frequency distribution, the scores classified within any interval lose their identity and are represented by the midpoint of that interval. This necessitates a slightly different procedure from that used with unorganized scores.

In Table A–2, section A, the midpoint of each interval is multiplied or "weighted" by the frequency which lies opposite it in the $f$ column. This gives the $fX$ column and the sum of this column (1100 in Table A–2) divided by $N$ (40) gives a mean of 27.50. The formula is

$$M = \frac{\Sigma fX}{N}$$

where $\Sigma fX$ is the sum of the products $f \times X$ and $N$ is the number of cases.

$M$ can always be computed by the "Long Method" just described, but it is generally computed by the Assumed Mean, or "Short Method." When $N$ is large, the Short Method reduces calculation and saves time. Moreover, the Short Method is mandatory when standard deviations and coefficients of correlation are later to be computed from the same data. Computation of $M$ by the Assumed Mean or Short Method is shown in Table A–2, Section B. Steps are as follows:

(1) Assume a mean, called the $AM$, near the center of the frequency distribution and if possible on the interval having the largest $f$. In our example, the $AM$ is taken at 27, midpoint of interval 25–29, and this interval also has the largest $f$.

## THE MEAN

### TABLE A–2
**Computation of the Mean from a Frequency Distribution**
*(Data are the forty scores in Table A–1.)*

#### A. LONG METHOD

| Intervals | Midpoints | $f$ | $fX$ |
|---|---|---|---|
| 40 – 44 | 42 | 3 | 126 |
| 35 – 39 | 37 | 4 | 148 |
| 30 – 34 | 32 | 8 | 256 |
| 25 – 29 | 27 | 10 | 270 |
| 20 – 24 | 22 | 9 | 198 |
| 15 – 19 | 17 | 6 | 102 |
| | | $N = 40$ | 1100 |

$$M = \frac{\Sigma fX}{N} = \frac{1100}{40} = 27.50$$

#### B. ASSUMED MEAN METHOD (SHORT METHOD)

| Intervals | Midpoints | $f$ | $x'$ | $fx'$ |
|---|---|---|---|---|
| 40 – 44 | 42 | 3 | 3 | 9 |
| 35 – 39 | 37 | 4 | 2 | 8 |
| 30 – 34 | 32 | 8 | 1 | 8 |
| | | | | 25 |
| 25 – 29 | 27 | 10 | 0 | |
| 20 – 24 | 22 | 9 | – 1 | – 9 |
| 15 – 19 | 17 | 6 | – 2 | – 12 |
| | | $N = 40$ | | – 21 |

$AM = 27.00$

$c = \dfrac{\Sigma fx'}{N} = \dfrac{4}{40} = .10$

$ci = .10 \times 5 = .50$

$M = AM + ci$
$\phantom{M} = 27.00 + .50$
$\phantom{M} = 27.50$

(2) In the column $x'$[1] lay off deviations from the $AM$ of 27 in units of interval. The midpoint of intervals 30–34—that is, 32—deviates five scores or one interval from 27; and the midpoint

---

[1] $x'$ denotes the deviation of a midpoint from the $AM$; that is, $x' =$ Mdpt. – $AM$. Deviations from $M$ are denoted by $x$.

of interval 35–39 deviates two intervals from 27, and so on. Below the $AM$, the deviations of the midpoints of the two intervals—22 and 17—are $-1$ and $-2$. The midpoint of the interval 25–29—that is, 27—is the assumed mean, and 0 is entered in the $x'$ column opposite this interval.

(3) Multiply each $x'$ by its $f$ and enter the product in the $fx'$ column. The sum of this column is $4-25-21$—from which the correction ($c$) is calculated. The formula is

$$c = \frac{\Sigma fx'}{N}$$

and $c = 4/40$ or .10 in our problem.

(4) Multiply $c$, the correction in units of interval, by the length of the interval or $i$, to give $ci$, the correction in score units. In our example, $ci = .10 \times 5 = .50$.

(5) Add the correction, $ci$, to the $AM$ to get $M$. In Table A–2, section B, the $M = 27.00 + .50$, or 27.50, thus checking the computation in A above.

### The Median, or $Mdn$

The median is defined as that point in the distribution below which and above which lie 50 percent of the distribution. The median is also described as the fiftieth percentile ($P_{50}$) and the second quartile ($Q_2$). Computation of the median in a frequency distribution is shown in Table A–3. (The $Q$, or quartile deviation, which is found in the same way as the median, is also computed in the table.) Steps are as follows:

(1) Take ½ of $N$ and count into the distribution from the low end until the interval containing the median is reached. In Table A–3, $N/2 = 20$, and counting into the distribution from interval 15–19, we locate the median on interval 25–29. The two lowest intervals contain $6 + 9$ or 15 $f$'s, and it is clear from this cumulated $f$ that the twentieth score must fall on interval 25–29.

## TABLE A–3
### Computation of the Median and Q from a Frequency Distribution
(*Data are the forty scores in Table A–1.*)

| Intervals | f | | |
|---|---|---|---|
| 40 – 44 | 3 | | |
| 35 – 39 | 4 | | |
| 30 – 34 | 8 | | |
| 25 – 29 | 10 | 25 | |
| 20 – 24 | 9 | 15 | |
| 15 – 19 | 6 | 6 | |
| | N = 40 | | |

$N/2 = 20 \qquad N/4 = 10 \qquad 3N/4 = 30$

By formula, Median $= 24.5 + 5 \left( \dfrac{20 - 15}{10} \right)$

$= 27.0$

By formula, $Q_3 = 29.5 + 5 \left( \dfrac{30 - 25}{8} \right)$

$= 32.63$

By formula, $Q_1 = 19.5 + 5 \left( \dfrac{10 - 6}{9} \right)$

$= 21.72$

$Q = \dfrac{32.63 - 21.72}{2}$

$= 5.46$

---

(2) Apply the following formula:

$$Mdn = l + i \left( \dfrac{N/2 - \text{cum } f_1}{f_m} \right)$$

in which
    $l =$ lower limit of interval on which $Mdn$ lies
    $N/2 =$ ½ of the number of scores
    cum $f_1 =$ sum of scores on intervals below $l$
    $f_m =$ frequency on the interval containing the $Mdn$
    $i =$ length of the interval

In our example in Table A–3, $l = 24.5$, lower limit of interval containing $Mdn$; $N/2 = 20$; cum $f_l = 15$; $f_m = 10$; $i = 5$. Substituting in the formula, we have

$$Mdn = 24.5 + 5 \left( \frac{20 - 15}{10} \right)$$
$$= 27.00$$

The median can be found by counting into the distribution from either end, but it is generally easier to start at the low end.

### The Mode

The mode is usually taken as the midpoint of the interval which contains the largest $f$. In Table A–3, the mode is simply 27, the midpoint of the interval 25–29. This "midpoint" mode is often called the crude mode. The mode may be calculated more accurately, but since it is usually a preliminary statistic it is hardly worthwhile to do so.

## COMPUTATION OF MEASURES OF VARIABILITY

The means or medians of two distributions are often the same or nearly so, but the spread or scatter of the scores around the central point is quite different. One class, for example, may show the same mean but a much greater range of talent than another. Knowing the variability of performance within a class may be more useful than knowing its average or typical performance.

There are three measures of variability all of which are used in mental testing: the *range*, the $Q$, and the $SD$ ($\sigma$).

### The Range

The range is the gap between the smallest and largest scores. The range is a useful statistic, but is often a rough measure. It is least efficient when there are several outstanding scores—either very large or very small. For example, suppose there is a gap of 20 points between 75, the highest score, and 55, the score next below it. Then if the lowest score in the set is 25, the single outstandingly high score will increase the range from 30 to 50. We had occasion to find the range in constructing the frequency distribution (page 258).

## The $Q$, or Quartile Deviation

$Q$, the quartile deviation, is defined as one-half the distance between the seventy-fifth and twenty-fifth percentile points in the distribution. To find these two percentiles, we must count into the distribution as we do to find the median. In Table A–3, for example, we count off ¾ of $N$ to get $Q_3$ (the third quartile or seventy-fifth percentile) and ¼ of $N$ to reach $Q_1$ (the first quartile or twenty-fifth percentile). The formula for $Q_3$ is

$$Q_3 = 1 + i \left( \frac{3N/4 - \text{cum } f_1}{f_m} \right)$$

and the formula for $Q_1$ is

$$Q_1 = 1 + i \left( \frac{N/4 - \text{cum } f_1}{f_m} \right)$$

in which

    1 = lower limit of the interval upon which the quartile point falls
    i = the interval
    cum $f_1$ = cumulated $f$'s up to the interval containing the quartile wanted
    $f_m$ = $f$ on the interval which contains the quartile

In Table A–3, ¾ of $N$ is 30. Counting into the distribution from the low end, twenty-five scores take us to 29.5, lower limit of 30–34, which is the interval containing $Q_3$. The $f$ on this interval is 8. Substituting in the formula, we have

$$Q_3 = 29.5 + 5\left(\frac{30-25}{8}\right)$$
$$= 32.63$$

To obtain $Q_1$ we count off ¼ of $N$ or ten scores as shown in Table A–3. Six scores take us to 19.5, lower limit of the interval 20–24, the interval which contains $Q_1$. The $f$ on this interval is 9. Substituting in the formula, we have

$$Q_1 = 19.5 + 5\left(\frac{10-6}{9}\right)$$
$$= 21.72$$

From the two quartile points, $Q_3$ and $Q_1$, we find $Q$ by substituting in the formula

$$Q = \frac{(Q_3 - Q_1)}{2}$$

and in our example, $Q = \left(\frac{32.63 - 21.72}{2}\right)$, or 5.46.

### The Standard Deviation, SD or $\sigma$ (sigma)

The standard deviation, or $\sigma$, is a measure of variability computed around the mean; hence it is usually calculated from the same frequency distribution as the mean. $SD$, or $\sigma$, is the most stable measure of variability within a group and so is regularly used in research problems which involve correlation and inference. The computation of $\sigma$ from a set of ungrouped scores was outlined on pages 22–23. Calculation of the $SD$ from a frequency distribution requires a somewhat different procedure. The method is illustrated in Table A–4 for the same forty scores tabulated in Table A–1. Steps are as follows:

(1) Find the deviation ($x'$) of each midpoint from the $AM$, as was done in Table A–2. Enter these figures as 1, 2, 3, 0, – 1, – 2–that is, in units of interval in the $x'$ column.

## TABLE A-4
### Computation of the Standard Deviation ($\sigma$) from a Frequency Distribution
(Data are the forty scores in Table A-1.)

| Intervals | f | $x'$ | $fx'$ | $fx'^2$ |
|---|---|---|---|---|
| 40 – 44 | 3 | 3 | 9 | 27 |
| 35 – 39 | 4 | 2 | 8 | 16 |
| 30 – 34 | 8 | 1 | 8 | 8 |
| 25 – 29 | 10 | 0 | $\overline{+25}$ | 0 |
| 20 – 24 | 9 | −1 | −9 | 9 |
| 15 – 19 | 6 | −2 | −12 | 24 |
| | $N = \overline{40}$ | | $\overline{-21}$ | $\overline{84}$ |

$$AM = 27.00 \quad c = \frac{\Sigma fx'}{N} = \frac{4}{40} = .10 \quad c^2 = .01$$

$$\sigma = i\sqrt{\frac{\Sigma fx'^2}{N} - c^2} = 5\sqrt{\frac{84}{40} - .01} = 5 \times 1.446$$

$$\sigma = 7.23$$

(2) Multiply each $x'$ by its $f$ to give the entries in the $fx'$ column.

(3) Multiply each $x'$ and its corresponding $fx'$ entry to give the entries in the $fx'^2$ column. For example, $x' = 3$ times $fx' = 9$ gives 27 as the $fx'^2$ entry.

(4) Sum the $fx'^2$ column to give $\Sigma fx'^2$.

(5) Compute the correction ($c$) as in Table A-2. Square $c$ to get $c^2$. Be sure that $c$ is left in units of interval.

(6) Find $\sigma$ from the following formula:

$$\sigma = i\sqrt{\frac{\Sigma fx'^2}{N} - c^2}$$

In our example, $i = 5$, $\Sigma fx'^2 = 84$, $N = 40$, and $c^2 = .01$. Substituting these values in the formula, we get $\sigma = 7.23$. It will be clear that in computing $\sigma$ we make use of the same quantities used in finding the mean; only the $\Sigma fx'^2$ is new.

## CORRELATION

Correlation (page 28) is the correspondence or relationship between two sets of test scores. Degree of relationship is expressed by a coefficient of correlation ($r$) along a scale which extends from $-1.00$ to $+1.00$ through .00. There are several methods of computing correlation, of which the product-moment method is the most often employed in dealing with test scores. Calculation of a product-moment $r$ is illustrated in Table A–5.

Table A–5 shows the computation of the correlation between test scores in reading and arithmetic achieved by ten children in the fifth grade. The sample is much too small to give an adequate indication of the relationship between these two variables, and our table must be taken as a much simplified illustration of correlational method.

TABLE A–5
*Correlation Between Reading and Arithmetic in the Fifth Grade*
($N = 10$)

| Pupils | Reading (X) | Arithmetic (Y) | $x$ | $y$ | $x^2$ | $y^2$ | $xy$ |
|---|---|---|---|---|---|---|---|
| John   | 60 | 26 |  7  |  5  |  49 | 25 |  35 |
| Carol  | 55 | 24 |  2  |  3  |   4 |  9 |   6 |
| Ann    | 63 | 18 | 10  | −3  | 100 |  9 | −30 |
| Betty  | 40 | 21 | −13 |  0  | 169 |  0 |   0 |
| Louise | 52 | 17 | −1  | −4  |   1 | 16 |   4 |
| Tom    | 61 | 20 |  8  | −1  |  64 |  1 |  −8 |
| Bill   | 43 | 15 | −10 | −6  | 100 | 36 |  60 |
| Joan   | 56 | 25 |  3  |  4  |   9 | 16 |  12 |
| Dick   | 44 | 23 | −9  |  2  |  81 |  4 | −18 |
| Carl   | 56 | 21 |  3  |  0  |   9 |  0 |   0 |
|        | 530 | 210 |     |     | $\Sigma x^2 = 586$ | $\Sigma y^2 = 116$ | $\Sigma xy = 61$ |

$M_x = 53.0 \quad M_y = 21.0$

$$r = \frac{61}{\sqrt{586 \times 116}} = .23$$

The coefficient of correlation in Table A–5 is .23, revealing a positive but quite low relationship between the two tests. The first test (reading) is designated X, and the second test (arithmetic) is Y. Note that, in order to compute the correlation, we must first find the deviation of each child's X-score from $M_X$ and the deviation of his Y-score from $M_Y$. Each deviation from $M_X$ (53) is entered in the $x$ column, and each deviation from $M_Y$ (21) is entered in the $y$ column. Each $x$ and $y$ is then squared and entered in the $x^2$ and $y^2$ columns, and the sums of these two columns are found. In the last column ($xy$), the $x$ and $y$ deviations of each pupil are multiplied with due regard for sign, and the sum of the $xy$ column is determined. Finally, the sum of the $xy$ column is divided by the square root of the product of the $\Sigma x^2$ and $\Sigma y^2$ to give the coefficient of correlation. The formula is

$$r = \frac{\Sigma xy}{\sqrt{\Sigma x^2 \cdot \Sigma y^2}}$$

The formula for $r$ may be written in a number of ways. The form selected for use will depend on the character of the data, size of the sample, purpose of the experimenter, and other considerations. Whenever $N$ is more than about 50, the correlation coefficient should be computed from a diagram (see references, Chapter 2).

## Appendix B

# PUBLISHERS OF MENTAL TESTS

Teachers who do much testing should write the publishers below for their catalogs.

Bureau of Publications, Teachers College, Columbia University, New York 27, New York.

California Test Bureau, Del Monte Research Park, Monterey, California.

Educational Test Bureau, 720 Washington Avenue, S.E., Minneapolis 14, Minnesota.

Educational Testing Service, Cooperative Test Division, 20 Nassau Street, Princeton, New Jersey.

Harcourt, Brace & World, Inc., 757 Third Avenue, New York 17, New York.

Houghton Mifflin Company, 2 Park Street, Boston 7, Massachusetts.

Psychological Corporation, 304 East 45th Street, New York 17, New York.

Public School Publishing Company, 345 Calhoun Street, Cincinnati 19, Ohio.

Science Research Associates, Inc., 259 East Erie Street, Chicago 11, Illinois.

C. H. Stoelting and Company, 424 North Homan Avenue, Chicago 24, Illinois.

**Stanford University Press,** Stanford, California.

# GLOSSARY

**achievement test**  A test designed to measure pupil performance in some school subject.
**age equivalent**  The chronological age assigned to an obtained score on a test representing the typical (average) age corresponding to the score. Example: reading age = 8–4.
**age norm**  Typical performance on a test expressed in age equivalents.
**alternate forms of a test**  Equivalent or parallel forms of a test.
**aptitude test**  A test designed to measure potential ability; specifically, a test to predict future success in a school subject or in a vocation.
**attitude test**  A test designed to measure likes or dislikes in a given area. Example: attitude towards war.
**battery**  A group of tests, often combined into a team, designed to measure a variety of abilities or aptitudes.
**biserial r**  A coefficient of correlation often used to measure the discriminative power of an item in analysis.
**central tendency**  A measure typical of a group of scores; a mean, median, or mode.
**chronological age (CA)**  Life age expressed in years and months. Thus, 10–4 means 10 years and 4 months.
**completion items**  Test questions in which the examinee must fill in blank spaces in a statement or sentence in order to complete the meaning.
**correlation**  The tendency for one test to be related (or unrelated) to another test.

**criterion**  Any measure of performance with which a test is compared in determining validity.

**deviation IQ**  A standard score found by converting raw scores into a distribution with a mean = 100 and a $\sigma$ of 15 or 16 points.

**diagnostic tests**  Tests designed to reveal pupil's strengths and weaknesses in school subjects.

**discriminating power**  A test item which separates good from poor students has discriminating power.

**distractor**  An incorrect option in a multiple-choice test.

**essay items**  Test items calling for a relatively free response.

**evaluation**  Appraisal of a pupil's performance; may include in-school and out-of-school behaviors.

**frequency distribution**  An arrangement of test scores into groups in order of size.

**grade equivalent**  The grade score assigned to a given obtained score on a test. Example: A score of 42 on an achievement test may have a grade equivalent of 6.5 (halfway through the sixth grade).

**graphic rating scale**  A rating device in which possession of a given degree of some trait is indicated by a check along a line.

**group test**  A test that may be administered to all members of a group or class at the same time.

**individual test**  A test administered to only one person at a time.

**IQ (intelligence quotient)**  Originally, the ratio of mental age to chronological age when mental age is obtained from an Age Scale. Often used loosely to mean any set of scores with a mean of 100. See deviation IQ.

**intelligence tests**  Tests designed to measure intelligence, which may be defined as mental alertness or ability to do well in school.

**inventory**  A test or checklist of a person's personal characteristics, attitudes, or interests.

**item**  A single question on a test.

**item analysis**  The process of determining the difficulty and validity of test items through statistical analysis.
**matching items**  Test items in which the members of one list are to be matched against the members of a second list.
**mean**  The arithmetic average of a set of test scores.
**median**  The point that divides a frequency distribution of scores into two equal parts.
**mental age (MA)**  The age for which an obtained score on an intelligence test is average or typical.
**mode**  The score which occurs most often in a distribution.
**multiple-choice items**  Test items which call for the selection of a correct answer from among several options.
**normal probability curve**  A theoretical distribution curve which many distributions of test scores approximate.
**norms**  Average performances for various groups—expressed as age or grade equivalents for school children, as percentiles, and in other ways.
**objective test**  A test answered by checking or circling a number or letter. Example: True-false test items.
**options**  Responses from among which an examinee must make a selection.
**percentile rank (PR)**  The equivalent to an obtained score on a scale of 100 points. Example: If a score of 86 has a percentile rank (PR) of 63, we know that 63 percent of the group scored below 86.
**personality test**  A test (often an inventory) designed to assess an individual's personal and social behaviors.
**power test**  A test designed to measure level of performance rather than speed.
**profile**  A graphic device for representing an examinee's scores on several tests.
**projective tests**  Devices for studying personality through the use of ink blots, pictures, designs.
**quartile deviation ($Q$)**  A measure of variability. $Q$ equals one-half of the range of the middle 50 percent of scores.

**questionnaire**  A systematic inventory of questions covering personality traits, attitudes, or interests.
**readiness test**  A measure of a child's readiness or maturity level. Often used in reading.
**reliability**  Consistency of test scores.
**reliability coefficient**  Correlation coefficient giving the self-correlation of a test.
**skewness**  The extent to which a distribution of scores is off center or biased.
**sociometry**  Measurement of interpersonal relations within a class or other group.
**split-half reliability**  Reliability coefficient found by splitting a test into halves. The two parts of the test usually consist of odd- and even-numbered items.
**standard deviation ($SD$ or $\sigma$)**  A measure of variability.
**standard error of a score**  An estimate of how close an obtained score is to its theoretical "true" value.
**standard score**  A converted or derived score found by expressing an obtained score as being so far above or below the mean in $SD$ units.
**standardized tests**  Printed tests for which there are norms on defined groups. Directions are carefully prescribed.
**test-retest reliability**  The correlation between scores made on the same test administered on two occasions.
**true-false items**  Test items which the examinee is to mark as true or false.
**T-score**  A normalized score.
**validity**  The degree to which a test measures what it purports to measure. There are several sorts of validity.
**z-score**  An obtained score expressed as a deviation from the test mean in terms of $\sigma$. When z-scores are converted into a frequency distribution with an assigned mean and $\sigma$, they are called standard scores.

# SUBJECT INDEX

Ability, meaning of, 47–48
Achievement tests, 108–112; definition of, 109; diagnostic uses of, 125–126; survey, 123–124; teacher-made, 224–225; value of, 110–112
Adjustment inventories, 176–177
Age norms, 42
Age scale, 33; value of, 34
American Council on Education Psychological Examination (ACE), 96
Aptitudes, meaning of, 141–142
Aptitude tests, art, 164; batteries of, 142–150; case studies of the use of, 244–252; clerical, 146–150; how to judge, 165; interpreting scores in, 166; mechanical, 143–146; music, 162; use of, in professional schools, 158–162
Army Alpha test, 8
Army Beta test, 8
Army General Classification Test (AGCT), 8–9
Art aptitude tests, 164–165
Arthur Point Scale, 76–79; use of, in schools, 79
Ascendance-Submission Reaction Study (Allport), 185–187
Attitudes, 184; questionnaires in study of, 185–187
Averages, computation of, 262–263

Bell Adjustment Inventory, 183
Bennett Mechanical Comprehension Test, 145–147
Bernreuter Personality Inventory, 180–181
Binet tests, characteristics of, 6–7
Biserial $r$, in item analysis, 232–233

California Achievement Tests, 118–119; characteristics of, 119
California Arithmetic Test, 226
California Test of Mental Maturity, 88; description of, 89–90
California Test of Personality, 177–179
Case studies, in evaluation, 246–252
Central tendency, meaning of, 20, 262
Clerical Aptitude Tests, 146–150
Columbia Research Bureau Spanish Test, 225–226
Combining test scores, methods of, 33–41
Completion-test items, 215–216; illustrations of, 216–217
Content analysis, 31, 126, 227–229
Cooperative French Test, 133
Cooperative General Achievement Tests, 119–121
Cooperative Mathematics Test, 131
Cooperative Science Test, 133–134
Correction for guessing, 204, 207; when to use, 207
Correlation, meaning of, 28–29
Correlation coefficient, computation of, 270–271
Criteria, in validity, 165–166

Diagnostic tests, clinical, 60–63, 80–81; differential, 150–154;

277

## SUBJECT INDEX

educational, 56, 58, 71–72, 74–76, 79–82
Diagnostic Tests of Achievement in Music, 162–164
Differential Aptitude Tests (DAT), 150–154

Educational achievement tests, 108–111; and intelligence tests, 109; compared with school examinations, 110–111; in school subjects, 127–134; how used in schools, 115–122; what to look for in, 135–138
Educational age, (EA), 137
Essay tests, characteristics of, 217–220; how to improve, 219–220; scoring in, 220
Evaluation and Adjustment Series, 131–132

Frequency distribution, 15–17; rules for constructing, 258–259
Frequency polygon, 16–19; how to construct, 259–261

Galton, Francis, role in testing movement, 6
General Clerical Test, 149–150
Gordon's Personal Profile and Personal Inventory, 181–183
Grade norms, 42–43
Group tests, of intelligence, 84–85; in guidance, 99–102; norms in, 104–105; reliability of, 103; scaling in, 104; use in schools, 99–103
Guidance, educational and vocational, 99–101, 124–126, 244–252

Halo effect in ratings, 172
Histogram, 17, 261; how to construct, 261

Individual differences, importance of, 3, 12
Intelligence, meaning of, 47–49; levels of, 48
Intelligence quotient (IQ), Stanford-Binet, 53–54; constancy of, 64–66; distribution of, 56–57; precautions in interpreting, 63–64; stability of, 59–60
Intelligence quotient (IQ), Wechsler, 69–71; in diagnosis, 71–72; range of, in population, 75
Intelligence tests, factors in the choice of, 103–106; group, 84–85; individual, 46–49; performance, 76–79
Interest inventories, 187–196
Iowa Silent Reading Tests, 130–131
IQ (intelligence quotient), 53–54; as standard score, 37–41; as ratio, 53
Item analysis, 230–235; short method of, 235–239
Item (test), difficulty of, 229–230; selection of, 227–229; validity of, 232–233

Kuder Preference Record, 191–193
Kuhlmann-Anderson Intelligence Tests, 93–94

Law School Admission Test, 160–161
Lorge-Thorndike Intelligence Test, 94–96

MacQuarrie Test of Mechanical Ability, 143–145
Matching items, 212–213; illustrations of, 213
Mean, 20; in frequency distribution, 263
Mechanical aptitude tests, 143–146
Median, 21; in frequency distribution, 265
Medical College Admission Tests, 158–160
Meier Art Judgment Test, 164–165
Mental age (MA), 33
Mental tests, classification of, 4–5; compared with physical, 2–3; history of, 5–12; uses of, in schools, 13
Metropolitan Achievement Tests, 115–117
Metropolitan Readiness Tests, 127–129

## SUBJECT INDEX

Minnesota Clerical Test, 148–149
Minnesota Paper Formboard Test, 154–156
Mode, 21, 266
Multiple-choice items, 206–211; illustrations of, 208–210
Multiple-response items, 211–212
Murphy-Durrell Diagnostic Reading Readiness Test, 156–157
Musical Aptitude Tests, 162–164

National Teacher Examination, 161–162
Nelson-Denny Reading Test, 226
Normal distribution, 18ff; uses of, in testing, 18–20
Normal probability curve, 18; areas under, 24–25
Norms, 42; age, 33–34, percentile, 34–36; standard scores as, 37–41

Objectives, educational, 108–109
Objective tests, 84–85; compared with essay, 199–202; item types in, 202–217
Occupational Interest Inventory, 189–190
Orleans Algebra Prognosis Test, 157
Otis Quick-Scoring Mental Ability Tests, 90–92

Percentile rank, 34–37; advantages of, 35–37; limitations of, 37; norms in terms of, 42–43
Percentile scale, 34
Performance tests, 76–79
Personality, meaning of, 168–169; inventories in the measurement of, 175–176; rating scales in the measurement of, 169–175; sociometric techniques in, 252–256
Personality inventories, 176–184; summary on the use of, 194–196
Pintner's Aspects of Personality, 179–180
Pintner-Cunningham Primary Tests, 86–88

Pre-engineering Ability Tests, 161
Profiles, use of, in comparing test results, 36, 91, 152
Projective tests, meaning of, 169

Quartile, meaning of, 25–26
Quartile deviation (Q), calculation of, 267–268
Questionnaires, 175–176

$r$, coefficient of correlation, 28–29; computation of, 270–271
Range of scores, 22, 266–267
Rating scales, 169–174; factors affecting, 173–174; improvement in, 174–175; summary on, 174
Reliability of a test, coefficient of, 29–31; parallel forms of, 30; split-half technique in, 240–242; test-retest in, 29–31

School College Ability Tests (SCAT), 121–123
Seashore Measures of Musical Talent, 162–163
Selection of tests, factors in, 103–106, 134–138, 165–166
Sequential Tests of Educational Progress, (STEP), 120–121
Sigma scores, meaning of, 37–41
Sociometric techniques, 252–256
Standard deviation (SD), 22–23; calculation of, in simple series, 23; in frequency distribution, 268–269
Standard error, of a score, 30–31
Standard scores, calculation of, 37–40; normalized or $T$-scores, 41
Standardized tests, 223–224
Stanford Achievement Tests, 112–115
Stanford-Binet Intelligence Scale, 49–55; reliability of, 59–60; scoring in, 52–54; uses of, in the schools, 55–58; validity of, 59–60
Strong Vocational Interest Blank, 193–194
Study of Values (Allport-Vernon-Lindzey), 186–187

Teacher-made tests, 223–224; directions for, 230–231; objectives in, 224–229; reliability of, 240–242; scoring of, 240; validity of, 242
Terman-McNemar Test of Mental Ability, 66
Test items, varieties of, 202ff
Thurstone Temperament Schedule, 183–184
True-False items, 202–206
$T$-score, 41
Turse Shorthand Aptitude Test, 157–158

Validity, of a test, 31–32; of test items, 231ff

Variability, of scores, 22–26; computation of measures of, 266–269
Verbal ability and performance abilities, 68–69, 200–201

Wechsler Adult Intelligence Scale, 67–69; in diagnosis, 69–70; in the schools, 71–72
Wechsler Intelligence Scale for Children, 72–74; compared with Stanford-Binet, 74; MA's in, 76; range and stability of IQ's in, 75–76

$z$-scores, 37

# AUTHOR INDEX

Anastasi, A., 13, 82, 138, 166, 196
Arthur, G. A., 82

Bean, K. L., 242

Cronbach, L. J., 82, 106, 166
Crow, L. W., 256
Crow, A., 256

Freeman, F. S., 13, 82, 106, 196

Garrett, H. E., 44
Gerberich, J. R., 221
Goodenough, F. L., 106
Greene, E. B., 166
Greene, H. A., 138

Hagen, E., 13, 44

Jørdan, A. M., 138, 196
Jorgenson, A. N., 138
Justman, J., 221

Lallas, J. E., 256

McNemar, Q., 82

Manuel, H., 44
Merrill, M. A., 82
Morgan, C. L., 221

Noll, V. H., 44, 106, 166, 242, 256

Remmers, H. H., 221
Robbins, I., 221
Ross, C. C., 13, 44, 221, 243
Ryden, E. R., 221

Stanley, J. C., 13, 44, 221, 243
Super, D. E., 256

Terman, L. M., 82
Thorndike, R. L., 13, 44
Travers, R. M., 196, 221, 243
Traxler, A. E., 138

Wechsler, D., 82
Wegner, K. W., 256
Wood, D. A., 221, 243
Wrightstone, J. W., 221

Zeran, F. N., 256